STREETWISE
MANDARIN
CHINESE

STREETWISE MANDARIN CHINESE

Speak and Understand Everyday Mandarin

RONGRONG LIAO, PH.D.
DAVID Y. DAI
JACK FRANKE, PH.D.

New York   Chicago   San Francisco   Lisbon   London   Madrid   Mexico City
Milan   New Delhi   San Juan   Seoul   Singapore   Sydney   Toronto

1 2 3 4 5 6 7 8 9 10 11 12 13 14 15 16 17 18 19 20 21   DOC/DOC   0 9 8

ISBN   978-0-07-147489-4 (book and CD set)
MHID   0-07-147489-7 (book and CD set)

ISBN   978-0-07-147490-0 (book alone)
MHID   0-07-147490-0 (book alone)

Library of Congress Control Number: 2005937445

McGraw-Hill books are available at special quantity discounts to use as premiums and
sales promotions or for use in corporate training programs. To contact a representative,
please visit the Contact Us pages at www.mhprofessional.com.

MP3 Disk

The accompanying disk contains MP3 recordings of all 30
Conversations in *Streetwise Mandarin Chinese*, as well as the
vocabulary lists in each chapter. These files can be played on all
MP3 players.

For optimum use on the iPod:
1. Open iTunes on your computer.
2. Insert disk into computer and open via My Computer.
3. Drag folder "Copy to iTunes Music Library" into Music in the
iTunes menu.
4. Sync your iPod with iTunes and eject iPod.
5. Locate recordings on your iPod by following this path:
Main menu: **Music**
Music menu: **Artists**
Artist menu: **Streetwise Chinese: By Chapter**
              (for conversations and vocabulary items)
              Streetwise Chinese: Vocab A-Z
              (for alphabetical ordering by pinyin of all vocabulary
              items)
Note: Conversation scripts (Simplified, Traditional, English) can be
located on the Lyric screen, if your iPod model has this feature.

This book is printed on acid-free paper.

Contents

Introduction

This book is for students who have completed one to two years' Chinese learning. The explanatory notes and vocabulary lists in the book also help students with relatively limited Chinese background to read the book and enjoy colloquial expressions and deeper culture that are not displayed in basic Chinese textbooks.

Immediately after students start to talk with native Chinese people, they will hear informal colloquial expressions. Although each word is familiar, they don't understand the whole meaning of the expression and don't know how to use it. These colloquial expressions are slang; they are familiar to their Chinese users and are used by them to replace well-known conventional synonyms. Just as English, where we encounter many expressions in popular culture, there are many manifestations of slang in Chinese. These can include sayings from folklore of China's rich historical and cultural background, local dialects, jargon, argot, and obsecenity. Once a student has mastered the basics, she can add slang to sound more native-like. Fortunately, Chinese is vast in the amount of slang, and many expressions can be used at the right time and place.

It is important to note that register plays an important role in the Chinese language. Once you go beyond expressions, such as 现在 or 目前 ("at the present"), a student might learn terms such as 眼下 or 这年头儿 ("at the present"). It is paramount that you understand the underlying meaning, and whether the slang term is informal, neutral, or vulgar. Were you to use these terms in the wrong context, this could result in a misunderstanding, at the best, and socio-cultural breakdown, at the worst. It is always better to err on the side of caution.

Most expressions that are explained in this book are used with high frequency by speakers of all subcultures, such as 爱...就... ("Do whatever you like.") and ...得了 ("Just ...."). The authors have chosen to include few taboo expressions; however, we have provided some cultural notes on obscenities. In addition, you can find additional documents on the CD to further enhance your knowledge. All of the dialogues, as well as the vocabulary, can also be found in CD-format and mp3 formats on the CD.

One feature of the book is that we have explained and used in exercises more than 80% of level 3 and level 4 colloquial items listed in the *Outline of Chinese Proficiency Level and Grammar Level* (汉语水平等级标准与语法等级大纲), which was drawn up by the office of China's central government that is in charge of teaching Chinese as a foreign language (国家汉办).

The layout of the book is as follows:

Chapter and conversations. There are fifteen chapters, each of which contains two conversations and focuses on certain functions in language. Slang entries are highlighted in the conversations.

Simplified and traditional characters. All conversations are printed first in simplified characters and then in traditional characters.

English translation. English translation of each conversation is provided.

Explanatory note (词语注释). After the English translation of each conversation, slang entries are briefly explained, and example sentences are provided with English translation.

Vocabulary list (词汇表). In each chapter, a vocabulary list for the two conversations is provided after the explanatory notes of the second conversation.

Exercises (练习) **and Answer keys** (答案). In each chapter, exercises and answer keys are provided after the vocabulary list.

Culture notes. One culture note is provided at the end of each chapter.

Slang Indexes. Two slang indexes are provided at the end of the book. Each index contains 570 slang entries that are sorted by pronunciation and by the corresponding chapter. There are two other indexes that contain the 48 slang entries that occur in the book *Outline of Chinese Proficiency Level and Grammar Level* (汉语水平等级标准与语法等级大纲).

We hope that *Streetwise Mandarin Chinese* will help students better understand Chinese people's daily spoken language and be able to express themselves in more natural Chinese.

本书献给克里斯、卢斯以及我们有缘且有幸认识的所有朋友。

We would like to thank Frank T. Dai who translated all conversations in the book from Chinese to English and edited explanatory notes in 12 chapters.

We would also like to thank the assistance of the following individuals from the Monterey Institute of International Studies for their support in voicing the CD: Dean Chuanyun Bao, Xiaoyan Shen, Ziyun Xu, and Yunhua Zhang.

STREETWISE
MANDARIN
CHINESE

就那样儿,成天瞎忙乎
哪阵风把你给吹到这儿来啦

GREETING PEOPLE
•
ASKING HOW THEY ARE
•
SAYING HOW YOU FEEL
•
ADDRESSING EACH OTHER

CONVERSATION A:

Simplified

李琳在百货商场里见到了正在那里上班的王文英。两人
一见面就聊了起来。

李琳: 阿姨,上班哪?

王文英: **呦**,是琳琳呀! 看我,**都没认出来**。

李琳: **好久没见**您了,您**挺好的吧**?

王文英: 挺好,挺好。哎呦,真是**女大十八变**,这么**水灵**
了!

李琳: **哪儿啊**,您家云云才水灵呢!

哪阵风把你给吹到这儿来啦? (lit: "What wind blew you here?")
Welcome! (to a friend or familiar person.) (See page 8)

At the mall, Li runs into Wang, who is working there. The two start chatting right away.

Li: Ma'am, are you working?

Wang: Hey, it's Lin! Look at me, I didn't even recognize you.

Li: It's been forever since I've seen you. Are you doing well?

Wang: Good, good. My, you've grown up; you're so pretty now!

Li: What are you talking about, I'm nowhere near as pretty as your daughter Yun.

王文英： 哎, 你妈还好吧?

李琳：   **就那样儿**, 成天**瞎忙乎**。昨儿她**还说起您来着**, 说要**上这儿来**买东西, 顺便看看您。

王文英： 你让她下礼拜**找个时候**过来, 你也来, 买完东西咱一块儿**聚聚**, 我请客。

李琳：   **行**, 我告诉她, 让她给您打电话

———■———

Traditional

李琳在百貨商場裏見到了正在那裏上班的王文英。兩人一見面就聊了起來。

李琳：   阿姨,上班哪?

王文英： **喲**,是琳琳呀！看我,**都沒認出來**.

李琳：   **好久沒見**您了,您**挺好的吧**?

王文英： 挺好, 挺好。哎呦,真是**女大十八變**,這麼**水靈**了！

李琳：   **哪兒啊**,您家雲雲才水靈呢！

王文英： 哎,你媽還好吧?

李琳：   **就那樣兒**,成天**瞎忙乎**。昨兒她**還說起您來著**,說要**上這兒來**買東西,順便看看您。

王文英： 你讓她下禮拜**找個時候**過來,你也來,買完東西咱一塊兒**聚聚**,我請客。

李琳：   **行**,我告訴她,讓她給您打電話。

Wang: Well, how's your mother?

Li: Same old, same old, busy everyday doing god knows
            what. She mentioned you yesterday, said she's going
            to come shopping here and drop by to see you.

Wang: You tell her to come over sometime next week. You
            come too – we can get together after shopping, my
            treat.

Li: Okay, I'll pass it on to her, and tell her to call you.

———————————— ■ ————————————

词语注释

- **呦**, 是琳琳呀!
  哟 (呦 [yōu] Hey!)
  This is an interjection that expresses surprise. 哎哟 and 哎呀 have
  a similar function. For example, 哟, 小明也来啦! 我还以为他
  不会来呢。"Hey, Xiaoming is here too. I thought he wouldn't
  come, and I was wrong."

- 看我, **都没认出来。**
  都没… "I couldn't even …." This is a pattern for emphasizing
  something in a negative form. For example, 她说得太快, 我都
  没听清楚。"She speaks so fast, I couldn't even hear clearly。"

- **好久没见**您了, 您挺好的吧?
  好久没见 Use either 好久没见 or 好久不见, which means:
  "I haven't seen you for a long time." The expression is used in greeting
  people and is usually followed by questions asking how they are. For
  example, 好久没见, 最近怎么样? 还那么忙吗? "Long time no
  see. How have you been recently? Are you still as busy as before?"

- 好久没见您了, 您**挺好的吧**?
  挺好的吧 "How is ... ?" This expression is often used with a greeting and shows consideration for the listener or other people. For example, 你去北京的时候见到你姐姐他们了吗? 他们都挺好的吧? "Did you see your sister and her family when you were visiting Beijing? How are they?"

- 真是**女大十八变**, 这么水灵了!
  女大十八变 "A girl's appearance changes fast." This is a fixed expression, often used with a positive comment on a girl's appearance as she changes from childhood to adulthood. The number 十八, literally "eighteen," refers to the pace or degree of the change. For example, 两年不见, 云云长得那么漂亮了, 真是女大十八变! "I haven't seen Yunyun for two years, and she has become such a beauty! No wonder people say that a girl's appearance changes fast."

- 真是女大十八变, 这么**水灵**了!
  水灵 (灵 [ling] clever; sharp)
  This word is used for describing girls and is a colloquial form of "bright and beautiful." For example, 那个小女孩儿长得多水灵啊! "That little girl is so pretty!"

- **哪儿啊**, 您家云云才水灵呢!
  哪儿啊 Here it conveys a modest expression: "No" or "I am not as pretty as you said." In general, 哪儿啊 is often used as a response to others that shows disagreement, meaning "No" or "It's not like what you said." For example, 妈妈问: "你见过他?" 女儿说: "哪儿啊, 我哪儿见过他, 我就见过他的照片。" "The mother asks: "You met him before?" The daughter says: "No, I never met him. I have only seen his picture.""

- **就那样儿**, 成天瞎忙乎。
  就那样儿 "It's just like that," "so-so," or "nothing special." It is often followed by further explanation. For example, 他呀, 就那样儿, 每天就想着上网玩儿游戏。"He is just like that; what he is interested in is playing games online."

- 就那样儿, 成天**瞎忙乎**。
  瞎忙乎 (瞎 [xiā] blind) This is a colloquial form of "bustle without plan or purpose." For example, 作这个有什么用呀? 他就喜欢瞎忙乎。"What's the use for him to do that? He just likes to be busy for no good reason."

- 昨儿她**还说起您来着**
  还…来着 This is a colloquial pattern meaning that something has happened relatively recently. For example, 上个星期他还给我打电话来着。"He only called me last week."

- 说要**上这儿来**买东西
  上…来 A colloquial form for "come to …." The similar pattern, 上…去, means: "go to …." For example, 他上咱们家来过吗? "Has he ever come to our home?" 你上她家去过吗? "Have you ever been to her house?"

- 你让她下礼拜**找个时候**过来
  找个时候 A colloquial form for "to find the time." For example, 咱们下个月找个时候去看看她怎么样? "How about we find a time to visit her next month?"

- 买完东西咱一块儿**聚聚**
  聚聚 (聚 [jù] get together)
  A colloquial way to say "to get together." For example, 咱们应该常在一块儿聚聚。"We should get together more often."

- **行**, 我告诉她

行 "All right," or "it's OK" For example, 我告诉他咱们要找他帮忙, 他说行。 "I told him that we might ask him for help, and he said that it's OK."

CONVERSATION B:

Simplified

张大朋跟马全山是同乡。这一天张大朋来到马全山工作单位办事, 碰到了马全山。

马全山：**张总,哪阵风把你给吹到这儿来啦?** 你可是大忙人儿。

张大朋：全子, 是你呀! **我当是谁呢! 还张总张总的**, 快别逗了!

马全山：**这年头儿**谁见了你不叫张总?

张大朋：那是班儿上**那伙儿人**。咱哥们儿**谁跟谁呀**, 还兴叫这个?

马全山：你**大小**也是个老总, 我哪能**当着大伙儿**叫你的小名儿!

张大朋：**那怕什么的?**

马全山：**再怎么也**得有个叫法。叫**先生,别扭**; 叫师傅, 也不合适。**还就得**叫你张总。

张大朋: **得**, 在这儿你**爱叫什么就叫什么**! 我可还是叫你小名儿, 还叫 "全子", **啊**?

马全山: **那没说的**, 你只**管**叫!

———◼———

Zhang and Ma are from the same village and are both working in Beijing. They haven't seen each other for a long time. Today, Zhang runs into Ma at Ma's workplace.

Ma:	Manager Zhang, what wind blew you here? You sure are a busy man.
Zhang:	Little Quang, it's you! I was wondering who it was! What is this "Manager Zhang," stop kidding around!
Ma:	These days who wouldn't call you Manager Zhang when they see you?
Zhang:	Those are the folks at work. We're old buddies. Why do we have to call each other those things?
Ma:	After all, you are a manager, I can't call you by your nickname in front of everyone!
Zhang:	What's there to be afraid of?
Ma:	No matter what, we have to call you something. "Mister" sounds awkward; "Master" doesn't fit. The only thing left is Manager Zhang.
Zhang:	Fine, over here you can call me whatever you want! But I'm still going to call you by your nickname, still "Little Quang," OK?
Ma:	Of course, go ahead!

———◼———

Traditional

張大朋跟馬全山是同鄉. 這一天張大朋來到馬全山工作
單位辦事, 碰到了馬全山.

馬全山： **張總, 哪陣風把你給吹到這兒來啦**？你可是
　　　　大忙人兒.

張大朋： 全子, 是你呀！**我當是誰呢！還張總張總的**,
　　　　快別逗了！

馬全山： **這年頭兒**誰見了你不叫張總？

張大朋： 那是班兒上**那夥兒人**. 咱哥們兒**誰跟誰呀**, 還
　　　　興叫這個？

馬全山： 你大小也是個老總, 我哪能**當著大夥兒**叫你
　　　　的小名兒！

張大朋： **那怕什麼的**？

馬全山： **再怎麼也**得有個叫法. 叫先生, **彆扭**；叫師
　　　　傅, 也不合適. **還就得**叫你張總.

張大朋： **得**, 在這兒你**愛叫什麼就叫什麼**！我可還是
　　　　叫你小名兒, 還叫 "全子", **啊**？

馬全山： 　　　**那沒說的**, 你只管叫！

———————■———————

词语注释 / NOTES

- **张总**, 哪阵风把你给吹到这儿来啦?
  ...总 (总 [zǒng] general manager; chief) This is an abbreviated
  form of the title "Chief …." For example, 张总, "Chief Zhang,"

could be the abbreviated form of the title 张总经理 "General Manager Zhang," or 张总工程师 "Chief Engineer Zhang."

- **张总, 哪阵风把您给吹到这儿来啦?**
  哪阵风把您给吹到这儿来啦 Literally, "What wind blew you over here?" This is a fixed expression that means: "How come I meet you here?" with the connotation: "I did not expect to meet you here." This expression is used between acquaintances, showing a little feeling of surprise. For example, 张明, 哪阵风把你给吹到这儿来啦? 你不是去日本了吗? "Hey, Zhang Ming, what wind blew you over here? I heard that you went to Japan. Is it true?"

- **你可是大忙人儿**
  可... "Very ... " In this pattern, 可 conveys the emphasis on the following words. For example, 那儿人可真多。 "There are so many people."

- **全子, 是你呀! 我当是谁呢!**
  我当是谁呢 (当 [dàng] thought) Literally, "I was wondering who this is." This is a fixed expression often used after the speaker realizes who the person in question is. For example, 我当是谁呢! 原来是他呀! "Oh, it's him! I was wondering who this is."

- **还张总张总的, 快别逗了!**
  还... ...的 (还 [hái] even) "Even say ..." One of the usages of 还 is to express feeling. In this pattern, "..." refers to other person's words, and the reduplicated form of "..." works together with 还 to show feeling. In the expression 还张总张总的, the feeling is "unexpected," and the connotation is: "You shouldn't be so polite. I am flattered." In the following example, the pattern is used to express the feeling of inpatience. 还别忙别忙的, 你快点儿行不行。 "You are even saying don't hurry. Why don't you hurry up?"

- 还张总张总的, 快**别逗了**!
  别逗了 (逗 [dòu] tease) "Don't tease me." For example, 那么冷
  的天还要去游泳? 别逗了。 "You want to swim in such cold
  weather? Come on, don't tease me."

- **这年头**儿谁见了你不叫张总?
  这年头 (年头 [niántóu] days, times) 这年头 or 那年头
  "These days" or "those days." The expression usually contains a
  negative connotation. For example, 这年头汽油那么贵, 你
  就别去旅行啦! "These days gas is so expensive, why don't you
  cancel the trip?"

- 那是班儿上那伙儿人
  那伙儿人 (伙 [huǒ] group, crowd, band) Also 这伙人。 This
  is a colloquial form for "the group of people." Sometimes 伙儿
  contains negative connotation. For example, 这伙人是从哪儿
  来的? "Where does this band of guys come from?"

- 咱哥们儿**谁跟谁呀**
  谁跟谁呀 Literally, "We, the buddies, who is talking to whom?"
  谁跟谁呀 or 谁跟谁啊 is usually put after 咱们 "we," 咱俩
  "the two of us," or 咱哥们儿 "the buddies," and this expression
  means: "Look how close we are, we don't need this!" "With the
  close relationship we have, there is no need to do this." For example
  咱俩谁跟谁呀, 你就不用付钱啦! "We are such good friends;
  you don't need to pay for this!"

- 还**兴**叫这个?
  兴 In context, 兴 stands for "become popular" or "encourage." 还兴
  叫这个 means: "How could we go in for this sort of address?" With

this meaning, 兴 could be used with either positive or negative connotation and in rhetorical questions. For example, 现在正兴这个。 "That's all the vogue now." 这儿不兴穿长裙! "People don't wear long skirts here."

- 你大小也是个老总
  大小 "At the very least." For example, 他大小也是个班长。 "His status is at least that of class leader." 这大小是一个生意。 "In any event, this is a deal."

- 我哪能当着大伙儿叫你的小名儿!
  当着… "In front of …"; "in one's presence." For example, 我不想当着她说那件事。 "I don't want to talk about that in her presence." 你的钱我是当着大家还给你的, 你怎么说没还呢? "I paid you back in front of everybody. How could you deny it?"

- 那怕什么的?
  This is a rhetorical question, meaning "It doesn't matter." For example, 你是说她不愿意参加? 那怕什么的? 没有她咱们也能作好。 "Are you saying that she doesn't want to join us? It doesn't matter. We can do well without her."

- 再怎么也得有个叫法。
  再怎么也 A colloquial form for "no matter what." In this pattern, 再怎么 means "in any case," and the words after 也 refer to the consequence or result. For example, 再怎么你们也得去! "You have to go no matter what happens!"

- 叫先生, **别扭**

  别扭 (别扭 [bièniu] uncomfortable, awkward) 别扭 is a colloquial word for "uncomfortable" or "awkward." For example, 他今天怎么这么别扭? 是在跟谁生气吧? "Why is he in a bad mood? Is he angry with someone?"

- **还就得**叫你张总。

  还就得 (得 [děi] have to) Both 还 and 就 convey the emphasis of the following word 得, "have to." For example, 这个活儿谁也干不了, 还就得我去。 "Nobody else can do this job; I have to do it."

- **得**, 在这儿你爱叫什么就叫什么。

  得 ([dé]) A colloquial form to indicate approval or prohibition, used when ending a statement. For example: 得, 就这么办。 "All right! Just go ahead." 得, 别再说了。 "That's enough. Let it go at that."

- 在这儿你**爱叫什么就叫什么**。

  爱…就… A colloquial pattern to express "do whatever you like." "…" is usually a verb or a verbal phrase, 就 is optional. For example: 你爱去就去, 我不管。 "Go ahead if you want, I do not care." 给你一百块钱, 你爱买什么买什么。 "Here is a hundred dollars for you, and you can buy whatever you like."

- 还叫"全子", **啊**?

  啊 (啊 [á] eh) This is an interjection that is used to ask opinions or to question closely. For example, 这么说你明天是不去了, 啊? "So you won't go tomorrow, eh?"

- **那没说的**, 你只管叫!

  那没说的 "Needless to say," "naturally," "of course." For example,

那没说的，这是我应该做的。 "No problem, it's what I should do."

- 那没说的,你**只管**叫！

  只管 A colloquial form for "Feel free to …"; "don't hesitate to …"; or "by all means." For example, 你想说什么只管说。 "Feel free to say anything you want to say." 既然你喜欢, 就尽管买好了。 "Don't hesitate to buy it since you like it." 你只管干下去。 "Go ahead by all means."

———◼———

▌ VOCABULARY

商场	shāngchǎng	market; bazaar
上班	shàngbān	go to work; on duty
聊	liáo	chat
阿姨	āyí	aunt or auntie (the form to call either mother's sister or a woman who is about the mother's age)
顺便	shùnbiàn	conveniently; in passing
礼拜	lǐbài	week
请客	qǐngkè	treat (at one's own expense)
同乡	tóngxiāng	a person from the same hometown
单位	dānwèi	unit (as an organization)
办事	bànshì	handle affairs; work
碰到	pèngdào	meet unexpectedly; run into
忙人	mángrén	busy person
咱	zán	we (including both the speaker and the listener)

哥们儿	gēmenr	brothers; buddies; pals
师傅	shīfu	master worker
小名儿	xiǎomíngr	childhood name

———————■———————

EXERCISES

A. Fill in the spaces with the appropriate words or phrases:

> 还去来着　　哪儿啊　　行　　　呦
> 挺好的吧　　瞎忙乎　　聚聚

1　你说我一定学过画画儿? _____,我根本没学过。

2　_____,都五点了,咱们要晚了,快走吧。

3　咱们班同学都好几年没见面了,这次一定要好好儿_____。

4　你们都想下个星期就去呀? _____,我听你们的。

5　你爸爸妈妈还在北京吗? 他们_____?

6　你看我打电话的时间都没有? 每天_____。

7　那个新电影院特别好,我前几天_____。

B. Choose the expression from the following list that best corresponds to the underlined words or phrases:

> 好久没见　　就那样儿　　都没带　　水灵
> 找个时候　　上我家来　　女大十八变

1　你看,那姐妹俩一个比一个长得<u>漂亮</u>。

2 我也喜欢滑冰,咱们<u>约个时间</u>一块儿去滑一回吧。

3 <u>几个月没看见你了</u>,怎么样? 还好吧?

4 我看那工作<u>没什么好</u>,成天对着电脑动也不能动。

5 <u>女孩儿变得好快</u>,两年不见就认不出来了。

6 看你着急的,连书包<u>也不带</u>就要去上学。

7 下个星期六你们都<u>来我这儿</u>,我请客。

C. Fill in the spaces with the appropriate words or phrases:

再怎么也　别逗了　　王总　　刘总刘总　　啊　　兴
爱去哪儿　哪阵风　　别扭　我当是谁呢　大　　小

1 现在就_____穿短衣服,你穿这件正合适。

2 我介绍一下,这位是_____,我们的老领导。

3 他_____也是你班长,你不应该对他不礼貌。

4 你说什么? _____? 你大声点儿。

5 你一叫我经理我就_____,还是叫我老刘吧!

6 _____,我有要紧事,没时间跟你开玩笑。

7 都说有个大人物要来,_____,原来是你呀!

8 你干了五个钟头了,_____该休息一会儿了。

9 你怎么那么客气? 跟我说话还_____的!

10 随便,你_____就去哪儿,你高兴,我就没意见。

11 老马,_____把你给吹到这儿来啦? 我都好久没
见着你了。

D. Choose the expression from the following list that best corresponds
   to the underlined words or phrases:

那怕什么的 谁跟谁呀 还就得 那伙人 只管
当着这么多人 那没说的 这年头 可有名了 得

1 邮局五点就下班, 你要寄包裹<u>只能</u>五点以前去。

2 <u>现在</u>什么都涨价, 你就少买点儿东西吧!

3 这主意不错, <u>行</u>, 就按你说的办。

4 今天你过生日, 你想买什么<u>尽量</u>买, 我来付钱。

5 你要我帮忙? <u>那好说</u>, 咱俩谁跟谁呀!

6 <u>那些人</u>一边看电影一边说话, 吵得我都没看好电
  影。

7 咱们<u>关系那么好</u>, 你就别跟我客气了。

8 他可能来不了? <u>那也没关系</u>, 咱们自己干吧。

9 你怎么<u>在这么多人面前</u>跟我说那件事啊?

10 这家饭馆<u>特别出名</u>, 我早就听说过了。

ANSWER KEY

Exercise A (Dialogue 1)

1 哪儿啊
2 呦
3 聚聚
4 行
5 挺好的吧
6 瞎忙乎
7 还去来着（还...来着）

Exercise B (Dialogue 1)

1 水灵
2 找个时候
3 好久没见
4 就那样儿
5 女大十八变
6 都没带（都没...）
7 上我家来（上...来）

Exercise C (Dialogue 2)

1 兴
2 王总（...总）
3 大小
4 啊
5 别扭
6 别逗了
7 我当是谁呢
8 再怎么也

9 刘总刘总（还......的）
10 爱去哪儿（爱...就...）
11 哪阵风（哪阵风把你给吹到这儿来啦）

Exercise D (Dialogue 2)

1 还就得
2 这年头
3 得
4 只管
5 那没说的
6 那伙人
7 谁跟谁呀
8 那怕什么的
9 当着这么多人（当着...）
10 可有名了（可...了）

▌ GREETING AND ADDRESSING: 招呼与称谓

Some linguists think that greeting people properly is one of the most complex things to learn when learning Chinese, not only because of its diversification, but also because of its rapid change. Generally speaking, there are several types of greeting in China today.

The first type is addressing: greeting people by name, by title, or by family member or relative. This type of greeting is usually used among acquaintances. Although addressing by full name is OK, it is seldom used among acquaintances. Usually people call each other either by first name or by last name by adding a "老" (elder or old), if he or she is younger, or "小" (younger or little), if he or she is older, before the last name, such as 老王 or 小赵. Another way of addressing is calling by profession, post, or official post title: such as 张厂长 (Factory Director Zhang); 赵经理 (Manager Zhao); 李教授 (Professor Li); 金医生 (Doctor Jin), etc. The third way of addressing is using the family member or relative terms, even by strangers: 大哥 (elder brother), 大姐 (elder sister), 大嫂 (elder sister-in-law), 叔叔/大爷 (uncle), 阿姨 (aunt), 爷爷 (grandfather), 奶奶 (grandmother), etc. When addressing an acquaintance, the last name could be added in front of the term: 王爷爷, 李奶奶.

The second type of greeting is asking questions. Friends or acquaintances will ask some questions to show their concern or caring, such as 吃过了吗? (Have you eaten yet?) 到哪儿去? (Where are you going?) or 干什么哪? (What are you doing?) Although in question format, these are really more greeting than question. Other questions are possible: 最近忙不忙? (Are you busy recently?) 你父母身体还好吧? (How are your father and mother?) 你怎么脸色不太好, 是不是病了? (How come you don't look well, are you sick?), etc. Generally speaking, the closer the relationship, the more personal the question. Affected by foreign influence, quite a few city people, especially intellectuals, like to use English style Chinese to greet each other, such as 早上好! (Good morning!) or even "你好

吗?" (How are you?). However, most Chinese are still not used to this kind of greeting. Even so, 你好! (Hi!, Hello! or How do you do?) is increasingly popular, especially for foreigners in China.

The third type of greeting is contextual talking: what the other party has done, is doing, or is going to do. For example, seeing a friend coming back from shopping, one would say 买东西去了? (You did some shopping?) Seeing an acquaintance going to school, one would say 上学去? (Going to school?) Seeing each other in the early morning, people will say 您早! (You are early!) or simply 早! (Early!) to each other. These seemingly meaningless contextual remarks are a very common way of greeting.

瞧这衣服，哪儿哪儿都露着
就怕越练越胖了

COMPLAINING
·
ENVY, ADMIRATION

CONVERSATION A:

Simplified

李琳在百货商场里跟正在那里上班的王文英聊天。王文英跟李琳的妈妈是朋友, 跟李琳也很熟。

王: 　唔, 你穿这衣服挺好看!

李: 　阿姨, 您这是**心里话**吗? 是不是看着**不顺眼儿**?

王: 　这孩子, **怎么说话儿哪?**

李: 　我还不知道您? 您跟我妈一样。她就成天儿**叨叨**: "瞧这衣服, **哪儿哪儿都露着**, 还露着肚脐儿!"

哪儿哪儿都露着 (lit: everywhere of the body is exposed.) It's so skimpy.

Li is in the mall chatting with Wang, who works there. Wang is friends with Li's mother, and knows Li well.

Wang: Hey, I like what you're wearing!

Li: Ma'am, are you telling the truth? Or do you not like the way I look?

Wang: Child, what are you talking about?

Li: How can I not know you? You're just like my mom. All she does all day long is nag: "Look at this, it's so skimpy, it's even showing your belly button!"

王: **得了**, 得了, **甭拿老眼光看人成不成**? 我跟你
妈可不一样, 她成天坐办公室, 我成天儿在这
儿站着。看多了, 就看顺眼儿了呗。

李琳: **您真行**, 还有看顺了眼儿的时候! 我妈**要也能
这么着就好了**!

王: 你多拉她去商场逛逛, 多看看就习惯了。

李: 我妈可**死心眼儿**了, 她哪儿像您**脑子那么活**!

王: 快别给我**戴高帽儿**了!

———◼———

Traditional

李琳在百貨商場裏跟正在那裏上班的王文英聊天王文英
跟李琳的媽媽是朋友, 跟李琳也很熟。

王文英: 唔, 你穿這衣服挺好看!

李琳: 阿姨, 您這是**心裏話**嗎? 是不是看著**不順眼
兒**?

王文英: 這孩子, **怎麼說話哪**?

李琳: 我還不知道您? 您跟我媽一樣。她就成天兒
叨叨: "**瞧這衣服, 哪兒哪兒都露著**, 還露著
肚臍兒!"

王文英: **得了**, 得了, 別拿**老眼光**看人**成不成**? 我跟你
媽可不一樣, 她成天坐辦公室, 我成天兒在這
兒站著。看多了, 就看順眼兒了唄。

Wang:	Now, now, don't judge everyone the same way, okay? I'm not like your mom at all. She sits in an office all day; I stand here all day. You see something a lot, and it starts looking nice.
Li:	Well, good for you, there are times you like what you see! If only my mom were like this too!
Wang:	Go drag her out to the mall; she'll get used to it once she sees it often enough.
Li:	My mom is so stubborn; you think she's as open-minded as you are?
Wang:	Now don't you flatter me!

———■———

李琳:	**您真行**, 還有看順了眼兒的時候! 我媽**要也能這麼著就好了**!
王文英:	你多拉她去商場逛逛, 多看看就習慣了。
李琳:	我媽可**死心眼兒**了, 她哪兒像您**腦子那麼活**!
王文英:	快別給我**戴高帽兒**了!

———■———

词语注释

- 您这是**心里话**吗

  心里话 "One's innermost thoughts and feelings." For example, 她是我的好朋友, 我已经把心里话都跟她说了. "She is my good friend, and I have spoken my mind to her." 说心里话, 我真是挺喜欢她。 "To tell you the truth, I really like her."

- 是不是看着**不顺眼儿**

  不顺眼 顺眼 means "pleasing to the eye." 不顺眼 means "be offensive to the eye," "be an eyesore." For example, 这衣服, 我越看越觉得不顺眼. "The more I look at the clothes, the more I feel that they're offensive to my eye."

- 这孩子, **怎么说话哪**?

  怎么说话哪? "How could you speak in this way?" This is a rhetorical question that is used to criticize the attitude of the speaker, or criticize how the speaker conducts himself or herself. This is the kind of criticism usually used by elders to younger people, or between close friends. For example, 看你, 怎么跟你妈说话哪? "Look at you, how could you talk to your Mom this way?"

- 她就成天儿**叨叨**

  叨叨 ([dāodao]) "Talk on and on;" "chatter away." For example, 那个老太太跟他叨叨了半天。 "The old woman talked to him on and on for a long time."

- 瞧这衣服, **哪儿哪儿都露着**

  哪儿哪儿都… "Anywhere is …." 哪儿哪儿 is a colloquial expression for "anywhere" or "everywhere." For example, 这地方怎么哪儿哪儿都是人啊? "Why are there people everywhere at this place?"

- **得了**, 得了, 别拿老眼光看人成不成?

  得了 "That's enough." "That's that." This is a colloquial expression to show prohibition. For example, 得了, 别聊个没完了. "That's enough. Don't keep chatting."

- 别拿**老眼光**看人成不成?

  老眼光 "Old ways of looking at things; " "old views." For ex-

ample, 你怎么还是拿老眼光看她? 她跟以前不一样了。
"How could you still judge her by what she used to be? She has changed."

- 别拿老眼光看人**成不成?**
  成不成 成 is a colloquial form for "OK" 成不成 means "Is it OK?" For example, 咱们早点儿去成不成? "Will it be alright if we go there earlier?"

- **您真行**, 还有看顺了眼儿的时候!
  真行 "Really capable"; "very competent"; "really terrific." For example, 这么多事儿都做完啦? 他真行。 "He has completed so much work. He is great."

- 我妈**要也能这么着就好了**!
  要是...就好了 This pattern is used to express wish in a subjunctive mood: "I wish ...." "It would be nice if ...." 要是, "if," is often shortened to 要 in colloquial form. For example, 你们要是跟我们同时放假就好了。 "I wish that we had vacation at the same time."

- 我妈要也能**这么着**就好了!
  这么着 "Like this"; "this way." For example, 要是这么着, 那咱们就明天再来。 "In that case, let's come again tomorrow." 这么着 is often used in imperative sentences. For example, 这么着, 我去接他, 你就在这儿等我们。 "Let's do it this way: I'll go pick him up, and you just wait for us here."

- 我妈可**死心眼儿**了
  死心眼 A colloquial expression for "stubborn" or "be set on one's purpose." For example, 跟我们一块儿看电影去吧, 着什么急作作业呀? 别死心眼儿了! "Come and watch a movie with us. Why should you worry about homework? Don't be stubborn."

- 她哪儿像您**脑子那么活**!

  脑子活 A colloquial expression: "have a quick mind." For example, 他脑子活, 看他有什么好主意。 "He has a quick mind; let's see if he has any good ideas."

- 快别给我**戴高帽儿**了!

  戴高帽儿 "Flatter"; "lay it on thick." For example, 他最喜欢别人给他戴高帽儿。 "He is fond of flattery from others." 他最喜欢给别人戴高帽儿。 "He is always ready to flatter other people."

———————————————————

CONVERSATION B:

Simplified

小王在健身房里遇见了小李。

小王: 小李, 都锻炼完啦?

小李: 嗯, 刚在跑步机上跑了三十来分钟。你看, 我衣服都汗湿了。

小王: 你真行! 你体形那么**瘦溜**, 还天天都来锻炼!

小李: 你不是也开始了吗? 多练练就也这样啦。

小王: 哎呀, 我可**没法儿**练成你那样儿。你就**跟个时装模特似的**, 我要是能有你的一半儿就**知足**了。

小李: 多练练对身体总会有好处。

小王: 哎, **你说**我都练了一个多礼拜了, 怎么一点儿都**不见瘦**啊?

小李:	哪能**说瘦就瘦**呢? 还不得练上**个把**月?
小王:	要这么久呀? 那可**麻烦**了。你看, 我这一运动, **体重没减不说, 饭量倒越来越大了。这么下去, 就怕**越练越胖了。
小李:	那倒不会。你运动量大了, 是可以稍微多吃一点儿补充能量。只要别吃太多, 哪会越练越胖?
小王:	我有时候想**干脆去减肥班得了**, 听说一天能减好几斤呢!
小李:	**没的事儿**, 哪儿有那么快! 去那儿, 人家也是**使劲让你运动**, 加上少吃东西, 你才能瘦下来。离开那儿以后, 你要是不练了, 马上就会长回去。
小王:	**怪不得**我们家邻居过一阵子就去一回减肥班, 我也没见他瘦下来。看这样儿, 我还是得靠自己慢慢儿练了, 也**省得**去交学费。

———————

Wang runs into Li in the gym.

Wang:	Li, all done with the workout?
Li:	Yeah, I ran on the treadmill for thirty something minutes. See, got sweat all over my clothes.
Wang:	Man, you're good. You're so fit, and you still come to work out every day!
Li:	Didn't you start, too? Work out some more and you'll be like this, too.

Wang: Aw, how can I be like you? You're like a fashion model. If I can get halfway there I'll be happy.

Li: Working out is always better for the body.

Wang: Oh, tell me why, after working out for over a week, I'm not slimming down?

Li: How can you slim down just like that? Have you been working out for a couple of months at least?

Wang: It takes that long? That's not good. See, once I started exercising, not only did I not lose any weight, but my appetite's getting bigger. If this goes on, I'm afraid that the more I work out the fatter I'll get.

Li: That won't happen. When you exercise more, you can eat a little more to recover energy. As long as you don't eat too much, how can you gain weight when you work out more?

Wang: Sometimes I think I might as well go on a weight loss program. I heard you can lose a few pounds a day!

Li: That's impossible. There's nothing that fast! If you go, they'll also keep telling you to work out. Plus they will make you eat less, and only then will you lose weight. And after you leave, if you stop working out, you'll gain it all back.

Wang: So that's why our neighbor goes to a weight loss program every so often, and I didn't see him getting any skinnier. If that's how things are, I will exercise patiently and save myself from paying for a program.

Traditional

小王在健身房裏遇見了小李。

小王：　小李，都鍛煉完啦?

小李：　嗯，剛在跑步機上跑了三十來分鐘。你看，我衣服都汗濕了。

小王：　你真行! 你體形那麼好，那麼**瘦溜**，還天天都來鍛煉!

小李：　你不是也開始了嗎? 多練練就也這樣啦。

小王：　哎呀，我可**沒法兒**練成你那樣兒。你就**跟個時裝模特似的**，我要是能有你的一半兒就**知足**了。

小李：　多練練對身體總會有好處。

小王：　哎，**你說**我都練了一個多禮拜了，怎麼一點兒都**不見瘦**啊?

小李：　哪能**說瘦就瘦**呢? 還不得練上**個把**月?

小王：　要這麼久呀? 那就**麻煩**了。你看，我這一運動，**體重沒減不說，飯量還越來越大了．這麼下去，就怕**越練越胖了。

小李：　那倒不會。你運動量大了，是可以稍微多吃一點兒補充能量。只要別吃太多，哪會越練越胖?

小王：　我有時候想**乾脆去減肥班得了**，聽說一天能減好幾斤呢!

小李： **沒的事兒**, 哪兒有那麼快! 去那兒, 人家也是
使勁讓你運動, 加上少吃東西, 你才能瘦下
來。離開那兒以後, 你要是不練了, 馬上就會
長回去。

小王： **怪不得**我們家鄰居過一陣子就去一回減肥班,
我也沒見他瘦下來。看這樣兒, 我還是得靠
自己慢慢兒練了, 也**省得**去交學費。

———————■———————

词语注释

- 你体形那么好, 那么**瘦溜**, 还天天都来锻炼!
  瘦溜 (瘦 [shòu] thin, lean; 溜 [līu] glide; smooth)
  A colloquial word: "slim." For example, 我要象你这么瘦溜就
  好了。"I wish that I could be as slim as you are."

- 哎呀, 我可**没法儿**练成你那样儿。
  没法儿 "There is no way out"; "can't help it." For example, 我
  今天早上头疼得厉害, 没法儿去上班。"This morning I
  had a bad headache, and couldn't go to work."

- 你就**跟个时装模特似的**, 我要是能有你的一半儿就知
  足了。
  跟...似的 "Seems to be ...." For example, 你怎么啦? 看见
  我就跟不认识似的, 一句话也不说。"What's happened to
  you? You don't talk to me as if you know me."

- 你就跟个时装模特似的, 我要是能有你的一半儿就**知
  足**了。
  知足 "Be content with one's lot." For example, 她说能有这么

好的工作, 她已经很知足了。 "She said that she is very satis-
fied to have such a good job."

- 哎, **你说**我都练了一个多礼拜了, 怎么一点儿都不见瘦
  啊?

  你说 Literally "you say." This pattern is usually used to introduce a
  question about opinions, similar to "what's your opinion about…?"
  For example, 你说今年选举谁能赢? "Who do you think will
  win this election?" 现在下这么大雨, 你说 我还要不要去
  呢? "Look, it's raining so hard; should I go or not?"

- 哎, 你说我都练了一个多礼拜了, 怎么一点儿都**不见瘦**
  啊?

  不见… "Does not look …." 见, "appear to be." For example, 大
  夫, 我感冒这么多天了, 怎么还不见好? "Doctor, I've had
  the flu for so many days; why have I not gotten better?"

- 哪能**说瘦就瘦**呢? 还不得练上个把月?

  说…就… "To … without delay"; "become … without delay."
  "…" is often a word or a phrase in this pattern. For example, 他们
  说干就干, 一会儿就把院子扫干净了。 "They act without
  delay and soon sweep the yard clean."

- 哪能说瘦就瘦呢? 还不得练上**个把**月?

  个把 "A couple of;" "one or two." For example, 我们那个会
  只开了个把小时就散了。 "Our meeting ended after only a
  couple of hours.

- 要这么久呀? 那就**麻烦**了。

  麻烦 "Troublesome"; "inconvenient." For example, 这可麻烦
  了, 我忘记带手机了。 "What a nuisance. I forgot to bring my
  cell phone with me."

- **体重没减不说, 饭量还越来越大了.**

  ...不说, 还... A colloquial way to express "not only...but also." For example, 今天下雨不说, 还刮大风。 "Today is not only rainy, but also windy." In the pattern, if the two portions do not share the same subject, the subject for the second portion should be inserted before 还.... For example, 这件毛衣式样新不说, 价钱还不贵。 "Not only is the style of the sweater new, but the price is not too high."

- **这么下去**, 就怕越练越胖了。

  这么下去 "This way"; "if this continues." In this expression, 下去 means "go on" or "continue." For example, 现在她每天练习弹钢琴, 这样下去, 她钢琴一定会弹得非常好。 "Now she practices piano every day. If she keeps doing so, she will be really good at playing the piano."

- 这么下去, **就怕**越练越胖了。

  就怕 "I am afraid"; "I suppose"; "perhaps." For example, 开车就怕没有你想的那么容易。 "I am afraid that driving is not as easy as you imagined."

- 我有时候想**干脆**去减肥班得了

  干脆 (脆 [cuì] crisp) "Simply"; "just." For example, 她干脆就不知道你要来。 "She simply doesn't know that you are coming."

- 我有时候想干脆**去减肥班得了**

  ...得了 "Just ...." This pattern is usually used in a declarative sentence to indicate affirmation. For example, 没预约也没关系, 你来就得了。 "Having an appointment doesn't matter; you just come."

- **没的事儿**, 哪儿有那么快!

  没的事儿 Similar to 没有的事儿, "nothing of the sort"; "it is impossible." For example, 谁说这本书没意思? 没有的事儿! "Who said that this book is boring? It is not true."

- 去那儿, 人家也是**使劲让你运动**,

  使劲... "Exert all one's strength to ...," "make efforts to ...." For example, 我们使劲快跑, 才追上了他们。 "Only by exerting ourselves to run fast did we catch up with the other runners." 他使劲让你去那儿, 可是他自己倒不去。 "He tried hard to push you to go there; but he, himself, didn't go."

- **怪不得**我们家邻居过一阵子就去一回减肥班,

  怪不得 (怪 [guài] find something strange; wonder at; blame.) "No wonder"; "so that's why"; "not to blame." Just like the use of "no wonder" in English, this expression is always used after knowing why. For example, 怪不得我最近总看见他, 原来他把家搬到这一带来了。 "No wonder I've been seeing him recently; he has moved to this neighborhood."

- 看这样儿, 我还是得靠自己慢慢儿练了, 也**省得**去交学费。

  省得 (省 [shěng] save) "So as to save (or avoid)." For example, 我得先给他打一个电话, 省得他着急。 "I need to call him first so that he won't worry."

---■---

VOCABULARY

聊天	liáotiān	chitchat; chat
成天	chéngtiān	all day long; all the time
瞧	qiáo	look; see
露	lòu	reveal; show
肚脐儿	dùqír	navel; belly button
顺眼	shùnyǎn	pleasing to the eye

逛	guàng	stroll; ramble; roam
习惯	xíguàn	be used to
健身房	jiànshēnfáng	gymnasium; gym
锻炼	duànliàn	take exercise
汗湿	hànshī	wet with sweat
体形	tǐxíng	bodily form; build
练	liàn	practice
时装	shízhuāng	fashionable dress
模特	mótè	(painting) model
运动	yùndòng	sports; exercise
胖	pàng	fat; stout; plump
稍微	shāowēi	a little; slightly
补充	bǔchōng	replenish; supplement; add
能量	néngliàng	energy
减肥	jiǎnféi	to lose weight
邻居	línjū	neighbor
一阵子	yīzhènzi	a period of time
靠	kào	depend on; rely on; lean against
学费	xuéfèi	tuition

EXERCISES

A Fill in the spaces with the appropriate words and phrases:

死心眼　　老眼光　　就好了　　叨叨

哪儿哪儿　不顺眼　　心里话

1　他总喜欢用 ＿＿＿＿＿＿ 看人, 不知道人是会变化的。

2　他那个男朋友, 我怎么看都＿＿＿＿＿＿＿ 。

3　就这么点事儿, 你怎么成天跟我＿＿＿＿＿＿＿啊, 烦不烦呀!

4　我说的都是＿＿＿＿＿＿＿, 你应该相信我!

5　我儿子可＿＿＿＿＿＿＿了, 他觉得打酱油的钱就不能买醋。

6　书房里＿＿＿＿＿＿＿都是书, 连个坐的地方都没有。

7　要是不下雨＿＿＿＿＿＿＿, 我们就可以去爬山了。

B. Choose the expression from the following list that best corresponds to the underlined words or phrases:

得了　真行　这么着　　脑子活

怎么说话哪　成不成　　戴高帽儿

1　他做生意做得好是因为<u>头脑灵活</u>。

2　<u>够了</u>, 不要再说了, 再说就该迟到了。

3　你又迟到了, 你要是<u>再这样</u>, 我就不理你了。

4　总经理就爱<u>听好话</u>, 所以大家见了他总说他好。

5　你跟你爸爸妈妈<u>不应该这么说话</u>。

6 她真能<u>王</u>, 第一次参加比赛就拿了冠军。

7 你别老叫我 "老王" <u>行不行</u>? 我和你岁数一样大。

C. Fill in the spaces with the appropriate words and phrases:

> 这么下去   瘦溜   你说   就怕   不说
> 说去就去   似的   干脆   怪不得

1 今天作业多, 没时间复习, _____明天考试要不及格了。

2 天气这么不好, _____ 咱们还去不去游泳呢?

3 你那块手表坏了多少次了? _____扔掉买块新的吧。

4 这几天小张急得吃不下饭, 睡不着觉, 总_____可不行。

5 _____你觉得累呢, 原来是昨天一夜没睡觉。

6 小王说人还是瘦一点好看, 作时装表演的人就都是_____的。

7 他学习不努力_____, 还天天迟到, 怎么可能学得好呢?

8 我一有困难他就帮助我, 就跟我哥哥_____。

9 她问我怎么还没去旅行, 我说哪能_____, 总得准备准备吧。

D. Choose the expression from the following list that best corresponds to the underlined words or phrases:

没的事儿　　没法儿　　知足　　省得　　麻烦
先去得了　　不见胖　　个把　　使劲

1 雨下得这么大, 路都不通了, 咱们今天<u>不能</u>回去了。

2 我现在的生活比大多数人都好, 我觉得很<u>满意</u>。

3 咱们虽然比他们多<u>一两个</u>人, 可事儿没他们作得多。

4 哎呀, 我忘了带机票和护照了, 这下可<u>难办</u>了!

5 我顺便替你把书买来吧, <u>不用</u>你自己去了。

6 谁说她病了? <u>不可能</u>! 她身体好着呢。

7 学外语, 只要<u>努力</u>学, 没有学不好的。

8 你什么都吃, 也<u>没变胖</u>, 我要是也这样就好了。

9 我还有不少事儿呢, 你<u>先走吧</u>, 不用等我了。

ANSWER KEY

Exercise A (Dialogue 1)

1 老眼光

2 不顺眼

3 叨叨

4 心里话

5 死心眼

6 哪儿哪儿（哪儿哪儿都...）

7 就好了（要是...就好了）

Exercise B (Dialogue 1)

1 脑子活

2 得了

3 这么着

4 戴高帽儿

5 怎么说话哪

6 真行

7 成不成

Exercise C (Dialogue 2)

1 就怕

2 你说

3 干脆

4 这么下去

5 怪不得

6 瘦溜

7 不说（...不说，还...）

8 似的（跟...似的）

9 说去就去（说...就...）

Exercise D (Dialogue 2)

1 没法儿

2 知足

3 个把

4 麻烦

5 省得

6 没的事儿

7 使劲（使劲...）

8 不见胖（不见...）

9 先去得了（...得了）

CONTEXT OF LANGUAGE

The Chinese language changes so rapidly and people use it so differently that it often makes Chinese learners confused. Let's take the greeting as an example. If you go to China, you will hear all kinds of different greetings: such as 同志 (comrade), 师傅 (master), 小姐 (Miss), etc. However, if you try to use 同志, you might be told that it's only used by some Chinese on formal occasions; if you use 师傅, you might be told that it's out-of-date already; if you use 小姐, the lady you addressed might be very angry since this also refers to a prostitute. Another example is the language of value or evaluation: while young girls think a fashionable cloth is 时髦 (modern), their parents might use 露肉 (exposing body) to criticize it; 瘦 (thin) is slender for young girls but weak or even sickly for the old. While 发福 (grow stout) is a flattering term when greeting the old, it might be perceived as mocking by the young. When you learn a Chinese phrase or slang expression, you will not feel confused if you pay attention to the context; i.e., at what time or occasion one uses it, and to whom and for what communicative purpose.

我都饿扁了
这车怎么还没影儿啊

GRUMBLING
•
TEASING

CONVERSATION A:

Simplified

李琳和男朋友方明到北京远郊区去爬山, 下午下山以后在长途汽车站等车。

李琳: 这儿的风景**好是好, 就是路太难走了. 哎哟,** 我都**饿扁了**。

方明: 我这儿还有点儿你不爱吃的那种饼干, 你要不要?

李琳: 要, 我先**垫点儿**。

方明: 哈, **嘴不刁啦**? 这叫**饥不择食**, 对不对?

李琳: **别罗嗦**! 快拿来!

发火 (lit: flare up; catch fire; ignite; detonate.) get angry; lose one's temper
(see p. 49)

Lin Li and her boyfriend, Xiaoming Fang, went hiking in the far
outskirts of Beijing and are waiting for a bus at the bus station. They
are hungry.

Li:	This place does have good scenery, but the roads are too hard to hike. Ah, I'm so hungry.
Fang:	I still have some of those crackers you don't like. Do you want some?
Li:	Yes, I'll have some.
Fang:	Ha, not picky anymore? This is called so hungry you could eat a horse, right?
Li:	Shush! Give them over!

方明: （笑）给。

李琳: 嗯。**呵**, 这么硬, 这么甜!

方明: **左也不是, 右也不是**, 你真**难伺候**。

李琳: **你尝尝看**, 这**也**太甜了! 怎么这么**舍得**放糖
啊!

方明: 快吃吧, 别**耍嘴皮子**了。

———————■———————

Traditional

李琳和男朋友方明到北京遠郊區去爬山, 下午下山以後
在長途汽車站等車.

李琳: 這兒的風景**好是好**, **就是**路太難走了。**哎喲**,
我都**餓扁了**。

方明: 我這兒還有點兒你不愛吃的那種餅乾, 你要
不要?

李琳: 要, 我先**墊點兒**。

方明: 哈, **嘴不刁啦**? 這叫**饑不擇食**, 對不對?

李琳: **別囉嗦**! 快拿來!

方明: （笑）給。

李琳: 嗯。**呵**, 這麼硬, 這麼甜!

方明: **左也不是, 右也不是**, 你真**難伺候**.

李琳: **你嘗嘗看**, 這**也**太甜了! 怎麼這麼**捨得**放糖啊!

方明: 快吃吧, 别**耍嘴皮子**了。

Fang:	(Laughs) Here.
Li:	'Kay. Oh, it's so hard, and so sweet!
Fang:	Damned if I do, damned if I don't. You're so hard to please.
Li:	You try it; this is way too sweet! Why are they so generous with the sugar!
Fang:	Hurry up and eat. Stop kidding around.

———— ■ ————

词语注释

- 这儿的风景**好是好，就是**路太难走了。
  好是好，就是 Also as 好是好，可惜… (可惜 [kěxī] It's a pity). "Although it is good, …" "It is good, but …" In this pattern, 好是好 functions as "although," and 就是 (or 可惜) functions as "but." For example, 这些水果好是好，就是太酸了。"Although these fruits are good, they are too sour." "这个怎么样？"

- **哎哟**，我都饿扁了。
  哎哟 (哎哟 [āiyō]) An interjection, expressing painful feelings, that is similar to English "Ouch" or "Ow." For example: 哎哟，我的脚怎么那么疼啊？"Ouch. How come my feet hurt so much?"

- 哎哟，我都**饿扁了**。
  饿扁了 (饿 [è] hungry; 扁 [biān] flat) This is a frequently used expression that is a shortened version of 肚子饿扁了。The literal meaning is "the belly becomes flat because of hunger," and the contextual meaning is "terribly hungry." For example: 你这儿有什么我都吃，我早就饿扁了。"I'll eat whatever food you have; I've been starved for a long time."

- 我先**垫点儿**。
  垫点儿 (垫 [diàn] fill up, pad) A colloquial way to say "to have light refreshments," evidently a humorous extension of a basic meaning of 垫, "to fill up," or "to pad." For example: 你看, 咱什么饭菜都没有了, 先垫点儿零嘴吧。 "See, we don't have any cooked food now. Let's have some junk food first."

- 哈, **嘴不刁啦**?
  嘴刁 (刁 [diāo] tricky, artful, sly) This is a commonly used idiom, "picky for food." For example: 他嘴真刁, 什么都不爱吃。 "He is so picky, and does not like any food." In the conversation, the question 嘴不刁啦? is asked with a teasing tone, "Are you not picky about food any more?"

- 这叫**饥不择食**, 对不对?
  饥不择食 (饥 [jī] be hungry; starve; 择 [zé] select, choose; 食 [shí] food) "A hungry person is not choosy about his food." This idiom is usually used in written form, but it is often used in colloquial style with special tones, as for teasing or joking. For example: 今天我是饥不择食了, 要不然我可不会吃这种东西。 "I am too hungry to choose foods today; I would never eat food like this."

- **别罗嗦**! 快拿来!
  别罗嗦 (罗嗦 [luōsuo] long-winded, troublesome) "Don't be troublesome." The expression is often used with an inpatient tone; however, it is used informally to tease. For example: 咱们快走吧, 你就别罗嗦了。 "Let's go now. Don't be troublesome."

- **呵**, 这么硬, 这么甜!
  呵 (呵 [hē] oh) This is a frequently used interjection for grumbling. For example, 你怎么走那么快呀? 呵, 比我跑还快呢! "Why are you walking so fast? Oh, even faster than my running!"

- 左也不是, 右也不是, 你真难伺候。
  ...也不是, ...也不是 This pattern expresses the meaning that no matter what happens, the situation will not change. For example, 她说得我不知道怎么办才好; 走也不是, 不走也不是。 "Her words made me wonder what I should do, and I don't know if I should leave or not." 左也不是, 右也不是 is an idiom in the general pattern of the paralleled structure ...也不是, ...也不是, and it is used to describe a person who is hard to please. In the idiom, 左, "left," and 右, "right," refers to a variety of ways to do things, and 是 means "right." For example, 左也不是, 右也不是, 你到底要我怎么办? "Damned if I do, damned if I don't. What on earth do you want me to do?"

- 左也不是, 右也不是, **你真难伺候。**
  难伺候 (伺候 [cìhou] wait upon, serve) The phrase literally means "hard to serve," but as an idiom, it means "hard to please," or "be fastidious." In the conversation, 难伺候 conveys a tone of teasing. For example, 这个客人特难伺候, 你小心点儿。 "This customer is very hard to please; you'd better be careful."

- 你**尝尝看**, 这也太甜了!
  ... ...看 "Try to ... and see." In the pattern, "..." is a verb or verb phrase, and 看 is used after a duplicated verb or verb phrase. The pattern expresses the meaning "try to do something" with the implication "see what will happen." For example, 这事应该不难办, 让我来试试看。 "This shouldn't be hard; let me have a try." 这是她最喜欢的音乐, 你听听看。 "This is her favorite song; you just listen."

- 你尝尝看, 这**也**太甜了!
  也 "too" or "so." 也 often conveys emphasis. For example, 这儿的天气也太奇怪了, 怎么这么早就下起雪来了呢。 "The weather is so strange here. How could it snow so early in the year?"

- 怎么这么**舍得**放糖啊!

   舍得 (舍得 [shěde] be willing to part with, not grudge) This word introduces a satirical note into the conversation. 舍不得, "begrudge," is the word that contrasts with 舍得。For example, 他很舍得给女朋友买礼物。"He is very willing to buy gifts for his girlfriend." 他做事就是这样, 舍不得花一分钱。"He does things just this way, and he begrudges spending a single cent."

- 快吃吧, 别**耍嘴皮子**了。

   耍嘴皮子 (耍 [shuǎ] play with; 皮 [pí] skin) 嘴皮子 is a colloquial word that refers to the lips of a glib talker. 耍嘴皮子 means "be a slick talker," or "mere empty talk." It is used in a teasing, conversational tone. For example, 他除了耍嘴皮子什么事儿也干不了。"He can do nothing except pay lip service."

———◼———

CONVERSATION B:

Simplified

李琳和方明还在长途汽车站等车......

李琳:　　**真要命**, 这车怎么还**没影儿**啊, 都等这么久了!

方明:　　会不会咱还没到它就提前来过了?

李琳:　　**那可缺德了。**这**前不着村后不着店**的, 咱怎么办哪?

方明:　　那就等着吧。

李琳:　　得等多久哇! 你**也真是**, 我说早一点儿来等车, 你就是不着急, **玩儿个没完**!

方明:　别, 别**发火**, 我**逗**你呢。**按说**这车只有晚点儿来晚点儿走, 不会提前到提前走. 它大概还没来呢。咱们才等了十来分钟, 再等等看。

李琳:　**坏蛋**! 看你, **吓我一跳**! 我还以为它真是走了呢。**倒也是,** 大概还没来呢。

———■———

Lin Li and Xiaoming are still waiting for a bus at the bus station. There is a bus at the station every two hours. It's already ten minutes past three, and the three p.m. bus is still not here.

Li:　What a nuisance! Why is there so no sign of the bus? We've been waiting forever!

Fang:　Could it have come early, before we got here?

Li:　That would be so mean. This is the middle of nowhere! What are we going to do?

Fang:　We just wait here.

Li:　Then how long should we wait? It's all your fault. I wanted to come here earlier to wait for the bus, but you just wouldn't hurry. You kept enjoying yourself.

Fang:　Don't get mad, I'm teasing you. Normally this bus arrives late and leaves late. It won't come and leave early. It probably hasn't come yet. We just waited a little over 10 minutes. Let's wait and see.

Li:　Bastard! See, you scared me! And I thought it really left. You're right, it probably hasn't come yet.

———■———

Traditional

李琳和方明還在長途汽車站等車......

李琳： **真要命**, 這車怎麼還**沒影兒**啊, 都等這麼久了!

方明： 會不會咱還沒到它就提前來過了?

李琳： **那可缺德了**。這**前不著村後不著店**的, 咱怎麼辦哪?

方明： 那就等著吧。

李琳： 得等多久哇! 你**也真是**, 我說早一點兒來等車, 你就是不著急, **玩兒個沒完**!

方明： 別, 別**發火**, 我**逗**你呢。**按說**這車只有晚點兒來晚點兒走, 不會提前到提前走。它大概還沒來呢。咱們才等了十來分鐘, 再等等看。

李琳： **壞蛋**! **看你, 嚇我一跳**! 我還以為它真是走了呢。**倒也是,** 大概還沒來呢。

———■———

词语注释

• **真要命**, 这车怎么还没影儿啊,
真要命 (要命 [yàomìng] drive somebody to his death)
In the expression, 要 means "demand" and 命 stands for "life." 真要命 or 要命 is a frequently used expression in a gripe or complaint, meaning "a nuisance." For example, 真要命, 天总是阴的。 "What a nuisance! It is always cloudy." 要命, 他又来了。 "What a nuisance! He's here again."

- 真要命, 这车怎么还**没影儿**啊,
没影儿 (影 [yǐng] shadow, reflection) 影儿 refers to the trace of a person's presence. 没影儿 means "no sign" or "vague impression." For example, 一下课, 他就没影儿了。 "As soon as the class was over, no one caught a glimpse of him." 她早忘得没影儿了, "She's completely forgotten it."

- 那**可**缺德了。
那可...了 "Then it will ...." This is a popular way of emphasizing a consequence. 那 means "then" or "in that case;" and 可 expresses emphasis on the event expressed by the following words. For example, 她要是来, 那可就麻烦了。 "Had she come, there would have been big trouble."

- 那可**缺德**了.
缺德 (缺 [quē] be short of, lack; 德 [dé] virtue) This is a colloquial expression with the literal meaning "virtueless." Its contextual meaning is "mean," "wicked," or "villainous." For example, 缺德话, "wicked words" or "vicious remarks." **缺德事** "offense," "rotten thing," or "mean trick." **真缺德!** "What a rotten thing!" "How dirty!" 他这么做太缺德了。 "It's so wicked of him to do this."

- 这**前不着村后不着店**的, 咱怎么办呀?
前不着村后不着店 (着 [zháo] touch; 村 [cūn] village; 店 [diàn] shop, inn) This is an idiom with the literaral meaning, "There is no village ahead and no inn behind." It refers to a remote or desolate place with the implication that it is hard to find people or get help there. For example, 这地方前不着村后不着店的, 有什么意思? "This place is in the middle of nowhere; how boring!"

- 你**也真是**, 我说早一点儿来等车, 你就是不着急, 玩儿个没完!

也真是 Also as 真是 or 真是的. The term 真是 is often used to express complaints, and 也 adds further emphasis on what is expressed by 真是. It is very similar to the English complaints: "Really" and "What a nuisance!" For example, 真是的, 这么晚了他还不来上班。 "Really, it's so late and he is still not at work."

- 你也真是, 我说早一点儿来等车, 你就是不着急, **玩儿个没完!**

  ...个没完 This pattern expresses the meaning "keep doing something," with the negative implication that the speaker does not like it. For example, 你看, 他说个没完。 "Look, he keeps on talking." (Not listening to others.)

- 别, 别**发火**, 我逗你呢。

  发火 A colloquial word for "get angry," "flare up," or "lose one's temper." For example, 别发火, 你先听我说。 "Don't be upset. Listen to me first."

- 别, 别发火, 我**逗**你呢。

  逗 (逗 [dòu]) "Tease"; "play with." This is a colloquial word for "tease." It usually refers to a friendly action. For example, 他老爱拿话逗他妹妹笑。 "He likes to make his younger sister laugh with jokes."

- **按说**这车只有晚点儿来晚点儿走。

  按说 (按 [àn] according to) A short form of 按理说, "according to reason" or "according to common sense." For instance, 按说我应该去看看她。 "It stands to reason that I should pay her a visit." 这种事按说不会有多少人关心。 "Normally there are few people who care about this kind of matter."

- **坏蛋**! 看你, 吓我一跳!
  坏蛋 (蛋 [dàn] egg) A very commonly used colloquial word for
  teasing. Its literal meaning is "bad egg," and its context meaning could
  be "scoundrel" or "bastard." For example, 你看那个小坏蛋, 一
  定又出了什么坏主意了。"Look at the little bastard; he must
  have had a wicked idea."

- 坏蛋! **看你,** 吓我一跳!
  看… "See what … did!" This pattern is often used for grumbling,
  followed by words to present the reason. For example, 看你, 把我
  的杯子打破了。"See, you broke my glass." 看我, 写错了好
  几个字。"See, I wrote several wrong characters."

- 坏蛋! 看你, **吓我一跳**!
  吓一跳 The expression means "scared." For example, 我吓了一
  跳, "I got scared." 她吓了我一跳, "She scared me."

- **倒也是,** 大概还没来呢。
  倒也是 (倒 [dǎo] used to denote a transition or concession)
  The idiom shows a hesitant or concessive agreement. It can be used
  as an independent phrase or as an adverbial phrase in the sentence.
  For example, 你说的倒也是对的, 不过他可能不这么想,
  "I suppose you're right, but *he* might not think so."

———■———

VOCABULARY

郊区	jiāoqū	suburbs; outskirts
长途	chángtú	long-distance
饼干	bǐnggān	cookie; cracker
硬	yìng	hard
甜	tián	sweet
班	bān	(measure word, similar to "number of times")
提前	tíqián	ahead of time; beforehand
多久	duōjiǔ	how long
着急	zháojí	worry; feel anxious
大概	dàgài	probably; most likely; presumably
以为	yǐwéi	think; believe; consider

EXERCISES

A. Fill in the spaces with the appropriate words and phrases:

耍嘴皮子　难伺候　嘴刁　呵

饥不择食　尝尝看　哎哟　也

1　我认识的人里, 还没有吃东西 这么＿＿＿＿的呢。

2 _____, 这么多脏衣服! 你多久没洗衣服了?

3 他们刚爬完山回来, 见着什么都要吃, 真是
_____了。

4 都说他_____, 我看他挺好的嘛。

5 你来得_____太晚了! 我们都 要回家了。

6 _____, 我腿疼得都走不了路了, 昨天真不该去
爬山。

7 小李, 今天咱没时间跟他_____, 那事儿明天再
说吧。

8 昨天你去农贸市场了吗? 这是我在那儿买的草莓,
你_____。

B. Choose the expression from the following list that best corresponds
to the underlined words or phrases:

饿扁了   就是   垫点儿   舍得
左也不是右也不是   别啰嗦

1 你要是<u>愿意</u>花时间, 我带你去一个好地方玩儿。

2 妈, 我都<u>快饿死了</u>, 咱们还不吃饭呀?

3 这儿有面包, 你<u>先吃点儿</u>, 咱们下了山就吃饭。

4 他让他妹妹<u>少说话</u>, 他妹妹气得什么都不说了。

5　我觉得电脑游戏好是好, <u>可惜</u>玩起来太费时间。

6　他对她那么好, 她还是那个样, <u>怎么都不高兴</u>。

C. Fill in the spaces with the appropriate words and phrases:

> 吓我一跳　看你　发火　那可　逗
> 前不着村后不着店　　　缺德　　也真是

1　快别_____他玩儿了, 让他睡觉吧, 明天早上还要早起呢。

2　你的钥匙不是在这儿吗? _____, 到处找!

3　你_____, 怎么就不给家里打个电话呢? 让一家人着急。

4　他说要来的, 怎么还不来呢? 要是真的不来, 可够_____的。

5　不知道为什么, 这几天她脾气特别坏, 为一点小事就_____。

6　你怎么一个人在这儿? 我还以为这儿没人呢, _____!

7　哎, 你看车坏了! 这地方_____的, 上哪儿去找人帮忙呀?

8　你的钱包真的丢了啊? _____麻烦了, 马上给警察局打电话吧。

D. Choose the expression from the following list that best corresponds to the underlined words or phrases:

> 聊个没完　　按说　　　真要命
> 没影儿了　　坏蛋　　　倒也是

1　你们这些小<u>东西</u>, 又想骗我, 是不是?

2　你的话<u>是对的</u>, 要是现在不去就没机会去了。

3　<u>真糟糕</u>, 我的作业呢? 是不是你们给藏起来了?

4　这门课挺容易, <u>应该</u>不会考不好。

5　我弟弟呀, 早就<u>不知道上哪儿去了</u>, 他才不在家里坐着呢!

6　他们是老朋友, 一见面就要<u>说上几个钟头的话</u>。

───■───

ANSWER KEY

Exercise A (Dialogue 1)

1　嘴刁

2　呵

3　饥不择食

4　难伺候

5　也

6　哎哟

7　耍嘴皮子

8　尝尝看（... ...看）

Exercise B (Dialogue 1)

1　舍得

2　饿扁了

3　垫点儿

4　别啰嗦

5 就是 (好是好，就是...)

6 左也不是右也不是 (...也不是...也不是)

Exercise C (Dialogue 2)

1 逗

2 看你 (看...)

3 也真是

4 缺德

5 发火

6 吓我一跳

7 前不着村后不着店

8 那可 (那可...了)

Exercise D (Dialogue 2)

1 坏蛋

2 倒也是

3 真要命

4 按说

5 没影儿了

6 聊个没完 (...个没完)

▌ MEN AND WOMEN

男女有别 (Between the sexes there should be a prudent reserve)

China has a long feudalist tradition, and until the middle of the last century relations between the sexes could be summed up by the expression 男女授受不亲 (It is improper for men and women to touch each other's hand in passing objects). Most Chinese still believe in and follow 男女有别 (Between the sexes there should be a prudent reserve). Nowadays, you can find all kinds of behavior and deportment in China. Male and female friends, colleagues, and relatives usually avoid touching and hugging. Except for those who admire and learn Western culture, even father and adult daughter seldom hug each other. Many Chinese would feel embarrassed to see people hugging or kissing in front of them. Men usually do not take the initiative to shake hands with women. Quite a few Chinese do not have the western concept of "ladies first": they do not open doors, pull out chairs, or help women into their coats. In social situations, the woman usually is expected to display the same etiquette as the male: she should stand up when she is introduced to others or offered a beverage.

人家不是那号人
还有人管他叫帅哥呢

GOSSIPING
•
DISBELIEF
•
OPINIONS ON CHARACTER

CONVERSATION A:

Simplified

李一丁跟朋友王小梅一起在一家酒吧聊天。

李一丁: 你看, 那边儿刚进来的是谁?

王小梅: 那不是李新平吗? **人家**现在**发**了。

李一丁: 跟他一块儿那女的是他老婆吧? **够精神的**!

王小梅: 不是, 我认识他太太。

李一丁: **瞧这亲热劲儿**! 还给他正衣领儿呢, 是小蜜还是二奶?

王小梅: 不可能。

傍大款 (lit: (a girl) lean on big money) Gold digging

Yiding Li and his friend Xiaomei Wang are chatting in a bar.

Li:	Look, who's that who just came in?
Wang:	Isn't that Xinping Li? He's rolling in money now.
Li:	Is that girl with him his wife? Pretty good looking!
Wang:	No, I know his wife.
Li:	They really like each other! She's adjusting his collar. Is she a mistress or wife number two?
Wang:	That's impossible.

李一丁：　**这不**, 他还**动手动脚**的, 给那女的弄头发呢,
　　　　　就差亲嘴儿了!

王小梅：　**你小子别瞎说**, 人家不是**那号人**!

李一丁：　现在的女孩儿, **傍大款儿的多的是**。他发财
　　　　　了, 还能没人找他? **不乱搞才怪呢**!

王小梅：　不会吧, 他挺正经的。

李一丁：　你看你, 大活人在你眼前表演你还不信!

王小梅：　哎, 这不又来了个男的, 还领着孩子呢。那女
　　　　　的跟他们准是一家子。

李一丁：　不会吧? 那她是李新平的什么人哪?

王小梅：　妹妹呗! 你仔细瞧瞧, 她长得多象李新平!

李一丁：　我这可是**乱点鸳鸯**了。我跟你说, 咱俩刚才
　　　　　说的话你可别告诉他。啊?

王小梅：　你呀, 怎么学得这么**事儿**了?

———————◼————————

Traditional

李一丁跟朋友王小梅一起在一家酒吧聊天。

李一丁：　你看, 那邊兒剛進來的是誰?

王小梅：　那不是李新平嗎? **人家**現在**發**了。

李一丁：　跟他一塊兒那女的是他老婆吧? **夠精神的**!

王小梅：　不是, 我認識他太太。

Li:	Look, he's making moves on her too! He's getting her hair done. The only thing left is making out!
Wang:	Get out of here, brat! He's not that kind of guy!
Li:	There are plenty of gold digging girls these days. He's rich; how can there not be someone after him? It'd be weird if he weren't cheating!
Wang:	That can't be. He's pretty straight-laced.
Li:	Look at you, a live performance right in front of you and you still don't believe it?
Wang:	Hey, see how another guy just joined them, and he's got a kid. Must be that girl's family.
Li:	Are you sure? Then what's her relationship with Xinping Li?
Wang:	It's his little sister! Look closely, she looks just like Xinping Li!
Li:	I just played matchmaker. Now let me tell you, you don't tell any of what I just said to him. Okay?
Wang:	Now really, since when did you become such a nag?

———■———

李一丁: **瞧這親熱勁兒**！還給他正衣領兒呢, 是小蜜還是二奶？

王小梅: 不可能。

李一丁: **這不**, 他還**動手動腳**的, 給那女的弄頭髮呢, **就差親嘴兒了**！

王小梅: **你小子別瞎說**, 人家不是**那號人**！

李一丁： 现在的女孩儿，**傍大款兒的多的是**。他發財了，還能沒人找他？**不亂搞才怪呢！**

王小梅： 不會吧，他挺正經的。

李一丁： 你看你，大活人在你眼前表演你還不信！

王小梅： 哎，這不又來了個男的，還領著孩子呢。那女的跟他們准是一家子。

李一丁： 不會吧？那她是李新平的什麼人哪？

王小梅： 妹妹唄！你仔細瞧瞧，她長得多象李新平！

李一丁： 我這可是**亂點鴛鴦**了。我跟你說，咱倆剛才說的話你可別告訴他。啊？

王小梅： 你呀，怎麼學得這麼**事兒**了？

———————■———————

词语注释

* **人家**现在发了。
  人家 This is a pronoun that can substituted for "he," "she," "they," or "I," and is usually used with a certain connotation, whether positive or negative. Here 人家 means "he" with a connotation of admiration. For example, 你大概还不知道，人家已经大学毕业了。"You might not know that he has graduated from college."

* 人家现在**发**了。
  发 Here this expression means "get rich." It's a colloquial form of 发财，"got rich." For example, 咱们同学中象他这么发的人不多。"Among our classmates, there are not many as rich as him."

- 跟他一块儿那女的是他老婆吧? **够精神的**!
  够...的 "quite" or "really." For example, 那本书够厚的。"That book is really thick."

- 跟他一块儿那女的是他老婆吧? 够**精神**的!
  精神 (精神 [jīngshen] vigorous) A colloquial version of "pretty," "beautiful," or "handsome" that can be applied to men and women. For example, 你弟弟长得真精神。"Your little brother is so handsome."

- **瞧这亲热劲儿**!
  瞧...劲儿 (瞧 [qiáo] look; 劲儿 [jìnr] manner; air)
  A colloquial pattern to express "Look, what a ... manner!" A pronoun and 这 or 那 are often put in front of 劲儿。 For example, 瞧你那傻劲儿! "Look, how stupid you are!"

- **这不**, 他还动手动脚的
  这不 "See" with the connotation of "I told you so!" For example, 我跟你说过他会来的, 这不, 他来了。 "I told you that he would come. See, he is here."

- 这不, 他还**动手动脚**的
  动手动脚 Literally, "to do things with one's hands and feet." The idiom is often used to blame a guy for being too fresh with a girl. For example, 别跟我动手动脚! "Don't touch me!"

- 还给那女的弄头发呢, **就差亲嘴儿了**!
  就差...了 "There's only ... left," meaning that things are almost to the point of .... For example, "你作业做完了吗?" "就差一点儿了。" "Have you finished your homework?" "There's only a little bit left." Another example, "他们夫妻俩关系怎么样?" "天天打架, 就差离婚了!" "How is the relationship between the couple?" "They fight every day; the only thing left is divorce."

- 还给那女的弄头发呢, 就差**亲嘴儿**了!
  亲嘴儿 A colloquial form of "kiss." For example, 他们怎么老在亲嘴儿啊? "Why are they always kissing?"

- **你小子**别瞎说
  你小子 (小子 [xiǎozi] boy; fellow; chap) 小子 This term is similar to "brat," and is a colloquial way to address a boy. Its connotation depends on the relationship between the speaker and the person who is called 小子. It can express intimacy, but can also be used to show contempt or to insult. In 你小子, 你 is in apposition to 小子, just like你们 "you," in 你们夫妻俩, "you and your wife." For example, 你小子怎么跑得这么快? "How did you run that fast, brat?"

- 你小子别**瞎说**
  瞎说 (瞎 [xiā] blind) "Talk irresponsibly"; "talk rubbish." For example, 别瞎说! "Don't talk nonsense!" 别瞎说 is often used like "be quiet" or "shut up." It is impolite, even a little rude, but it is not offensive between close friends. 我叫你别瞎说, 你怎么不听啊? "I told you not to spout nonsense. Why don't you ever listen?"

- 人家不是**那号人**!
  那号人 The colloquial form of "that kind of person." For example, 他可不是你说得那号人. "He is not that kind of person."

- 现在的女孩儿, **傍大款儿**的多的是。
  傍大款儿 (傍 [bàng] depend on; attach oneself to; 款 [kuǎn] money) Literally "attach oneself to a rich person." This idiom means "to be a gold digger." For example, 她才不会去傍大款呢。 "She'll never go gold digging."

- 现在的女孩儿, **傍大款儿的多的是.**
  ...多的是 "There are a lot of …." For example, 这儿好电影多的是, 你要看哪个? "There are a lot of good movies here. Which one do you want?"

- **不乱搞才怪呢!**
  不...才怪呢 "It will be strange if not …." This is a pattern used to emphasize the certainty that "…" will be true. For example, 这天气, 不下雨才怪呢。"With this weather, it'd be strange if it didn't rain."

- **不乱搞才怪呢!**
  乱搞 "to act promiscuously." One meaning of **搞** is "to carry on an affair with somebody" or "be promiscuous." For example, 这人年纪也不轻了, 怎么还乱搞? He's not young anymore, why is he still fooling around?

- **我这可是乱点鸳鸯了。**
  乱点鸳鸯 (鸳鸯 [yuānyang] mandarin duck; an affectionate couple) "to make a mistake about the romantic involvement of others." For example, 你不知道他有没有女朋友, 就别乱点鸳鸯了。"You don't know if he has a girlfriend, so stop playing matchmaker."

- **你呀, 怎么学得这么事儿了?**
  事儿 often serves as an adjective that means "wordy" or "troublesome." It also means "meddlesome." For example, 那个人可事儿了, 什么都管。"That person is so meddlesome, she pokes her nose into everything."

CONVERSATION B:

Simplified

星期五晚上, 周云和刘芳在宿舍里说话。

周云:　小莉呢? 我正要叫上她跟咱们一块儿去看电影呢, 怎么**一转眼儿**就不见了?

刘芳：　她才不跟咱们一块儿去呢?

周云：　咱们怎么她啦? 我是怕她**一个人闷得慌**, 才说叫上她。

刘芳：　人家有**心上人**啦, 哪会跟咱一块儿去!

周云：　真的? 是谁呀? 我怎么一点儿也不知道? 你没搞错吧?

刘芳：　我也才听说, 说得**有鼻子有眼儿**的。**说是**她跟英语系的林山**好上了**。就是那个**大个子**。

周云：　还有人**管他叫帅哥**呢, 我可**看不出他有什么帅的**。

刘芳：　对, 就是他! 听说他还跟别人好着呢, 就又来**勾小莉**!

周云：　他的**底儿**我最清楚了, 我们在一个班上过课。他除了个子大, **要什么没什么**, 又没人品, 又没本事。

刘芳：　听说他**特能说**, 特会甜言蜜语。

周云：　**就是**, 所以挺**招女生喜欢**。他今儿追这个, 明儿追那个, 过不了多久又**跟人家吹**。

刘芳：　这人也太**差劲**了!

周云：　就是! 小莉可别**上他的当**! 咱得跟小莉说说, 让她小心点儿。

刘芳：　人家要是好上了, 你的话她才**听不进去**呢。还以为你是**吃醋**了呢。

周云: 别瞎说! 我这可是为她好。

刘芳: 我看咱**还是少管闲事儿好**。

周云: 小莉**要人品有人品, 要相貌有相貌**, 学习又**拔
尖儿**。 林山哪儿**配得上她**? 她这不是**鲜花插
在牛粪上了吗**? 太可惜了!

刘芳: 等小莉回来, 咱**先问问他们到底是怎么回事
儿再说**吧。

---■---

It's Friday night. Yun Zhou and Fang Liu are talking in the dorm.

Zhou: Where's Xiaoli? I was just about to invite her to the
movie with us, so how come I turn around and she's
gone?

Liu: She's not going to go with us!

Zhou: What did we do to her? I was afraid she'd be lonely
by herself, that's why I was going to take her.

Liu: She's going out with someone. How can she go
anywhere with us!

Zhou: Really? Who? How come I don't know anything?
You're not mistaken, are you?

Liu: I just heard it myself, and they were very specific. It's
Lin from the English department. That tall guy.

Zhou: And there are people calling him cute—I don't see
anything cute about him.

Liu: Yeah, that's him! I heard he's still going out with
someone, and now he's seducing Xiaoli!

Zhou: Nobody knows better than me what kind of person he is, as we took the same class. Besides being big, he's got nothing else—no character, no ability.

Liu: I heard he knows what to say; he's really good at sweet talk.

Zhou: No wonder that's why the girls like him. Today he chases this one, tomorrow that one, and then breaks up not long after that.

Liu: What a creep!

Zhou: Yeah! We can't let Xiaoli get fooled by him! We gotta talk to her, tell her to be careful.

Liu: If she's into him, she's not going to listen to anything you say. She'll just think you're jealous.

Zhou: Don't say that! I'm looking out for her.

Liu: I think we should mind our own business.

Zhou: Xiaoli's a good person, she's pretty, and she gets good grades. You think Lin deserves her? Isn't she like a flower on a dung-hill? It's a pity!

Liu: Let's first ask Xiaoli what's going on.

Traditional

星期五晚上, 周雲和劉芳在宿舍裏說話。

周雲: 小莉呢？我正要叫上她跟咱們一塊兒去看電影呢, 怎麼**一轉眼兒**就不見了？

劉芳: 她才不跟咱們一塊兒去呢？

周雲: 咱們怎麼她啦？我是怕她**一個人悶得慌**，才說叫上她。

劉芳: 人家有**心上人**啦，哪會跟咱一塊兒去！

周雲: 真的？是誰呀？我怎麼一點兒也不知道？你沒搞錯吧？

劉芳: 我也才聽說，說得**有鼻子有眼兒**的。**說是**她跟英語系的林山**好上了**。就是那個**大個子**。

周雲: 還有人**管他叫帥哥**呢，我可**看不出他有什麼帥的**。

劉芳: 對，就是他！聽說他還跟別人好著呢，就又來**勾**小莉！

周雲: 他的**底兒**我最清楚了，我們在一個班上過課。他除了個子大，**要什麼沒什麼**，又沒人品，又沒本事。

劉芳: 聽說他**特能說**，特會甜言蜜語。

周雲: **就是**，所以挺**招女生喜歡**。他今兒追這個，明兒**追那個**，過不了多久又**跟人家吹**。

劉芳: 這人也太**差勁**了！

周雲: 就是！小莉可別**上他的當**！咱得跟小莉說說，讓她小心點兒。

劉芳: 人家要是好上了，你的話她才**聽不進去**呢。還以為你是**吃醋**了呢。

周雲: 別瞎說！我這可是為她好。

劉芳：　我看咱**還是少管閒事兒好**。

周雲：　小莉**要人品有人品**,**要相貌有相貌**,學習又**拔尖兒**。林山哪兒**配得上**她？她這不是**鮮花插在牛糞上**了嗎？太可惜了！

劉芳：　等小莉回來,咱**先問問他們到底是怎麼回事兒再說**吧。

———◼———

词语注释

- 怎么**一转眼儿**就不见了
  一转眼 (转 [zhuǎn] turn) Literally "A turn of the eye." This idiom is a shortened version of 一转眼的功夫, meaning "in an instant." For example, 一转眼就作完了。"It was done in a moment."

- 我是怕她**一个人**待着闷得慌
  一个人 "Alone"; "by oneself." For example, 她就喜欢这样一个人坐在家里。"She just likes to sit at home alone in this way."

- 我是怕她一个人**闷得慌**
  …得慌 (慌 [huāng] flurried, confused) This pattern means "awfully …," or "unbearably …" For example, 她觉得饿得慌。"She felt awfully hungry."

- 人家有**心上人**啦,
  心上人 "Sweetheart" or "lover." For example, 她就是你的心上人吧? "She is your sweetheart, right?"

- 说得**有鼻子有眼儿**的
有鼻子有眼儿 Literally "complete with nose and eyes," this idiom means "in great detail." It also carries a connotation that the story is second hand. For example, 他说的这事儿可能是真的, 有鼻子有眼儿的。 "His story might be true, since it contains great detail."

- **说是**她跟英语系的林山好上了
说是 "It was said." This idiom is used to relate a story told by others. For example, 我听说过这事儿, 说是他们都常去体育馆, 所以就成了朋友了。 "I heard the story, too. It was said that both of them often went to the gym. So they became friends."

- 说是她跟英语系的林山**好上了**
好上了 Literally "become good with each other." Without context, the idiom means: "have become lovers." With context, the idiom could mean: "have become friends with each other." For example, 你知道吗? 丽丽 跟(小华)好上了。 "Do you know that Lili and Xiaohua have become lovers?" 小弟 跟 小妹, 刚才还吵架呢, 现在又好上了。 "My younger brother and younger sister have become friends again after their quarrel moments ago."

- 就是那个**大个子**
...个子 "... fellow." 大个子has the same meaning, "tall fellow," as in 高个子, 大个儿, or 高个儿。 In this pattern, ... can be 大, 小, 高, or 矮; and 个子 can also be 个儿。 They are all commonly used colloquial terms. 个子 or 个儿, which means "height," can also combine with 小 or 矮 to mean "small fellow." For example, 那个大个子和那两个小个子都是我们班同学。 "The tall fellow and the two small fellows are all my classmates."

- 还有人**管他叫帅哥**呢
  管…**叫**… "to call… …" For example, 我管他妹妹叫小王。 "I call his younger sister 'Little Wang.'" 管 serves as a preposition here and functions similar to 把. In this pattern, the " " usually refers to person.

- 我可**看不出他有什么帅的**
  看不出… 有什么… 的 A frequently used expression: "don't see anything … about …" For example, 我看不出这游戏有什么好玩儿的。 "I don't see anything interesting about this game."

- 听说他还跟别人好着呢，就又来**勾**小莉!
  勾 is a colloquial form of "to seduce" with negative connotations. For example, 他最会勾女孩儿了, 你得小心点儿。 "He's very good at picking up girls, so you had better be careful."

- 他的**底儿**我最清楚了
  底儿 "Somebody's past"; "somebody's unsavory background." For example: 他可不想让别人知道他的底儿。 "He doesn't want others to know about his past."

- 他除了个子大，**要什么没什么**
  要什么没什么 literally "to have nothing one needs," this idiom means "to have no good qualities." This expression is the negative form of the expression 要什么有什么 "to have everything one needs." 什么 can refer to either material items or abstract items according to the context.

- 听说他**特能说**
  特能说 特 is a colloquial equivalent of 特别 or 很. 特能说 means "to be a smooth talker." For example, 我还以为他不太会说话呢, 其实他特能说。 "I thought he wasn't good at talking, but he is actually a smooth talker."

- **就是**, 所以挺招女生喜欢。

  就是 A colloquial response showing agreement with other people's opinion: "exactly," "right," "precisely." For example, 我说 "这个周末过得太没意思了, 咱们不该来这儿。" 她说: "就是, 以后不来了。" I said: "This weekend is way too boring. We shouldn't have come here in the first place." She said: "Right, we're not coming back."

- 就是, 所以挺**招女生喜欢**。

  招...喜欢 (招 [zhāo] attract; provoke) "to attract (someone)" This pattern is used to describe clever, cute, or attractive traits in human beings or animals. For example, 看, 那个孩子多可爱啊! 真招(人)喜欢! "Look, what a cute baby! He's so attractive!"

- 他**今儿**追这个, **明儿**追那个

  今儿..., 明儿... Literally "today ..., tomorrow ...," this parallel pattern suggests a changing variety of states or actions. Here it has a negative connotation, suggesting infidelity in love because the subject is chasing a different girl everyday. The pattern has a positive connotation in another example: 你们的活动可真多啊, 今儿去爬山, 明儿去野营。 "You guys have so many things to do, hiking today, camping tomorrow."

- 过不了多久又**跟人家吹**。

  跟...吹 "break up with (somebody)" The colloquial term 吹 means "to break off" or "to screw up." The pattern 跟...吹 means "to break up with ...." For example, 我相信李丽不会跟张明吹。 "I believe that Lili will not break up with Zhang Ming."

- 这人也太**差劲**了!

  差劲 (差 [chà] short of; 劲 [jìn] strength) "disappointing," "of low quality" For example, 我没想到这个人会这么差劲。 "I didn't expect him to be such a creep."

- 小莉可别**上他的当**!

  上...的当 "Be fooled by ...." 上当 is a colloquial word that means "to be fooled." For example, 你这可不是第一次上她的当了。 "This is not your first time to be fooled by her."

- 人家要是好上了, 你的话她才**听不进去**呢。

  听不进去 "Does not want to hear it." 她从来听不进我的话去。 "She never wants to hear your words."

- 还以为你是**吃醋**了呢。

  吃醋 A colloquial form of "to be jealous." This idiom usually means: "to be jealous of a rival in love." For example, 看见丽丽跟那个男孩在一起, 她就吃醋了。 "She was jealous when she saw that Lili was with the boy." 吃醋 can be used in the pattern of 吃(...的)醋, "to be jealous of ...." For example, 看见丽丽跟那个男孩在一起, 她就吃丽丽的醋了。 "She was jealous of Lili when she saw Lili was with the boy."

- 我看咱**还是少管闲事儿好**

  还是...好 "Had better..." or "Should...." This pattern expresses a preference for an alternative. For example, 你还是先给他打个电话再去好。 "You'd better call him before you go there." 都那么晚了, 还是不去的好。 "It's already so late; you'd better not go."

- 我看咱还是**少管闲事儿好**

  管闲事 (管 [guǎn] bother about; 闲事 [xiánshì] other people's business) Also as in 多管闲事, "poke one's nose into other people's business." 少管闲事 is often used in an imperative sentence: "Mind one's own business." For example, 她总喜欢管闲事。 "She always likes to poke her nose into other people's business." 你能不能少管点儿闲事儿? "Could you mind your own business?"

- 小莉**要人品有人品, 要相貌有相貌**
要...有..., 要...有... This is a parallel structure that means "have both ... and ...." For example, 这地方真漂亮, 要山有山, 要水有水。 "The scenery here is so pretty; there's both mountain and river." The negative form of this pattern is 要...没..., 要...没...,"to have neither ... nor ...." For example, 那儿风景一点儿也不好, 要山没山, 要水没水。 "The scenery there is not good at all; there is neither mountain nor river."

- 学习又**拔尖儿**
拔尖儿 "Tiptop." For example, 她是这个班上最拔尖儿的学生。 "She is the top student of the class."

- 林山哪儿**配得上**她?
配得上 (配 [pèi] deserve) "Deserving," "worthy." For example, 她的表演完全配得上她的名气。 "Her performance befits her reputation."

- 她这不是**鲜花插在牛粪上**了吗?
鲜花插在牛粪上 "flower on a dung hill," "a bad match." This idiom describes a situation where a woman is married to someone undeserving of her. For example, 她怎么就跟他结婚了呢? 真是鲜花插在牛粪上。 "How could she have married him? It's just like a flower on a cow patty!"

- 咱**先问问**他们到底是怎么回事儿**再说**吧。
先...再说 Literally, "First ..., then talk about it." With the connotation, "put the matter aside for the time being," the idiom means: "first ...." For example, 你累了吧? 先休息休息再说。 "You must be very tired. Please take a rest first."

VOCABULARY

瞧	[qiáo]	look; see
亲热	[qīnrè]	intimate
劲儿	[jìnr]	manner; air
小蜜	[xiǎomì]	Cutie-pie; little sweetie
二奶	[èrnǎi]	mistress; illegal spouse
动手动脚	[dòngshǒudòngjiǎo]	move one's hands and feet; touch
弄	[nòng]	manage; handle
亲嘴	[qīnzuǐ]	kiss
傍	[bàng]	depend on; attach oneself to
大款	[dàkuǎn]	rich person; big wheel
发财	[fācái]	get rich; make a fortune
乱搞	[luàngǎo]	carry on an affair with somebody
怪	[guài]	strange
挺	[tǐng]	very; rather
正经	[zhèngjǐng]	decent; respectable; honest
活人	[huórén]	a living person
眼前	[yǎnqián]	before one's eyes
表演	[biǎoyǎn]	perform
领着	[lǐngzhe]	lead; bring
准是	[zhǔnshì]	certainly; for sure
待着	[dāizhe]	stay
闷	[mèn]	bored; in low spirits
心上人	[xīnshàngrén]	sweetheart; lover
大个子	[dàgèzi]	tall fellow
帅哥	[shuàigē]	handsome young chap

勾	[gōu]	seduce
底儿	[dǐr]	past; unsavory background
除了	[chúle]	except; besides
人品	[rénpǐn]	moral quality; character
本事	[běnshì]	ability
甜言蜜语	[tiányánmìyǔ]	sweet words and honeyed phrases
招	[zhāo]	attract; provoke
追	[zhuī]	chase (or run) after; pursue
吹	[chuī]	break off; break up
差劲	[chàjìn]	disappointing
上当	[shàngdàng]	fooled
吃醋	[chīcù]	be jealous (of a rival in love)
瞎说	[xiāshuō]	talk irresponsibly
管	[guǎn]	bother about
闲事	[xiánshì]	other people's business
相貌	[xiàngmào]	facial features; appearance
拔尖儿	[bájiānr]	tiptop; top notch
配	[pèi]	deserve; be worthy of
鲜花	[xiānhuā]	fresh flowers
插	[chā]	insert
牛粪	[niúfèn]	cow dung
可惜	[kěxī]	it's a pity; it's too bad
到底	[dàodǐ]	finally; after all

EXERCISES

A. Fill in the spaces with the appropriate words or phrases:

> 动手动脚　发了　就差　你小子　精神
> 乱点鸳鸯　这不　乱搞　亲嘴儿　傍大款儿

1 今天早上我就告诉你要下雨，_____，现在已经下了。

2 他爱跟女孩子_____，所以女孩子们都不愿意理他。

3 有人说年轻漂亮的女孩子都喜欢_____，这可真是瞎说。

4 老王现在_____，你看他买了辆那么贵的车。

5 他太太和他离婚了，因为他老是在外面_____。

6 _____ 真厉害，居然得了全校第一名!

7 小王的女朋友不是丽丽,小李的女朋友也不是云云,你别_____。

8 他什么坏事都干过,_____杀人放火了。

9 小李的女朋友长得可_____了,你见过她吗?

10 他们俩怎么老爱当着那么多人_____呀?

B. Choose the expression from the following list that best corresponds to the underlined words or phrases:

> 不发财才怪呢　那号人　瞎说　人家
> 瞧这高兴劲儿　多的是　事儿　够热闹的

1 你不清楚的事情别<u>乱说</u>, 要不就该有麻烦了。

2 她的话你都听见了, 你说我是她说的<u>那种人</u>吗?

3 好玩儿的地方<u>多极了</u>, 你想去哪儿? 我带你去。

4 他们都说那个老太太可<u>爱管闲事</u>了, 什么都要管。

5 别开玩笑! <u>我</u>跟你说要紧事呢。

6 今天<u>可真热呀</u>, 坐着不动还出汗。

7 你们队是不是赢他们队了? <u>这么高兴</u>!

8 他那么会做生意, <u>怎么会不发呢</u>!

C. Fill in the spaces with the appropriate words or phrases:

> 有鼻子有眼儿　大个子　　心上人　　就是　　　底儿
> 要资金有资金　特能说　　有什么　　一个人　勾

1 情人节又快到了, 大家都在想着要给自己
　的_____买礼物。

2 我根本不认识他, 可他说跟我一起打过球, 还说
　得_____的。

3 我说今天人真多。她说: "_____, 人太多了, 咱们
　回去吧。"

4 那小子_____, 所以女孩子都喜欢他, 咱可比不了
　他。

5 你看, 这个班的女生不理他了, 他就去_____那个
　班的女生。

6 咱们班同学都知道他的_____, 他才骗不了咱们
　呢。

7 我女朋友胆小，_____在家害怕，所以我常去她那儿陪着她。

8 一般来说，篮球队员都是_____，足球队员可不一定。

9 那个公司_____，要人才有人才，所以发展得很快。

10 我看不出西餐_____好吃的，我就爱吃中国饭。

D. Choose the expression from the following list that best corresponds to the underlined words or phrases:

> 上坏人的当　　管他叫　　一转眼　　再说　　说是
> 要什么没什么　　管闲事　　闷得慌　　差劲　　好上了

1 这个饭馆儿的服务真好，你刚点完菜，<u>一会儿</u>就端上来了。

2 你知道小李的事儿吗？<u>听说</u>他酒后开车让警察抓起来了。

3 他不但每天上课都迟到，而且还不作作业，<u>真不象话</u>。

4 老张常告诉自己的家人少<u>管别人的事</u>。

5 那地方真穷，<u>什么都没有</u>，我没去过那么穷的地方。

6 你看，我们班的林木跟李丽<u>交起朋友来了</u>。

7 他是你爸爸的弟弟，你应该<u>叫他</u>"叔叔"。

8 你要是一个人呆着没事干<u>觉得闷</u>，就出去散散步。

9 她总怕<u>坏人骗她</u>，所以很少跟不认识的人说话。

10 该准备旅行了, 我看还是先订机票后作别的事吧。

E. Fill in the spaces with the appropriate words or phrases:

配得上　　　　　拔尖儿　　招人喜欢　明儿　吹
鲜花插在牛粪上　听不进去　吃醋　　　还是

1 这些十五六岁的中学生, 就是_____父母的话。

2 她特别爱_____, 一看见女孩子跟她丈夫说话就生气。

3 一个人的能力有限, 就是天才, 也不会什么都_____。

4 只有象他那样有成就的人才_____得这么大的奖。

5 她那么好, 怎么就跟这么坏的人结婚了呢? 真是_____了。

6 小孩子都是挺可爱的, 可是一打起架来就不_____了。

7 你今儿要买这个, _____要买那个, 咱哪儿有那么多钱啊?

8 她这几天那么不高兴, 是不是跟男朋友_____了。

9 有人爱看电影, 有人爱运动, 可我觉得_____上网最好玩儿。

ANSWER KEY

Exercise A (Dialogue 1)

1　这不
2　动手动脚
3　傍大款儿
4　发了(发)
5　乱搞
6　你小子
7　乱点鸳鸯
8　就差（就差...了）
9　精神
10　亲嘴儿

Exercise B (Dialogue 1)

1　瞎说
2　那号人
3　多的是
4　事儿
5　人家
6　够热的（够...的）
7　瞧这高兴劲儿（瞧...劲儿）
8　不发财才怪呢（不...才怪呢）

Exercise C (Dialogue 2)

1　心上人
2　有鼻子有眼儿
3　就是
4　特能说
5　勾

6　底儿
7　一个人
8　大个子（...个子）
9　要资金有资金（要...有...，要...有...）
10　有什么（看不出 ... 有什么 ... 的）

Exercise D (Dialogue 2)

1　一转眼
2　说是
3　差劲
4　管闲事
5　要什么没什么
6　好上了（...跟...好上了）
7　管他叫（管...叫...）
8　闷得慌（...得慌）
9　上坏人的当（上...的当）
10　再说（先...再说）

Exercise E (Dialogue 2)

1　听不进去
2　吃醋
3　拔尖儿
4　配得上
5　鲜花插在牛粪上
6　招人喜欢（招...喜欢）
7　明儿（今儿...，明儿...）
8　吹（跟...吹）
9　还是（还是...好）

WHY THE CHINESE ASK SO MANY PERSONAL QUESTIONS?

语言点: 映照性文化 Reflective Culture

You might have heard or noticed that some Chinese like to ask personal questions, even the first time they meet each other. They do not only ask questions like "How old are you?" "Are you married?" or "Do you have a girlfriend?" but also, "How much is your salary?" It's surprising that Chinese people will answer these seemingly offensive questions sincerely. One explanation is that Chinese communication is "reflective" (映照性文化): people like to compare themselves with others through communication and socialization. They think they will be able to talk or behave more properly if they know each other well. For example, some areas have the custom of using the terms of family members to address each other. People can decide to call you either " 大哥"(elder brother) or "老弟"(younger brother) only after knowing your age. People are also able to avoid offensive language or behavior better when they know what would make you unhappy. So, the real purpose of the seemingly offensive questions is to avoid any offending.

Why do Chinese people have to bother about with this constant "reflection" or "comparison?" On the one hand, everybody lives within the human relations of a society: you are the son of your father, father of your son, husband of your wife, citizen of your country, etc. On the other hand, according to the traditional Chinese value system, the individual is always the least important one in this relational society. The country is the most important, then your patriarchal clan, and then your family, and, finally, yourself. Your proper behavior or speaking must take into account your status, capacity, and position in relation to the people around you.

咱俩好像在哪儿见过嘀，说爱就爱上了

MAKING FRIENDS WITH A GIRL
•
FLATTERING A GIRL
•
SELF-INTRODUCTION
•
EXPRESSING LOVE AND AFFECTION

CONVERSATION A:

Simplified

在酒吧里, 高山先生和张小姐, 两个二十出头的年青人谈了起来。

高山： 你好! 我看你怎么这么面熟啊? 咱俩好像在哪儿见过。

张小姐： 是吗? 你肯定没看错吗?

高山： 不敢肯定。其实以前见没见过也**不要紧**, 现在咱就认识一下儿吧. 我叫高山, 请问你贵姓?

张小姐： **免贵姓张**。

高山： 张小姐, 能认识你, 太高兴了!

情人眼里出西施 (lit: "There is a beauty in the lover's eyes.") Everything appears better to a lover's eyes. (See page 95)

In a bar, Mr. Gao and Miss Zhang, two twenty-something's, talk

Gao:	Hi! Why do you look so familiar? I think we met somewhere.
Zhang:	Really? You sure you're not mistaken?
Gao:	I'm not positive. But it's okay even if we haven't met; let's get to know each other right now. I'm Gao, and your noble name?
Zhang:	I'm Zhang, without the nobility.
Gao:	Miss Zhang, I'm very pleased to meet you!

张小姐: 这儿到处都是人, 你**干吗**就要认识我呀?

高山: 你的气质特别好, 我进来**一眼就看见你了**, 再说你又挺面熟的。这儿**人多是多, 就是谁也比不上你**。

张小姐: 光看气质哪儿成! 俗话说 **"知人知面不知心"**。

高山: **话是这么说, 可我一见着你就觉得你不错,** 所以**说什么也得交个朋友**。

张小姐: 你不是一看见气质不错的女孩儿就想交朋友吧?

高山: 看你**说到哪儿去了!** 我跟不认识的女孩儿交朋友, 这可是头一回。**说实话,** 我的朋友都是慢慢儿认识的。

张小姐: **我吧,** 不随便交朋友。不过今儿咱**算认识了,** 以后**说不定**还会再碰上呢。

高山: 以后你就知道了, 我这人**好说话儿好共事儿,** 朋友有难处我准帮忙。**日久见人心,** 你准不会后悔有我这么个朋友。**对了,** 咱们**先交换个手机号码再接着聊**怎么样?

Zhang: There are so many people here, why did you come meet me?

Gao: You looked like a good person. I noticed as soon as I walked in here, and you looked familiar. There are a lot of people here, but no one to compare to you.

Zhang: I look like a good person? They say, "Know the person, know the face, but not the heart."

Gao: That's what they say, but I liked you as soon as I saw you. That's why we have to be friends, no matter what.

Zhang: Do you try to make friends with every girl who looks like a good person?

Gao: Now look where you're going with that! I don't make friends with just any girls I don't know; this is the very first time. Honestly, even my friends I got to know slowly.

Zhang: Me, I don't make friends with just anyone. But you can say that we know each other now. We might see each other somewhere.

Gao: Just so you know, I'm easy to talk to and fun to be with. I never let down friends in trouble. You get to know people after a while, and you won't regret having me as a friend. Oh yeah, how about we exchange cell phone numbers and then talk some more?

Traditional

在酒吧裏, 高山先生和張小姐, 兩個二十出頭的年青人談了起來。

高山: 你好! 我看你怎麼這麼面熟啊? 咱倆好像在哪兒見過。

張小姐: 是嗎? 你肯定沒看錯嗎?

高山: 不敢肯定。其實以前見沒見過也**不要緊**, 現在咱就認識一下兒吧。我叫高山, 請問你貴姓?

張小姐: **免貴姓張**。

高山: 張小姐, 能認識你, 太高興了!

張小姐: 這兒到處都是人, 你**幹嗎**就要認識我呀?

高山: 你的氣質特別好, 我進來**一眼就看見你了**, 再說你又挺面熟的。這兒**人多是多, 就是誰也比不上你。**

張小姐: 光看氣質哪兒成! 俗話說 "知人知面不知心"。

高山: **話是這麼說, 可我一見著你就覺得你不錯**, 所以**說什麼也得交個朋友**。

張小姐: 你不是一看見氣質不錯的女孩兒就想交朋友吧?

高山: 看你**說到哪兒去了**! 我跟不認識的女孩兒交朋友, 這可是頭一回。**說實話**, 我的朋友都是慢慢兒認識的。

張小姐: **我吧**, 不隨便交朋友。不過今兒咱**算認識了**, 以後**說不定**還會再碰上呢。

高山: 以後你就知道了, 我這人**好說話兒**好**共事兒**, 朋友有難處我准幫忙。**日久見人心**, 你准不會後悔有我這麼個朋友。**對了**, 咱們**先交換個手機號碼再接著聊**怎麼樣?

———————————

词语注释

*   其实以前见没见过也**不要紧**
    不要紧 "It doesn't matter." For example, 你不会不要紧, 我来教你。"It doesn't matter if you don't know how to do it; I can tell you."

*   **免贵姓张**
    免贵姓… Literally, "Dismiss the honorable and my last name is Zhang." It's a polite form to answer the question: 请问您贵姓? "May I ask your honorable surname?"

*   你**干吗**就要认识我呀?
    干吗 ([gàn má]) "Why on earth." This is a colloquial form for asking why. For example, 今天不上课, 你干吗背书包呀? "We do not have class today; why do you carry your bag?"

*   我进来**一眼就**看见你了
    一眼就… "See … at first glance." For example, 昨天在街上我一眼就认出他来了。"Yesterday on the street I recognized him at first glance."

- 这儿人**多是多**,**就是谁也比不上你**.

  ...是...,就是... This is a pattern of concession, which means "... all right, but ...." For example, 这块手表好看是好看, 就是太贵了。 "The watch looks good all right, but it is too expensive." 我去是去, 就是得晚一点儿。 "I'm certainly well on my way, but I'll be a little bit late."

- 这儿人多是多, 就是谁也**比不上你**。

  比不上 "not to hold a candle to"; "cannot compare with"; "no match for." 比得上 "comparable"; "can be compared with." For example, 你住的那所房子比得上比不上这栋? "Is your house comparable with this one?"

- 俗话说 **"知人知面不知心"**

  知人知面不知心 This is an idiom that means: "We may know a man's exterior but not his heart." "It is impossible to judge a man's heart from his face." For example, 他昨天还是模范教师呢, 今天就因为性骚扰被关进监狱了, 真是知人之面不知心啊! "He was a model teacher yesterday, and now he's in jail for sexual harassment." "Really, you can know a person's face, but not his heart!"

- **话是这么说,** 可我一见着你就觉得你不错

  话是这么说, 可... "Although you could say that, but..." "You can say this, but..." Also as 说是这么说. This expression is usually followed by an adversative clause that is lead by 可是 or 可. A sentence with **话是这么说** expresses a different opinion with a softened tone. For example, 你说得对, 我有病就应该在家休息。 话是这么说, 可是这店里不能没有人, 我只有来上班! "Sure, if I'm sick I should stay home. You could say that, but this store can't be left alone."

- 话是这么说, 可我**一见着你就觉得你不错**

  一见着...就... "As soon as one sees..., (B)." 见着 is the colloquial form of 见 or 看见, so this pattern can be expressed as 一见...就... or 一见着...就....For example, 我家的狗一见着猫就要追, 怎么拦也拦不住。 "My dog will chase the cat as soon it sees one; I just cannot stop it no matter how hard I try."

- 所以**说什么也得交个朋友**

  说什么也得... This is a colloquial pattern for "have to ... no matter what." Here 说什么也 means "in any case" or "whatever happens." For example, 我今天说什么也得去开这个会。 "I have to attend the meeting no matter what." For example, 现在说什么也来不及了。 "It's too late now no matter what happens."

- 看你**说到哪儿去了!**

  说到哪儿去了 This is a mild negative form for "what you said is wrong." 想到哪儿去了 is also often used, which is a mild negative form for "What you are thinking is wrong." For example, if a wife asked her husband: 你是不是有情人了, 不爱我了? "Do you have another lover, and don't you love me anymore?" The husband could answer: 看你想到哪儿去了! "What are you talking about?"

- **说实话**, 我的朋友都是慢慢儿认识的。

  说实话 (实话 [shíhuà] truth) "Tell the truth"; "speak frankly." For example, 跟你说实话, 我已经不相信你了。 "To tell you the truth, I do not believe you anymore."

- **我吧**, 不随便交朋友。

  我吧 When the particle 吧 is used in the middle of a sentence, it needs a pause and often contrasts to somebody or something. For example, 我吧 is used to emphasize on 我 and contrast to other people. For example, 你喜欢上网? 我吧, 就喜欢看电影。 "You like to go online? As for me, I just like to watch movies."

- 不过今儿咱**算**认识**了**

  算… "Regard as …"; "count as …." For example, 他可以算一个作家。"He can be counted as a writer." 你算有运气, 赶上了最后一班汽车。"You can consider yourself lucky enough to catch the last bus."

- 以后**说不定**还会再碰上呢。

  说不定 "Perhaps "; "maybe." For example, 说不定他已经走了。"Maybe he's already left." 明天说不定会下雨。"It might rain tomorrow."

- 我这人**好说话儿**好共事

  好说话儿 "good-natured"; "amiable"; "easy to deal with." For example, 他好说话儿, 谁找他帮忙他都答应。"He is very obliging; he will help whoever asks him."

- 我这人好说话好**共事儿**

  共事 "Work together (at the same organization)"; "be fellow workers." 好共事, "easy to get along with." For example, 那个人脾气很坏, 不好共事。"That man is ill-tempered and not easy to get along with."

- **日久见人心**, 你准不会后悔有我这么个朋友。

  日久见人心 "Time will tell a true friend from a false one." "Time reveals a man's heart." For example, 虽然他现在还不了解咱们, 可是日久见人心, 他迟早会知道咱们是什么样的人。"Although he doesn't know us well now, time reveals a man's heart. He'll know what kind of people we are sooner or later."

- **对了**, 咱们先交换个手机号码再接着聊怎么样?

  对了 "Oh, ah, by the way." 对了 is a parenthesis here, used to change the subject when the speaker suddenly thinks of something. For example, 该开会了。对了, 你还没吃午饭呢。你先去把饭

吃了再来开会吧。 "It's time for our meeting. Oh, you haven't had your lunch yet. Go have your lunch first before the meeting."

- 对了, 咱**先交换个手机号码再接着聊**怎么样?
先…再… "First … then …." 早上起床后, 我总是先喝一杯水再吃饭。 "I always drink a cup of water first after getting up in the morning, and then I have my breakfast."

———————■———————

CONVERSATION B:

Simplified

刘芳和周云在宿舍里聊天。

刘芳: 我爱上篮球队的小王了, 你说我该不该马上告诉他?

周云: 篮球队里姓王的好像不只一个吧?

刘芳: 就是那个浓眉大眼的。别跟我**装傻**, 你不会对他没印象。

周云: **噢**, 我知道了, 就是那个**个儿**最矮的。**嘀**, 说爱就爱上了, 真够快的。

刘芳: 什么 "个儿最矮的?" 打篮球哪儿有个儿矮的? 他个儿可高了! 球队里**数**他长得最帅。

周云: 要不怎么说 "**情人眼里出西施**" 呢? 怪不得这两天你一下课就往球场跑, 原来是有了心上人了。

刘芳：　我也**不知怎么的**，一见他就心跳。我觉得他**对我也挺有意思**的，他看我的眼神跟别人不一样，打招呼也有点儿特别。

周云：　这就是**来电**啦!

刘芳：　可能是吧。原来见他也没什么感觉，可现在**怎么看怎么好**。你知道吗? 他人也**没得挑**，可会**疼人**了，还**没脾气**。

周云：　这就是 "来电" 的效果。你们约会过吗?

刘芳：　还没呢，就说过一两次话。我想今儿晚上就把他约出来跟他**挑明**了，你说怎么样?

周云：　快了点儿吧。要不你再了解了解?

刘芳：　交朋友又不是结婚，说明白了更好了解。

周云：　那你准备怎么跟他说呢?

刘芳：　这还不简单? 我就告诉他我喜欢他，愿意跟他交朋友，因为他长得帅气，人又好，球也打得没得说。然后我就约他每天晚上见一面。

周云：　**好你个刘芳**，真够痛快的。可是，**话又说回来了**，第一次约会，**哪有像你这么单刀直入的**。要是人家觉得你太厉害了，**给你个软钉子碰**，那你怎么下台?

刘芳：　**什么下台不下台的**，我**才不在乎呢**。找朋友这种事，宁愿碰钉子也别误了。我说什么也得让他知道我爱上他了。

Fang Liu and Yun Zhou are chatting in their dorm.

Liu: I'm in love with Wang on the basketball team; you think I should tell him right away?

Zhou: There's more than one Wang on the basketball team, right?

Liu: The one with the thick brows and big eyes. Don't play dumb with me; you have to know who I'm talking about.

Zhou: Ah, I know, the one who's the shortest. Hah, fell in love just like that, that was quick.

Liu: What "shortest?" How can there be any short people playing basketball? He's really tall! He's the cutest one on the whole team.

Zhou: Everything appears better to a lover's eyes. So that's why you keep running off to the basketball court after class these days. You've got your eyes on someone.

Liu: I don't even know why, but my heart jumps every time I see him. I think he feels something for me too; he looks at me differently from other people, and he greets me differently, too.

Zhou: That's love!

Liu: Maybe. Before I didn't feel any different when I saw him, but now he's perfect no matter how I look at him. You know, he's a good person, too. He knows how to make you feel special, and he's nice.

Zhou: That's the effect of falling in love. Have you guys dated?

Liu: Not yet, we just talked once or twice. I want to ask him out tonight and own up, what do you think?

Zhou: A bit fast. Why don't you get to know him a bit better?

Liu:　　　　　Dating isn't like marriage. It's easier to know him better after I tell him.

Zhou:　　　　Then what are you going to say to him?

Liu:　　　　　Isn't that obvious? I'll tell him I like him, want to go out with him, because he's cute, he's a good person, and he plays great basketball. Then I'll ask him to spend some time with me every day.

Zhou:　　　　Really now Liu Fang, that's really direct of you. But, after all, it's your first date. How can you just put it in front of him like that? If he thinks you're too aggressive, and politely tells you no thanks, how are you going to save face?

Liu:　　　　　Face schmace, I don't care at all. For things like dating, getting rejected is better than missing the chance. Whatever I do, I have to let him know I like him.

———■———

Traditional

劉芳和周雲在宿舍裏聊天。

劉芳:　　我愛上籃球隊的小王了, 你說我該不該馬上告訴他?

周雲:　　籃球隊裏姓王的好像不只一個吧?

劉芳:　　就是那個濃眉大眼的。 別跟我**裝傻**, 你不會對他沒印象。

周雲:　　**噢**, 我知道了, 就是那個**個兒**最矮的。 **呵**, 說愛就愛上了, 真夠快的。

劉芳： 什麼 "個兒最矮的?" 打籃球哪兒有個兒矮的? 他個兒可高了! 球隊裏**數**他長得最帥。

周雲： 要不怎麼說 "**情人眼裏出西施**" 呢? 怪不得這兩天你一下課就往球場跑, 原來是有了心上人了。

劉芳： 我也**不知怎麼的**, 一見他就心跳。我覺得他**對我也挺有意思**的, 他看我的眼神跟別人不一樣, 打招呼也有點兒特別。

周雲： 這就是**來電**啦!

劉芳： 可能是吧。原來見他也沒什麼感覺, 可現在**怎麼看怎麼好**。你知道嗎? 他人也**沒得挑**, 可會**疼人**了, 還**沒脾氣**。

周雲： 這就是 "來電" 的效果。你們約會過嗎?

劉芳： 還沒呢, 就說過一兩次話。我想今兒晚上就把他約出來跟他**挑明**了, 你說怎麼樣?

周雲： 快了點兒吧。要不你再瞭解瞭解?

劉芳： 交朋友又不是結婚, 說明白了更好瞭解。

周雲： 那你準備怎麼跟他說呢?

劉芳： 這還不簡單? 我就告訴他我喜歡他, 願意跟他交朋友, 因為他長得帥氣, 人又好, 球也打得沒得說。然後我就約他每天晚上見一面。

周雲： **好你個劉芳**, 真夠痛快的。可是, **話又說回來了**, 第一次約會, **哪有像你這麼單刀直入**

的。要是人家覺得你太厲害了, **給你個軟釘子碰,** 那你怎麼下臺?

劉芳: **什麼下臺不下臺的,** 我**才不在乎**呢。找朋友這種事, 寧願碰釘子也別誤了。我說什麼也得讓他知道我愛上他了。

词语注释

- 別跟我**裝傻**
  裝傻 "Pretend not to know"; "feign ignorance"; "make a pretense." 他刚才还说知道呢, 现在又装傻说不知道了. "He said he knew it a moment ago. Now he fakes ignorance and says he doesn't know."

- **噢,** 我知道了, 就是那个个儿最矮的。
  噢 (噢 [ō] Oh!) "Oh!" This is an interjection that is used to express understanding. For example, 噢, 原来是这样! "Oh, that's why." 噢, 我明白了。 "Oh, I see."

- 噢, 我知道了, 就是那个**个儿**最矮的。
  个儿 "size" or "height" of a person. For example, 你们班谁个儿最高? "Who is the tallest in your class?"

- **嗬,** 说爱就爱上了, 真够快的。
  嗬 (嗬 [hē] ah, oh) "Ah"; "oh." This is an interjection that is used to express surprise. For example, 嗬, 真吓人了! "Oh, how scary." 嗬, 这么漂亮! "Ah, it's so beautiful!"

- 球队里**数**他长得最帅
  数 (数 [shǔ] be reckoned as exceptionally) Here the meaning of 数 is: "be reckoned as exceptionally (good, bad, etc.)" For example, 全校数他最高。 "He is the tallest in the school."

- 要不怎么说"**情人眼里出西施**"呢?
  情人眼里出西施 (情人 [qíng rén] lover, sweetheart) **西施** (西施 [xī shī] the name of a famed beauty in Chinese history, synonymous with beauty) This fixed expression means "beauty lies in the lover's eyes." For example, 王东总说他的女朋友是他认识的最漂亮的女孩儿, 这可真是"情人眼里出西施"啊。 "Wang Dong always says that his girlfriend is the most beautiful girl that he knows, which reminds me of the saying, 'Beauty lies in the lover's eyes.'"

- 我也**不知怎么的**
  不知怎么的 "Don't know why (that)" For example, 不知怎么的, 我这几天晚上睡觉都做恶梦。 "I don't know why, I've had nightmares for the past several nights."

- 我觉得他**对我也挺有意思**的
  对...有意思 "be disposed to be in love with ...." For example, 上大学那几年, 我一直对她有意思, 可是她对我一点儿意思都没有。 "During our college years, I wanted to date her, but she was not interested in me at all."

- 这就是**来电**啦
  来电 Literally "electrify," which means "feel chemistry" or "feel a spark" when used to describe the feelings between boyfriend and girlfriend. For example, 我跟他在一块儿的时候, 一点儿来电的感觉都没有, 所以不可能交朋友。 "When I was together with him, I didn't feel a spark at all, so it's impossible for me to be together with him."

- 原来见他也没什么感觉, 可现在**怎么看怎么好**。
  怎么...怎么... A colloquial pattern to express "no matter what one does... the result is always ..." "..., it always leads to ...." In this pattern, the first "..." is a verb, and the second "..." is often the

result. 怎么, an interrogative pronoun, is used in this pattern to indicate the general nature, condition, or manner. For example, 她唱得好极了,怎么唱怎么好听。 "She sings extremely well; no matter what she sings it always sounds wonderful."

- 他人也**没得挑**, 可会疼人了, 还没脾气。
  没得挑 (挑 [tiāo] nitpick) This expression means "flawless." Telling somebody 没得挑 means "It's flawless, even if you are picky." For example, 这桔子真是没得挑。 "You couldn't find better oranges anywhere else." 他的服务态度没得挑。 "His attitude toward serving people couldn't be better."

- 他人也没得挑, 可会**疼**人了, 还没脾气。
  疼 A short form of 疼爱, "love dearly," or 心疼, "dote on." For example, 老王最疼小女儿。 "Lao Wang dotes on his younger daughter more than anyone else." 这孩子挺招人疼的。 "This child is really lovable."

- 他人也没得挑, 可会疼人了, 还**没脾气**。
  没脾气 (脾气 [pí qi] bad temper, irritable disposition, temper) "to not have a bad temper"; "to have a good temper." For example, 我们老师没脾气, 她从来不急躁。 "Our teacher has a nice personality and never gets angry." 老王可不是没脾气的人。他常常发脾气, 一发起脾气来就拿孩子出气。 "Lao Wang has a bad temper. He often gets angry and takes it out on his children."

- 我想今儿晚上就把他约出来跟他**挑明**了
  挑明 "No longer keep it back"; "let it out." The expression means "to speak frankly or openly and make one's intention's clear." It comes from the phrase 挑灯, "raise the wick of an oil lamp and make it brighter." For example, 我跟你挑明了吧, 我不同意这

么作。"I'll be frank with you: I don't agree with this." 这事不便挑明。"We'd better not state it so explicitly."

- **好你个芳芳**,真够痛快的。
  好你个… This expression is usually used at the beginning of an imperative sentence to express either dissatisfaction or admiration. 好 could be used at the beginning of a sentence or a clause to express disapproval. … is usually a person's name. For example, 好你个张英,居然敢跟我顶嘴。"How dare you, Zhangying! You dare to talk back to me!"

- 可是,**话又说回来了**
  话又说回来 "On the other hand." This is an adversarial expression, usually used at the beginning of a sentence as a parenthesis to introduce a different opinion or situation. For example,他这个人能力是差点儿, 可是话又说回来, 你能干又怎么样呢? "Yes, he is not very capable; however, even if you are capable, what can you do?"

- **哪有像你这么**单刀直入**的**
  哪有像…这么…的 有…这样…的吗? This is a rhetorical question, in which the first "…" is usually a pronoun and the second "…" is a verb. It means "Who on earth does … like … does" For example,哪有像你这么做生意的。"Who on earth runs a business like you did?" This pattern can also be expressed as: 有…这样…的吗? For example,你也真是, 有你这样谈恋爱的吗? "Really, is it even possible to date someone like you did?"

- 要是人家觉得你太厉害了,**给你个软钉子碰,**那你怎么下台?
  碰软钉子(碰 [pèng] bump, hit; 软 [ruǎn] soft; 钉子 [dīngzi] nail)碰钉子 means "meet with a rebuff"; "hit (or strike, run against) a snag." 软钉子, literally "a soft nail," means a mild or tact-

ful refusal or refutation. 给你个软钉子碰 means "Reject you politely." For example, 昨天我去跟跟小张借书, 结果碰了个软钉子。 "Yesterday I went to borrow a book from Xiao Zhang and was mildly rebuffed."

- 要是人家觉得你太厉害了, 给你个软钉子碰, 那你怎么下台?

  下台 Literally, "to step down from the stage or platform." The contextual meaning is: "to get out of a predicament or an embarrassing situation." This expression is often used in a negative form: 下不来台, 下不了台, 没法下台 or 不好下台, "be unable to back down with grace." For example, 你想当着那么多人跟他说这件事, 他要是不同意你的意见, 你就没法下台了。 "You want to discuss this matter with him in front of so many people. If he does not agree with your opinion, you will be unable to back down with grace."

- **什么下台不下台的**

  什么...不...的 A colloquial pattern used to express "I don't care" or "It doesn't matter." For example, when somebody says that it is too far to go somewhere, one could answer: 什么远不远的, 我去定了。 "No matter how far it is, I'll go there anyway." When somebody says that it is too difficult to learn something, one could answer: 什么难学不难学的, 我保证学会。 "No matter how hard it is, I'll learn how to do it." And when somebody thanks a person for paying for a meal, the person could say: 什么钱不钱的, 咱们好朋友不用说这些。 "Don't mention it; we are good friends."

- **我才不在乎呢**

  才...呢 "Just don't ...." This pattern shows emphasis or stress. For example, 他要是不知道才怪呢。 "It would be strange if he didn't know." 他是说今天会热吗? 今天才不热呢。 "Did he say that it would be hot today? It's not hot at all."

- 我才**不在乎**呢
  不在乎 "Don't care" or "don't mind." For example, 他不在乎别人怎么说他。 "He does not mind what people say about him."

▌ VOCABULARY

面熟	miànshú	look familiar
肯定	kěndìng	sure; positive; definite
其实	qíshí	actually; in fact
到处	dàochù	everywhere
非得	fēiděi	have got to; must
气质	qìzhì	temperament; disposition
再说	zàishuō	what's more; besides
俗话	súhuà	common saying; proverb
随便	suíbiàn	random; carelessly
不过	bùguò	but; however
难处	nánchu	difficulty; trouble
后悔	hǒuhuǐ	regret; repent
交换	jiāohuàn	exchange
手机	shǒujī	cell phone
号码	hàomǎ	number
马上	mǎshàng	immediately; right away
不只	bùzhǐ	not only; not merely

浓眉大眼	nóngméidàyǎn	thick eyebrows and big eyes
印象	yìnxiàng	impression
要不	yàobù	otherwise; or else
怪不得	guàibùde	no wonder; so that's why
原来	yuánlái	so; it turns out
心跳	xīntiào	palpitation; rapid heartbeat
眼神	yǎnshén	expression in one's eyes
打招呼	dǎzhāohū	greet somebody; say hello
感觉	gǎnjué	feeling; sensation
效果	xiàoguǒ	effect; result
约会	yuēhui	date
帅气	shuàiqì	handsome
痛快	tòngkuai	straightforward
单刀直入	dāndāozhírù	come straight to the point
厉害	lìhài	aggressive; fearlessness
宁愿	nìngyuàn	would rather; better
碰钉子	pèngdīngzi	meet with a rebuff
误	wù	miss

———————◼———————

EXERCISES

A. Fill in the spaces with the appropriate words or phrases:

日久见人心　　说不定　　一见着　对了　算

知人知面不知心　免贵姓李　比不上　我吧　再

1   香港买东西便宜, 因为不用上税, 这一点哪儿都
    _____香港。

2   你们都去呀? _____, 其实也挺想去的, 可是实在
    没时间。

3   这房子在这儿不_____大, 要是在我老家可就是
    大房子了。

4   他常常买彩票, 他说_____哪天运气好就能中大
    奖。

5   你要去爬山呀? _____, 你得带上伞, 天气预报说
    今天有雨。

6   他好不好现在还不知道, 不过, _____, 时间长了
    咱们就了解他了。

7   你别以为那些人都是好人, _____, 谁知道他们心
    里想的是什么。

8   医生说, 这种药, 得先吃些东西以后_____吃, 要
    不然对胃不好。

9   我问他:"请问您贵姓? 他说:"_____。"

10 他_____喜欢的东西就买, 完全不管有用没用。

B. Choose the expression from the following list that best corresponds
    to the underlined words or phrases:

    话是这么说 说实话 共事 好说话儿   不要紧
    说什么也得 好是好 干吗 说到哪儿去了   眼

1   你刚开始学, 做错了<u>也没关系</u>, 一回生, 二回熟嘛。

2   天气预报说今天不下雨, 你<u>怎么</u>拿着雨伞呢?

3   那两个跟你<u>一起工作</u>的人好不好相处?

4 他们去游泳,<u>其实</u>我也挺想去,可是我感冒了,不能去。

5 你找他一块儿租房没错儿,<u>他人很好</u>,跟谁都能交朋友。

6 你说吸烟有害,应该戒烟,<u>这话是对的</u>,可是真要戒就难了。

7 他跟我借钱,我以为他又要吸毒。他说:"你<u>说错了</u>,我是要买车。"

8 刚才买东西,人家找给我几张票子,我<u>一下子</u>就看出有一张是假的。

9 他说,每天一块儿去运动<u>是挺好</u>,可是得花不少时间。

10 明天是我太太生日,这次我<u>怎么也</u>得给她买件好一点的礼物。

C. Fill in the spaces with the appropriate words or phrases:

话又说回来　装傻　下台　噢　好你个　　　数
危险不危险　来电　个儿　嗬　情人眼里出西施

1 他可会说假话了,知道的事情他常常＿＿＿＿＿＿说不知道。

2 ＿＿＿＿＿＿,你是在哪儿买的这么漂亮的衣服?

3 ＿＿＿＿＿＿,现在我明白了,你是在跟我开玩笑。

4 那个店里卖的冰淇凌,就＿＿＿＿＿＿这种最好吃,所以卖得最快。

5 他说要是你从来没有过＿＿＿＿＿＿的感觉,那就是从来没喜欢过谁。

6   在课上, 你要是回答不出老师的问题, 会不会觉得不好_____?

7   你们兄弟几个谁的身材最好? 谁的_____最高?

8   _____王成, 真够厉害的, 居然得了全校冠军!

9   这次考试是难了点儿, 不过_____, 不难点儿怎么考得出水平?

10 不管别人怎么样说, 他总觉得她特别漂亮, 要不怎么说_____呢。

11 我爸爸说我一个人去爬山太危险, 我说, 什么_____的, 我不怕。

D. Choose the expression from the following list that best corresponds to the underlined words or phrases:

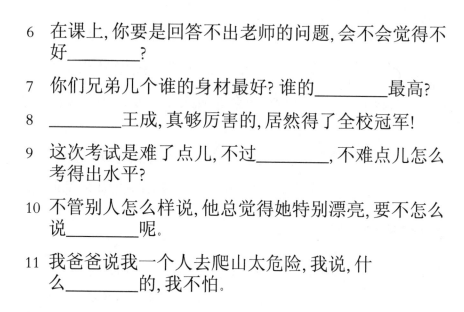

碰了个软钉子   不知怎么的   没脾气   没得挑
挑明   疼

哪有像你这么   对她有意思   不在乎   才不笨呢
怎么买怎么

1   性格和健康有关系, 有的人平常<u>不爱生气</u>, 可是一生病就变了。

2   我喜欢旅游, 只要有好玩儿的地方我就去, 从来<u>不管</u>远近。

3   他在他们家最小, 所以全家人都特别<u>关心</u>他。

4   你有话就<u>明白说出来</u>吧, 不要这么躲躲闪闪的。

5   这双鞋样式和价钱都合适, <u>一点毛病都找不出来</u>。

6   考试的时候, 我<u>不知道为什么</u>就什么都忘了, 所以没及格。

7 你说他笨? 他一点儿都不笨! 他就是学习不用功。

8 你问我和我太太谁先爱上谁的? 我先喜欢上她的。

9 股市好的时候, 买什么都赚钱, 可是现在, 买什么都赔钱。

10 他去借钱, 结果被人家客客气气地找借口拒绝了。

11 你怎么是这么作生意的! 一开始就把顾客都吓跑了!

ANSWER KEY

Exercise A (Dialogue 1)

1 比不上

2 我吧

3 算 (算…)

4 说不定

5 对了

6 日久见人心

7 知人知面不知心

8 再 (先…再…)

9 免贵姓李 (免贵姓…)

10 一见着 (一见着…就…)

Exercise B (Dialogue 1)

1 不要紧

2 干吗

3 共事

4 说实话

5 好说话儿

6 话是这么说

7 说到哪儿去了

8 一眼 (一眼就…)

9 好是好 (…是…, 就是…)

10 说什么也得 (说什么也得…)

Exercise C (Dialogue 2)

1 装傻

2 嗬

3 噢

4 数

5 来电

6 下台

7 个儿

8 好你个 (好你个…)

9 话又说回来

10 情人眼里出西施

11 危险不危险 (什么…不…的)

Exercise D (Dialogue 2)

1 没脾气

2 不在乎

3 疼

4 挑明

5 没得挑

6 不知怎么的

7 才不笨呢（才…呢）

8 对她有意思（对…有意思）

9 怎么买怎么（怎么…怎么…）

10 碰了个软钉子（碰软钉子）

11 哪有像你这么（哪有像…这么…的）

CULTURE NOTES

When talking about marriage and friendship, the Chinese often mention the Buddhist concept 缘, "predestined relationship." China has a long tradition of Buddhism, and today a lot of Chinese still believe that 缘 is one of the most important concepts of Buddhism. There is no exact equivalence for Buddhist 缘 in English. Some people suggest it means the combination of karma, fate, and destiny. 缘 is an abbreviation of 因缘 which means "cause" or "principal and subsidiary causes." According to Buddhism, there is no phenomenon without cause. Everything has its 缘起 "genesis or origin." That is everything is in a certain kind of relationship, and is limited or conditioned by other phenomena. Accordingly, all the relationships you have with other people have "cause." Even if you met a stranger unexpectedly at some corner of the world, it must be because you have the 一面之缘 "predestined relationship to meet once." So you meet your girlfriend the first time is because you have the 缘分 "lot or luck by which people are brought together." You get married to your wife because you two have the 姻缘 "predestined marriage." You get divorced because your 缘分已尽 "lot has been exhausted or finished."

这他也是一把好手
我有眼光吧?

ACCLAIMING; PRAISING; COMMENDING
•
BEING PROUD OF SOMETHING
•
SHOWING AFFECTION

CONVERSATION A:

Simplified

小东和小强在看篮球赛, 是他们学校跟别的学校比赛。

小东: 新平真行, **一投就中**。

小强: **那是**。别说他**在篮筐跟前儿投篮**, 绝对**没说的**, 就连远投, 也是一投一个准儿。

小东: 我还真**没怎么看过**他打球呢。

小强: 那你等着, 看他给你**露一手**的。这不, 你看他怎么传球。

小东: 嘿, 传得**绝了**! 哎呀, 三号**怎么搞的**, 把球让人家队给抢走了。

小强: 呦, 他们投篮呢。好, 没中!

脸上有光 (lit: "the face is shining.") Look good. (see page 120.)

Dong and Qiang are watching a basketball game; their school is playing against another school.

Dong: Xinping is so good, he sinks every shot.

Qiang: Of course. He's shooting right in front of the basket, so it's no problem at all. You haven't seen his long shots; he also makes all of them.

Dong: I really haven't seen him play much at all.

Qiang: Then just you wait; he'll show you a move. See, look at that pass.

Dong: Ah, nice pass! Aiya, what's up with number 3. He got the ball they stole.

小东：　　这哪儿有咱新平投得好!

小强：　　就是, 没法儿比。看新平抢球, 这他也是**一把好手**。你看他多灵, 谁也抢不过他。好, 远投, 又中一个!

　小东：　这**接二连三**地进球, 咱们学校又该拿冠军了。

小强：　　**那还用说**! 都拿了两届冠军了。**我打保票**, 今年还要拿。这几年, 每场比赛我都看了, 一场也没**落下**。

小东：　　你可真**下功夫**! 怪不得都管你叫球迷呢。

小强：　　**反正**除了念书也没什么事儿要干, 看看球赛多**过瘾**哪!

———■———

Traditional

小東和小強在看籃球賽, 是他們學校跟別的學校比賽。

　小東：　新平真行, **一投就中**。

　小強：　**那是**。別說他**在籃筐跟前兒**投籃, 絕對**沒說的**, 就連遠投, 也是**一投一個準兒**。

　小東：　我還真**沒怎麼看過**他打球呢。

　小強：　那你等著, 看他給你**露一手**的。這不, 你看他怎麼傳球。

Qiang: Yo, they're shooting. Good, missed!

Dong: Nothing compared to our Xinping's shots!

Qiang: That's right, no comparison at all. Look at Xinping steal. He's an expert at this too. Look how fast he is. No one out steals him. Alright, long shot, sank another one!

Dong: With all these shots, our school should get the championship again.

Qiang: Does it even need to be said? We've been the champs for the past two seasons. I guarantee same goes for this year. These last few years, I've seen every game; I haven't missed a single one.

Dong: You really put in the time! No wonder everyone says you're a basketball fan.

Qiang: Besides schoolwork, there's nothing to do anyhow. There's nothing like watching a ball game.

———————■———————

小東: 嘿, 傳得**絕了**! 哎呀, 三號**怎麼搞的**, 把球讓人家隊給搶走了。

小強: 呦, 他們投籃呢。好, 沒中!

小東: 這哪兒有咱新平投得好!

小強: 就是, 沒法兒比。看新平搶球, 這他也是**一把好手**。你看他多靈, 誰也搶不過他。好, 遠投, 又中一個!

小東: 這**接二連三**地進球, 咱們學校又該拿冠軍了。

小強: **那還用說!** 都拿了兩屆冠軍了。**我打保票**,今年還要拿。這幾年,每場比賽我都看了,一場也沒**落下**。

小東: 你可真**下功夫!** 怪不得都管你叫球迷呢。

小強: **反正**除了念書也沒什麼事兒要幹,看看球賽多**過癮**哪!

———■———

词语注释

- 新平真行, **一投就中**
一...就... "Once ..., then ... must happen." This pattern shows that ... is a natural or inevitable result of .... For example: 你真聰明, 一学就会。"You are so smart. Whenever you learn something, you get it immediately."

- **那是**
A colloquial form for "Sure it is." or "I could not agree more." For example, "太胖对健康不利。""那是, 所以大家才要减肥嘛。" "Being overweight is bad for your health." "Sure, that's why people want to lose weight."

- 他**在篮筐跟前儿投篮**, 绝对没说的
在...跟前 "In front of ..."; "close to ...." For example, 他就住在我们跟前。"He lives right next to us." 你在我跟前儿不要不好意思。"Don't be shy in front of me."

- 他在篮筐跟前儿投篮, 绝对**没说的**
没说的 "Unimpeachable"; "really good." This has the same meaning as 没得说. For example, 小王的中文没说的。"Xiao Wang's Chinese is really good." 这儿的天气没得说。"Can't complain about the weather here."

- 就连远投, 也是**一投一个准儿**。
  一...一个准 "Whenever ... happens, he (or she) hits the target." This
  is a colloquial form for the pattern 一...就..., and emphasizes "..." more.
  For example, 他打抢打得好极了, 一打一个准。 "He shoots
  extremely well, and he never misses the target."

- 我还真**没怎么看过**他打球呢
  没怎么... This pattern could also be expressed as不怎么....
  When the question word 怎么 is used together with 没 or不, it
  means "not quite" or "not much." For example, 这几天没怎么
  下雨。 "It didn't really rain these past few days." 我不怎么熟悉
  这个地方。 "I don't really know much about this place."

- 那你等着, 看他给你**露一手**的
  露一手 (露 [lòu] show) This expression means to show off one's
  mastery in something. For example, 他唱歌唱得不错， 一有
  机会就爱在人们面前露一手。 "He sings well and likes to
  show off in front of others whenever he gets an opportunity."

- 嘿, 传得**绝了**!
  绝了 (绝 [jué] superb; unique; matchless) A colloquial form for
  "superbly good," used when praising someone's skills. For example,
  他的画画得绝了。 "His paintings are superbly good."

- 三号**怎么搞的**, 把球让人家队给抢走了。
  怎么搞的 "What is wrong with (somebody)?" This expression is
  often used to show dissatisfaction or blame rather than to a question, and it carries a connotation that "it shouldn't be like this."
  For example, 你怎么搞的, 这么晚了还没做作业。 "What is
  wrong with you? It's so late, and you still haven't done your homework."

- 这他也是**一把好手**
  一把好手 "A good hand"; "able man." For example, 他干活真是一把好手。"He has such a good hand for work."

- 这**接二连三**地进球, 咱们学校准赢了。
  接二连三 "One after another"; "in quick succession." For example, 好消息接二连三地传来。"Good news came in quick seccession."

- **那还用说!** 都拿了两届冠军了。
  那还用说 "That goes without saying." An often-used expression for emphasis. It carries the meaning "of course" or "it does not need to be mentioned." For example, "要是你得了病，就该去看医生。" "那还用说，不过我现在没得病。""You should see a doctor if you are sick." "Of course, but I am not sick."

- 我**打保票**, 今年还要拿。
  打保票 Same as 打包票, "vouch for"; "to guarantee." For example, 我敢打保票, 他今天一定会来。"I guarantee that he will come today." 这件事你可不能给人打保票。"This isn't something you can guarantee."

- 每场比赛我都看了, 一场也没**落下**。
  落下 (落 [là] be missing; leave behind; lag behind). "Leave out;" "be missing." For example, 他病了, 落下了一个星期的课。"He missed a week of lessons because of illness."

- 你可真**下功夫**!
  下功夫 The same as 下工夫, "devote time and energy"; "concentrate one's efforts." For example, 不下功夫是学不好外语的。"You cannot learn a foreign language well without effort."

- 反正除了念书也没什么事儿要干。

  反正 A colloquial word used to express reasoning or certainty with the meaning, "anyway"; "anyhow;" or "in any case." 不管怎么说, 你今天反正得做作业。 "You must do your homework today no matter what." 反正得去一个人, 就让我去吧。 "Since someone has to go anyway, let me go." 反正我不同意。 "Anyhow, I do not agree."

- 看看球赛多过瘾哪!

  过瘾 (瘾 [yǐn] addiction; strong interest (in a sport or pastime) "Satisfy a craving"; "enjoy oneself to the fullest." For example, 这次旅行玩儿得真过瘾。 "This trip really did the trick." 今天的足球赛看得真过瘾。 "I really enjoyed watching today's soccer game."

CONVERSATION B:

Simplified

星期天上午, 芳芳和丈夫文立在逛商场。

芳芳: 这是新开的服装商场, 咱进去看看吧?

文立: **闹了半天**, 是把我骗出来跟你逛服装店来了! 行啊, **逛就逛吧! 谁让我是你老公呢?**

芳芳: 真是好老公! 你可得**说话算数**, 别逛一会儿就**不干了**。

文立: 没问题, 你爱逛多久就逛多久! 今儿我陪你逛上一整天。我可是模范丈夫!

芳芳: 得了吧, 又**说大话**! 我可**没那么大瘾**。逛上个把钟头就行了, 省得你又假装头疼。

文立： 哎, 这还**差不离儿**!...(B) 这边儿生意这么**火**! 卖什么哪?

芳芳： 毛衣。你看, 那是新式样儿。

文立： 要不要**来**一件? 瞧, 这件颜色多**棒**! 你穿上它, 咱俩一块儿出去, 我**脸上也有光**。

芳芳： 又**耍贫嘴**! 来, 我穿穿看。你瞧, 怎么样?

文立： 不错。**我有眼光**吧? 一眼就看上这件了!

芳芳： 嗯, **有两下子**! 不过, 这价钱挺贵... (B)其实, 我毛衣够多的了。

文立： 不想买? 看我多**有福气**, 太太又漂亮又**会过日子**! 不过逛了半天哪能**空着手**回去? 别人该以为是我不让你买东西了呢。

芳芳： 谁也**管不着**咱们的事儿。

文立： 对了, 情人节快到了, 我正**发愁**该给太太买什么礼物呢。得, 就算你替**我拿主意**了。来, 我**掏腰包**!

芳芳： 哈哈! 你**倒**挺会**省事儿**的!

———————————■————————————

It is Sunday morning, and Fang fang and her husband Wenli are at the mall.

　　Fang:　　　　This clothing store just opened. Let's go in and check it out.

Wen:	So all that fuss and it was to fool me into going shopping for clothes with you? Fine, you wanna shop, let's shop! That's what I get for being your husband, right?
Fang:	That's my husband! You'd better keep your promise, and not flake out on me after a little while.
Wen:	No problem, you can shop for as long as you want. I will go with you all day long. I'm a model husband!
Fang:	Knock it off. Bragging again! I'm not that addicted. Shopping for an hour or so is plenty; you don't have to pretend to have a headache.
Wen:	Well, that's more like it! …. Business here is hot. What are they selling?
Fang:	Sweaters. Look, that's the new style.
Wen:	Do you want one? Look, the color of this one is great! If you wear it and the two of us go out, I'd look good standing next to you.
Fang:	Teasing again! Here, let me try. See, how is it?
Wen:	Not bad; do I have taste or what? Picked it out with one glance!
Fang:	Oh, impressive! But, it's expensive… Actually, I have enough sweaters.
Wen:	Don't want to buy it? Look how lucky I am, my wife's pretty and thrifty! But how could we go back empty handed? Others will think that I don't allow you to buy things.
Fang:	No one should be concerned with our business.
Wen:	But, then again, Valentine's Day is almost here, I was just worrying about what present to get you. Well, let's just say you gave me the idea. Here, I'll pay.
Fang:	Ha-ha! You really know how to save yourself trouble.

Traditional

星期天上午, 芳芳和丈夫文立在逛商場。

芳芳: 這是新開的服裝商場, 咱進去看看吧?

文立: **鬧了半天**, 是把我騙出來跟你逛服裝店來了! 行啊, **逛就逛! 誰讓我是你老公呢?**

芳芳: 真是好老公! 你可得**說話算數**, 別逛一會兒 就**不幹了**。

文立: 沒問題, 你愛逛多久就逛多久! 今兒我陪你逛 上一整天。我可是模範丈夫!

芳芳: 得了吧, 又**說大話**! 我可**沒那麼大癮**。逛上個 把鐘頭就行了, 省得你又假裝頭疼。

文立: 哎, 這還**差不離兒**! ...(B)這邊兒生意這麼**火**! 賣什麼哪?

芳芳: 毛衣。你看, 那是新式樣兒。

文立: 要不要**來**一件? 瞧, 這件顏色多**棒**! 你穿上它, 咱倆一塊兒出去, 我**臉上也有光**。

芳芳: 又**耍貧嘴**! 來, 我穿穿看。你瞧, 怎麼樣?

文立: 不錯。**我有眼光**吧? 一眼就看上這件了!

芳芳: 嗯, **有兩下子**! 不過, 這價錢挺貴…(B)其實, 我毛衣夠多的了。

文立:　不想買? 看我多**有福氣**, 太太又漂亮又**會過日子**! 不過逛了半天哪能**空著手**回去? 別人該以為是我不讓你買東西了呢。

芳芳:　誰也**管不著**咱們的事兒。

文立:　對了, 情人節快到了, 我正**發愁**該給太太買什麼禮物呢。得, 就算你替我**拿主意**了。來, 我**掏腰包**!

芳芳:　哈哈! 你**倒**挺會**省事兒**的!

———————————

词语注释

- **闹了半天**, 是把我骗出来跟你逛服装店来了!
  闹了半天 (闹 [nào] go in for; do; make.) Literally, "after went in for it for such a long time," this expression is usually used when someone suddenly realizes someone's reason or purpose after something had been going on for a while. For example, 这几天你一直说我不关心你, 闹了半天, 是想让我送你件生日礼物啊。 "You've been blaming me for not caring about you over the last few days. All this time, you wanted me to get you a birthday gift."

- 行啊, **逛就逛吧**!
  ...就...吧 "Ok, ..." This pattern usually conveys a sense of resignation. For example, 不去就不去吧, 反正没什么重要的事情。 "Fine, don't go. There's nothing important going on anyway."

- **谁让我是你老公呢**?

  谁让...呢 This is a rhetorical question that carries a connotation that "there is no alternative because of ....." It usually precedes the reason why something has to be done. For example, 今天我们只好不去了, 谁让天下雨了呢? "We can't go today, because it is raining."

- **你可得说话算数**

  说话算数 This is the same as 说话算话: "honor one's word"; "mean what one says." The negative form is 说话不算数 or 说话不算话。For example, 这个人一向说话算数, 很可靠。"This person is very reliable; he always means what he says." 别信她的, 她从来说话不算话。"Don't trust her. She never honors her words."

- **别逛一会儿就不干了**。

  不干了 A colloquial expression: "Quit." One usage of 干 carries the meaning of "willing." For example, 我儿子不喜欢数学, 每次都是做一会儿作业就不干了。"My son doesn't like math. He always quits after a little while."

- **得了吧, 又说大话**!

  说大话 "Talk big"; "brag"; "boast." For example, 他的缺点是爱说大话。"His shortcoming is that he likes to talk big."

- **我可没那么大瘾**。

  没那么大瘾 "Not that crazy about it." This expression is used to show lack of interest in doing something. For example, 你以为他会来呀? 他才没那么大瘾呢。"You think that he's coming? He's not crazy about coming here."

- 这还**差不离**儿!

  差不离 A colloquial way to express "more like it" or "not bad." For example, 你上次考试得D 实在说不过去了。这回才差不离了, 得了个B。 "There's no excuse for the 'D' you got on the last test. This time is more like it; you got a 'B'."

- 这边儿生意这么**火**, 卖什么哪?

  火 A colloquial abbreviation of 红火: "flourishing" or "prosperous." For example, 他的饭馆儿越办越火了。 "His restaurant is really taking off."

- 要不要**来**一件?

  来... Often used colloquially as a substitute for another verb. For example, 给我来盘宫爆鸡丁吧。 "I'll get the Kung Pao Chicken." Here 来 is used to substitute for the verb "order." 你歇歇, 我来。 "You take a break, I'll get this." Here 来 is used as a substitute for the verb "do."

- 这件颜色多**棒**!

  棒 A colloquial form for "excellent," "fine," or "strong." For example, 他的字写得棒极了。 "His handwriting is excellent."

- 我**脸上也有光**。

  脸上有光 Literally, "light up the face," and the contextual meaning is "to be beaming." The negative form of the expression, 脸上无光, means "to lose face." For example, 他有这么好的儿子, 觉得脸上有光。 "He feels proud having such a wonderful son."

- 又**耍贫嘴**!

  耍贫嘴 (耍 [shuǎ] play; 贫嘴[pín zuǐ] garrulous; loquacious) This is a colloquial expression that means "to be garrulous." For example, 他要是跟你耍贫嘴, 你就别理他。 "Don't talk to him if he is garrulous."

- 我有**眼光**吧?
  有眼光 "Have foresight." For example, 他是个有眼光的政治家。"He is a statesman."

- 嗯,**有两下子**!
  有两下子! A colloquial expression for "having real skill"; "know one's stuff." For example, 那个大夫看病有两下子。"That doctor is really good."

- 看我多**有福气**,
  有福气 (福气 [fú qi] good luck; good fortune)
  "To be fortunate." 你真有福气,孩子这么听话。"You are really fortunate to have such obedient children."

- 太太又漂亮又**会过日子**!
  会过日子 "Knowing how to make ends meet"; "good at getting along." For example, 同样的工资,会不会过日子大不一样。"With any given salary, it makes a big difference whether or not you know how to make ends meet."

- 不过逛了半天哪能**空着手**回去?
  空着手 "Empty-handed"; "without taking anything." For example, 你不是去买衣服的吗? 怎么空着手回来啦? "Didn't you go shopping for clothes? Why did you come back empty-handed?" 她从来不空着手去看我妈。"She never visits my mother empty-handed."

- 谁也**管不着**咱们的事儿。
  管不着 (管 [guǎn] bother about; be concerned about; intervene.)
  "Have no right to intervene." "It's none of your business." For example, 那是我们几个人的事儿,你管不着。"That is something between us; it's none of your business."

- 我正**发愁**该给太太买什么礼物呢。

  发愁 "Worry"; "be anxious." For example, 光发愁没用, 我们得赶快想办法。 "It won't help just being anxious. We have to think of a way out."

- 得, 就算你替我**拿主意**了。

  拿主意 (主意 [zhú yi] decision; idea; plan) This is a colloquial expression for "make a decision." For example, 到底跟不跟他结婚, 我一时拿不定主意。 "Now I just can't decide whether or not to marry him."

- 来, 我**掏腰包**!

  掏腰包 "Pay out of one's own pocket." A colloquial expression used in talking about who will pay for something. For example, 今天这顿饭, 我掏腰包。 "Today's meal is on me." 昨天送给老板的礼物是谁掏的腰包? "Who paid for the boss' gift yesterday?"

- 你**倒**挺会省事儿的!

  倒 Also as 倒是, "although." This word is often used to indicate contrast or concession. For example, 你说得倒轻松, 可是做起来就不容易了。 "It's easy for you to say it, but it's not so easy to do it." 小李倒是来了, 可是小王没来。 "Although Xiao Li has come, Xiao Wang has not."

- 你倒挺会**省事儿**的!

  省事 (省 [shěng] save; omit; leave out) "Save trouble"; "simplify matters." For example, 跟旅行团去玩儿省事儿。 "It's more convenient to travel by joining a touring party." 他作事不负责, 只图自己省事。 "He is irresponsible in his work and just tries to save himself trouble."

VOCABULARY

篮球赛	lánqiúsài	basketball game
比赛	bǐsài	match; competition
别说	biéshuō	let alone; no need to mention
投篮	tóulán	shoot a basket
绝对	juéduì	absolutely
打球	dǎqiú	play ball
传球	chuánqiú	passed ball
抢	qiǎng	snatch; grab
灵	líng	quick; clever
冠军	guànjūn	champion
届	jiè	(measure word, similar to "number of sessions")
球迷	qiúmí	(ball game) fan
服装	fúzhuāng	dress; clothing
陪	péi	accompany
模范	mófàn	model; fine example
丈夫	zhàngfu	husband
个把	gèbǎ	one or two
省得	shěngde	so as to save (or avoid)
假装	jiǎzhuāng	pretend
头疼	tóuténg	headache
生意	shēngyi	business; trade
式样	shìyàng	style
漂亮	piàoliàng	pretty; beautiful
情人节	qíngrénjié	Valentine's Day

EXERCISES

A. Fill in the spaces with the appropriate words or phrases:

一把好手　　一来就　　过瘾　　反正　　那是

怎么搞的　　露一手　　绝了　　落下

1　我说,要是警察叫你停车你就停。他说: "_____,
　要不然就会罚你。"

2　你怎么也应该去趟九寨沟,那儿的风景真是_____。

3　你们上次爬山把我_____了,这次可得记住叫我
　一起去。

4　下雨了,咱们去饭馆儿吃饭吧,_____不能在外面
　野餐了。

5　听说你是咱们学校的乒乓球冠军,哪天有时间给我
　们_____吧?

6　这家饭馆不错,这顿海鲜大餐吃得真_____!

7　今天你_____,先把门钥匙忘在家里,然后又把车
　钥匙锁在车里。

8　他不但篮球打得好,游泳也是_____.

9　这么大的困难你_____解决了,你真行!

B. Choose the expression from the following list that best corresponds to the underlined words or phrases:

　　没怎么吃　打保票　　没说的　　　一个准

　　那还用说　接二连三　　跟前儿　　　下功夫

1　你学英文有问题可以去问老张, 他的英文<u>特别好</u>。

2　中国人乒乓球打得真好, 在世界比赛中<u>一个连一个</u>地拿冠军。

3　我说王文准能考上个好大学。李立说:"<u>那当然</u>, 绝对没问题。"

4　医生说能不能治好这病虽然不能<u>保证</u>, 但他会尽最大努力。

5　你要是想在比赛中得第一, 就得<u>花时间和精力</u>反复练习。

6　今天报上说, 有个小偷在警察<u>眼前</u>把一辆车偷走了.

7　我家那只小花猫特别会抓老鼠, 一抓就<u>抓到</u>。

8　你今天作的饭太少了, 咱们还<u>没吃多少</u>呢就没了!

C. Fill in the spaces with the appropriate words or phrases:

去就去吧　有两下子　　耍贫嘴　　说大话　有眼光　发愁
没那么大瘾　脸上有光　闹了半天　管不着 你爸爸　省事

1　买股票一定要_____, 否则肯定赔钱。

2　结婚是件大事, 婚礼可不能怎么_____怎么办。

3　这孩子怎么这样? 自己考不上大学也不_____, 就知道玩儿。

4 你一会儿说忙, 一会儿说头疼, _____, 你是不想
   去啊。

5 他是个老实人, 说话负责, 从来不_____。

6 能参加世界奥林匹克运动会比赛的运动员
   都_____。

7 我儿子学演讲没学会, 倒学会了_____。

8 上班的时候你听他的, 下了班在家里干什么, 他
   就_____了。

9 你想让我早上五点就跟你一块儿去钓鱼呀? 我
   可_____。

10 要是你们家孩子偷东西让警察抓走了, 你们家人会
   觉得_____吗?

11 既然你一定要跟我们一起去, 那_____。

12 看来这辆车我是一定得给你买了, 谁让我
   是_____呢。

D. Choose the expression from the following list that best corresponds
    to the underlined words or phrases:

会过日子   空着手   差不离   不干了   棒   火
说话算数   掏腰包   有福气   拿主意   倒是   来

1 这种式样的衣服最近卖得可<u>不错</u>了, 大家都抢着买.

2 这次考试很多人不及格, <u>我虽然</u>及格了, 但只得了六
   十一分。

3 他英文水平太差, 他的日文倒还<u>可以</u>。

4 那儿的风景特<u>好</u>, 去玩儿的人都舍不得走。

5 从前, 多数中国人都觉得孩子越多越<u>幸福</u>。

6 我儿子本来挺高兴的, 可是一听说要带他去医院看病就<u>不愿意了</u>。

7 王刚对朋友挺大方, 每次一块儿吃饭都是他<u>出钱</u>。

8 去什么地方旅游, 得大家一起商量, 不能就一个人<u>决定</u>。

9 我从前不<u>会有计划地用</u>钱, 每个月的工资半个月就花完了。

10 你去人家家吃饭不能<u>不带点儿东西</u>去。

11 我什么事都是<u>说到做到</u>, 从来不骗人, 不信你问问他们。

12 "您今天想吃点什么?" "先给我<u>拿</u>瓶啤酒, 然后我再点菜。"

ANSWER KEY

Exercise A (Dialogue 1)

1 那是
2 绝了
3 落下
4 反正
5 露一手
6 过瘾
7 怎么搞的
8 一把好手
9 一来就（一…就…）

Exercise B (Dialogue 1)

1 没说的
2 接二连三
3 那还用说
4 打保票
5 下功夫
6 跟前儿（在…跟前）
7 一个准（一…一个准）
8 没怎么吃（没怎么…）

Exercise C (Dialogue 2)

1 有眼光
2 省事
3 发愁
4 闹了半天

5 说大话
6 有两下子
7 耍贫嘴
8 管不着
9 没那么大瘾
10 脸上有光
11 去就去吧（…就…吧）
12 你爸爸（谁让…呢）

Exercise D (Dialogue 2)

1 火
2 倒
3 差不离
4 棒
5 有福气
6 不干了
7 掏腰包
8 拿主意
9 会过日子
10 空着手
11 说话算数
12 来（来…）

█ CULTURE NOTES

Chinese people like the word 福, which means "good fortune,"
"blessing," or "happiness," and often use expressions that contain 福 in
both spoken and written forms. For instance, the mascot of the 2008
Olympic Games is called 福娃, which means "good luck dolls." Also
the Chinese often put a large character of 福 upside down on a door
to show the wish of having a good luck. This is because "福"倒了
("the '福' is upside down,") is a homophony of "福"到了 ("the '福'
has come" or "our good luck has come.") The two expressions have the
same pronunciation in some dialects. The following lists are Chinese
words and phrases that containing 福. Those in group (1) are basically
in colloquial style, and those in group (2) are in literary style.

Group (1)

福气	happy lot; good fortune
福分	good fortune; good luck
福相	face's appearance shows good fortune.
口福	luck to have good food
托福	\<polite\> thanks to you
享福	enjoy a happy life; live in ease and comfort
眼福	the good fortune of seeing something rare or beautiful
发福	grow stout; put on weight
全家福	a photograph of the whole family; hotchpotch (as in a dish)

Group (2)

福利	material benefits; well-being; welfare
福星	lucky star; mascot
福音	Gospel; glad tidings
纳福	(elderly people) enjoy a life of ease and comfort

幸福	happiness; well-being; happy
造福	being benefit to; benefit
祝福	blessing; benediction
祸福相依	stuck through thick and thin
祸福与共	share trials with somebody
有福同享,有祸同当	share joys and sorrows; stick together through thick and thin

进了村儿，
顺路往南走不了多远
这点儿小意思，说什么您也
得收下

ASKING AND GIVING DIRECTIONS
•
SAVING FROM GETTING LOST
•
ASKING FOR A PERSON
•
EXPRESSING GRATITUDE
•
MAKING MODEST REMARKS
•
MAKING A FRIEND

CONVERSATION A:

Simplified

新平去北京远郊区爬山迷路了, 正在向遇到的一个老人问路。

新平：   大爷，**跟您打听个路。**

心里直发毛 (lit: "the heart is hairy.") To be scared. (see page 138.)

Xinping goes to a rural area to hike and gets lost. Seeing an old farmer, he asks for directions.

Xinping: Sir, let me ask you for some directions.

老大爷: 噢, 你要去哪儿?

新平:　　我来这儿爬山, **糊里糊涂**走错路了。本来要回县城住旅馆的, 可**这会儿**天都快黑了, 要能就近找个住处**凑合**一晚上就好了。

老大爷: 这儿离县城三十多里地呢, 你就**甭去了**。前边儿不远儿就是我们村儿, **不愁找住处**.

新平:　　**都这么晚了**, 我心里**直发毛**, **亏得碰上您了**。

老大爷: 别愁, 我**这不正要回去吗?** 你就跟上我走吧。

新平:　　那太谢谢您了! 村儿里有吃饭的地方吗?

老大爷: 有! **有的是**。你上村儿里去找个家庭旅馆, 一宿30块, 吃饭、洗澡、住处全包了。

新平:　　太好了! 能麻烦您给介绍一个吗?

老大爷: **不瞒您说**, 我家也办了一个。**要是不嫌弃**, 住我家就行。

新平:　　**是吗? 那再好不过啦!** 这可什么问题都解决啦!

老大爷: 前边儿就是我们村儿, 看见没? 进了村儿, **顺路往南**走不了多远, **往东拐**过去, 再**走几步**就是我家了。

Old Man:	Oh, where do you want to go?
Xinping:	I came here to hike, and stupidly got lost. I was going to go back to town to stay at the hotel, but now that it's almost dark, if I can I'll just find some place to crash for a night.
Old Man:	It's thirty li to town, so don't go. Up ahead just a little ways is our village. Don't worry about finding a place to stay there.
Xinping:	It was getting so late, I was getting scared. Thank goodness I ran into you.
Old Man:	Don't worry; I'm going back there right now. Just follow me.
Xinping:	Thank you very much! Is there a place to eat in the village?
Old Man:	Yes! There's plenty. Go to the village and find a family hostel. For 30 yuan a night, food, bath, and lodging are all included.
Xinping:	That's great! Can you please recommend one?
Old Man:	Actually, my family runs one. If you think it's good enough, you can just stay at my place.
Xinping:	Really? That's wonderful! All my problems are solved!
Old Man:	Up ahead is our village, you see it? Go into the village, walk along the road to the south for a little bit, turn to the east, and my home's a few steps away.

———————■———————

Traditional

新平去北京遠郊區爬山迷路了， 正在向遇到的一個老人問路。

新平： 大爺, **跟您打聽個路。**

老大爺： 噢, 你要去哪兒?

新平： 我來這兒爬山, **糊裏糊塗**走錯路了。本來要回縣城住旅館的, 可**這會兒**天都快黑了, 要能就近找個住處**湊合**一晚上就好了。

老大爺： 這兒離縣城三十多里地呢, 你就**甭去了**。前邊兒不遠兒就是我們村兒, **不愁找住處。**

新平： **都這麼晚了, 我心裏直發毛, 虧得碰上您了。**

老大爺： 別愁, 我**這不正要回去嗎?** 你就跟上我走吧。

新平： 那太謝謝您了! 村兒裏有吃飯的地方嗎?

老大爺： 有! **有的是。** 你上村兒裏去找個家庭旅館, 一宿30塊, 吃飯、洗澡、住處全包了。

新平： 太好了! 能麻煩您給介紹一個嗎?

老大爺： **不瞞您說,** 我家也辦了一個。**要是不嫌棄,** 住我家就行。

新平： **是嗎? 那再好不過啦!** 這可什麼問題都解決啦!

老大爺： 前邊兒就是我們村兒, 看見沒? 進了村兒, **順路往南**走不了多遠, **往東拐**過去, 再**走幾步**就是我家了。

———— ■ ————

词语注释

- **跟您打听个路。**

  跟你打听… "I'd like to ask you about …." "…" is often a measure word or a noun. This is a colloquial pattern for asking for information. For example, 小王, 跟你打听件事。"Wang, let me ask you about something."

- **糊里糊涂**走错路了。

  糊里糊涂 (糊涂 [hútu] muddled; confused) This is an idiom with the meaning, "muddleheaded." For example, 他昨天晚上喝醉了, 今天上午还糊里糊涂的, 什么事都干不成呢。"He was drunk last night, and this morning he was still muddleheaded and couldn't do anything."

- 可**这会儿**天都快黑了,

  这会儿 A colloquial form for "now." For example, 我刚给他打过电话, 她这会儿不在家。"I just called her, and she is not at home now."

- 要能就近找个住处**凑合**一晚上就好了。

  凑合 A colloquial expression: "make do." For example, 这儿就这么一家小饭馆, 咱就凑合一顿吧。"There is only this small restaurant here; let's make do for a meal."

- 这儿离县城三十多里地呢, 你就**甭去**了。

  甭… (甭 [béng] don't; needn't) A colloquial form for "don't …" or "needn't …." This pattern is usually used in the imperative mood, when asking somebody not to do something. For example, 他作事就那样儿, 你甭跟他生气。"He always does things like this, so please don't be upset with him."

- 前边儿不远儿就是我们村儿，**不愁找住处。**
  不愁... (愁 [chóu] worry; be anxious) "Not to have to worry about ...," "it shouldn't be hard to ...." For example, 这儿是旅游区，不愁找导游。"This is a travel area, so it shouldn't be hard to find a tour guide."

- **都这么晚了，**我心里直发毛
  都...了 "Already ...."This pattern is usually followed by a consequential fact or opinion. For example, 我都三年没回中国了，今年一定要回去一次。"It's already been three years since I went back to China, so I have to go back this year."

- 我心里**直发毛**
  直... A colloquial form for "continuously ..." In this pattern, ... is a verb, and 直 is an adverb. For example, 听说那个大学录取了她，她激动得心直跳。"When she was told that she was accepted by the university, her heart was pounding with excitement." 他踩了我一脚，直说对不起。"He stepped on my foot and apologized several times."

- 我心里直**发毛**
  发毛 A colloquial form of "scared" or "frightened." For example, 一听说今天有考试，他心里就发毛，因为他昨天一点也没复习。"He was frightened when he learned that there would be a test today, because he didn't review at all yesterday."

- **亏得碰上您了。**
  亏得... (亏得 [kuīde] fortunately, luckily) 亏得 is a colloquial form of "fortunately" or "luckily." 亏得..., "luckily ...," is usually used to explain the reason for saying something. For example, 这种汽车毛病那么多，亏得我没买，我去年差一点就要买了。"This car has so many problems. I almost bought one last year —luckily I didn't buy one."

- 别愁, 我**这不正要回去吗?**
这不…吗? This is one pattern for rhetorical questions, which is used to provide definite information … or confirm a fact …. The meaning is often: "Isn't … true?" "Doesn't somebody …?" 这不 is a short form of 这不是, so the pattern can also be expressed as 这不是…吗? For example, 我没说错吧? 她这不(是)已经来了吗? "Wasn't I right? Hasn't she come already?"

- 有! **有的是**。
有的是… "Have a plenty of …," "There's no lack of …." For example, 你想逛商店啊? 没问题, 这儿有的是商店, 咱们一起去逛。 "You want to go window shopping? Sure, there are plenty of stores here. Let's go together." This pattern can be simplified as 有的是, when the content of … is clear from the context. For example, 你问这儿有没有中国饭馆啊? 有, 有的是。我带你去。 "Are you asking if there are any Chinese restaurants here? Sure, there are plenty. I'll take you to them."

- **不瞒您说,** 我家也办了一个。
不瞒您说 (瞒 [mán] hide the truth from) "To tell you the truth." This expression is often used by a speaker to provide personal information. For example, 说到弹钢琴, 不瞒您说, 我从五岁起就开始弹钢琴了。 "Talking about piano, to tell you the truth, I began playing when I was five."

- **要是不嫌弃,** 住我家就行。
要是不嫌弃 (嫌弃 [xiánqì] dislike and avoid; cold-shoulder) "If you don't mind, …." This colloquial pattern is in a very polite tone, and is often used to make offers. 要是不嫌弃 shows the politeness, and … represents what is offered. For example, 我们家房子是挺旧, 不过还有间客房。您要是不嫌弃, 就在我们家凑合几天, 省得住旅馆了。 "Although my house is quite

old, there is a guest room. If you don't mind, just stay at my home, and don't bother going to a hotel."

- **是吗**? 那再好不过啦!
  是吗 This is a colloquial form for responding to others in a conversation, and it is similar to the English "oh" in many ways. For example, 王:" 我买了辆新车。" 李: "是吗? 是什么车? Wang: "I bought a new car." Li: "Oh, really? What kind of car?"

- 是吗? **那再好不过啦!**
  那再好不过啦 "That would be superb!" For example, 王:"你刚才说的那本书正好我有。你不用去图书馆借了,就用我的吧。" 李:"是吗? 那就再好不过啦! Wang: "I happen to have the book that you just mentioned. You could save a trip to library, and just use my book." Li: "Oh, really? That would be superb!"

- **顺路往南**走不了多远,
  顺路往… This is a pattern for giving directions:"Toward … along the road." … refers to the direction. For example, 你顺路往西走, 过一个红绿灯就到了。 "Walk toward the west along the road, and you will get there after passing a traffic light."

- **往东拐**过去,
  往…拐 This is a pattern for giving directions: "Turn …." … refers to the direction. For example, 你往前走, 往右拐。 "You walk ahead, and turn right."

- 再**走几步**就是我家了。
  走几步 "Walk for a short distance." 几步 refers to a short distance, although its literal meaning is: "a few steps." For example, 你看, 再走几步就到了。 "See, we are only a few steps away now."

CONVERSATION B:

Simplified

高山丢了皮包,齐子华拣到了它,通过派出所把它还给了高山。高山到齐子华工作的地方找他,向他表示感谢。

高山: 请问**哪位**是齐子华?

齐子华: 我就是,您是...(B)?

高山: 我叫高山,昨天您拣的皮包是我的。我是来谢您的。

齐子华: 哦,**没什么**,没什么,那是我该做的事儿。您还**专门跑一趟!**

高山: 我皮包里**又是几千块钱,又是护照、证件**,还有我明天出国的机票。**要不是您拾金不昧,我可就有得麻烦了。**

齐子华: 我也丢过东西,知道丢了要紧东西的**滋味儿**。**将心比心**,所以一拣着就送到派出所去了,嘱咐他们快点儿找着您。

高山: 您这可是救了我的命了,要不今儿我们家就该**乱套**了,我哪儿能像现在这么**没事儿人似的**呀? 您看,这五百块钱是我的一点儿**小意思**,请您收下。

齐子华: 这我可不能收! **我不过是做了件该做的事儿,也没费什么劲儿。**

高山: 可您**帮了我大忙**了!这点儿小意思,说什么您也得收下。要不,我心里**过意不去**。

齐子华: 做了件该做的事儿就收人家钱,我成什么人了?

高山: 这钱您怎么也得收。您要是不收,今天我就不走了。

齐子华: 我看您是**诚心诚意**的,就不**跟您客气**了。这么着,咱俩交个朋友,以后我要有**求得着**您的事儿,您给我**帮把手**。这钱呢,您先留着,出国**办事儿**正是用钱的时候。

高山: 能交上您这样的朋友是我的运气。说实话,**五百块钱**也是少了点儿。既然您一定不收,那等我回来以后咱一块儿吃顿饭,您看行不行?

齐子华: **没问题,**您回来以后咱一块儿聚聚。

———— ■ ————

Shan Gao lost his bag. Zihua Qi found it and returned it to Shan Gao through the police station. Shan Gao finds Zihua Qi's workplace and thanks him.

Gao: Excuse me, which one is Zihua Qi?

Qi: I am; you are?

Gao: I'm Shan Gao. The bag you found yesterday was mine. I came to thank you.

Qi: Oh, it's nothing; it's nothing, just what I was supposed to do. And you came all the way just for that!

Gao: In the bag there were several thousand yuan, and my passport and papers, and also my plane ticket tomorrow to leave the country. If it weren't for your honesty, I'd be in deep trouble.

Qi: I've lost things too; I know what it is like to lose something important. I imagined what I would have felt, so I came straight to the police station, and told them to hurry up and find you.

Gao: You saved my life, or else my family would be in a great mess, and I wouldn't be acting as if I've got nothing to worry about. Here, this 500 yuan is a small token of my appreciation. Please take it.

Qi :   I can't take this! I just did the right thing, and it didn't take anything on my part.

Gao: But you helped me in a huge way! This little gift, you have to accept it no matter what. Or else, my mind won't give me any peace.

Qi: Taking money for doing the right thing, what does that make me?

Gao: You have to take the money, whether you want it or not. If you don't, I'm not leaving today.

Qi: I see that you mean it, so I'll be frank. Let's do this, let's get acquainted, and if I have anything to ask of you later on, you give me a hand. This money, you keep it for now. You'll be needing money now that you're going abroad.

Gao: It's my luck to have a friend like you. Honestly, 500 yuan is really not enough. Since you persist in not taking it, then let's eat together when I come back, what do you say?

Qi: Sure, we'll get together after you come back.

Traditional

高山丟了皮包,齊子華揀到了它,通過派出所把它還給了
高山。高山到齊子華工作的地方找他,向他表示感謝。

高山：　　請問**哪位**是齊子華?

齊子華：我就是,您是…(B)?

高山：　　我叫高山,昨天您揀的皮包是我的。我是來謝
　　　　　您的。

齊子華：哦,**沒什麼**,沒什麼,那是我該做的事兒。您還
　　　　　專門跑一趟!

高山：　　我皮包裏**又是幾千塊錢,**又是護照、**證件**,還
　　　　　有我明天出國的機票。**要不是您拾金不昧,我
　　　　　可就有得麻煩了。**

齊子華：我也丟過東西,知道丟了要緊東西的**滋味兒**。
　　　　　將心比心,所以一揀著就送到派出所去了,囑
　　　　　咐他們快點兒找著您。

高山：　　您這可是救了我的命了,要不今兒我們家就
　　　　　該**亂套**了,我哪兒能像現在這麼**沒事兒人似
　　　　　的**呀?您看,這五百塊錢是我的一點兒**小意思**,
　　　　　請您收下。

齊子華：這我可不能收! **我不過是做了件該做的事兒,
　　　　　也沒費什麼勁兒。**

高山：　　可您**幫了我大忙**了! 這點兒小意思,說什麼您
　　　　　也得收下。要不,我心裏**過意不去**。

齊子華: 做了件該做的事兒就收人家錢,我成什麼人了?

高山:　　這錢您怎麼也得收。您要是不收,今天我就不走了。

齊子華: 我看您是**誠心誠意**的,就不**跟您客氣**了。這麼著,咱倆交個朋友,以後我要有**求得著**您的事兒,您給我**幫把手**。這錢呢,您先留著,出國**辦事兒**正是用錢的時候。

高山:　　能交上您這樣的朋友是我的運氣。說實話,**五百塊錢也是少了點兒**。既然您一定不收,那等我回來以後咱一塊兒吃頓飯,您看行不行?

齊子華: **沒問題,**您回來以後咱一塊兒聚聚。

———————◼———————

词语注释

• 请问**哪位**是齐子华?
  哪位 A polite way of saying "who." For example, 您找哪位? "Who are you looking for?"

• 哦,**没什么**,没什么,那是我该做的事儿。
  没什么 "It's nothing." "Don't mention it." This expression is often used as a modest way to reply to praise. For example, 王:"你帮了我这么多忙!" 李:"没什么,我没帮上什么忙。Wang: "You helped me a lot!" Li: "Don't mention it; I didn't help much."

- 您还**专门跑一趟**!
  专门... With the literal meaning "especially ...," this pattern is often used to express appreciation. For example, 你对他真好, 还专门给他作这么多菜。 "It's very nice of you to make so many dishes for him."

- 我皮包里**又是几千块钱, 又是护照、证件,**
  又是..., 又是... This pattern is often used to express the meaning that there are both ... and .... For example, 这条路怎么这么挤? 又是人又是车! "Why is this street is so crowded? It's full of both people and cars."

- **要不是您拾金不昧, 我可就有得麻烦了.**
  要不是..., 可就...了 This pattern is used to indicate that if ... would not happen, then the consequence would be .... If ... and ... do not share the same subject, the subject of ... should occur before 可就...了. For example, 今天早上要不是你叫醒我, 我可就迟到了。 "If you hadn't woken me up this morning, I would have been late for sure." 要不是你提醒他这么作, 可就麻烦了。 "If you hadn't reminded him to do so, there would've been big trouble."

- 要不是您拾金不昧, 我可就**有得麻烦了**
  有得...了 This pattern is used to suggest that something negative will happen. ... can be either a word or a phrase that refers to the negative situation. For example, 看你把她的车撞成这样! 这可有得啰嗦了。 "Look, you crashed her car! You will be in big trouble."

- 知道丢了要紧东西的**滋味儿**。
  滋味儿 (滋味 [zīwèi]) "Taste"; "flavor." 滋味 often refers to a negative experience. For example, 他身体特别好, 他说他就不知道生病是什么滋味的。 "He is very healthy, and he said that he doesn't even know what getting sick feels like."

- **将心比心**, 所以一拣着就送到派出所去了,
  将心比心 (将 [jiāng] take) "Put oneself in another's shoes." For example, 谁都会碰到难办的事, 咱们将心比心想一想, 就帮帮他吧。 "Anyone can run into difficulties. Let's compare his feeling with ours, and help him."

- 要不今儿我们家就该**乱套**了,
  乱套 "Muddle things up." For example, 你们每个人要是都想怎么办就怎么办, 那可就乱套了。 "If each one of you acts as you please, everything would be in a muddle."

- 我哪儿能像现在这么**没事儿人似的**呀?
  没事儿人似的 "Seems indifferent." For example, 不管别人怎么说他, 他都跟没事人似的。 "No matter how much other people criticize him, he always looks unconcerned."

- 您看, 这五百块钱是我的一点儿**小意思**,
  小意思 "A small token of one's regard." For example, 这是一点儿小意思, 给你作个纪念。 "This is a small token of my esteem, just a little keepsake for you."

- **我不过是做了件该做的事儿,**
  不过是... "It's only ...." ... is usually a phrase. For example, 我不过是开个玩笑, 你别不高兴。 "I only made a joke. Please don't feel unhappy."

- **也没费什么劲儿.**
  费... (费 [fèi] consume too much, expend something too quickly, be wasteful) There are several fixed expressions for the verb-object structure, 费..., such as 费劲, "need or exert great effort"; 费事, "give or take a lot of trouble"; 费钱, "cost a lot"; and 费心, "give a lot of care." For example, 他费了好多事才把那个电脑修好。

"He went to a lot of trouble to get the computer repaired." 让您费心了, 谢谢您! "Thanks a lot for taking all the trouble."

- 可您**帮了我大忙**了!
  帮了…大忙 "Give … a lot of help." "Be of a great help to …."
  For example, 这件事, 他帮了我们大忙。 "He helped us a lot in this matter."

- 要不, 我心里**过意不去**。
  过意不去 This is a fixed expression, "feel apologetic" or "feel sorry." For example, 这事花了他那么多时间, 我觉得很过意不去。 "I feel very sorry that he has spent so much time on this matter."

- 我看您是**诚心诚意**的,
  诚心诚意 (诚 [chéng] sincere; honest) This is a fixed expression meaning, "earnestly and sincerely." For example, 你这么诚心诚意地帮助他, 他一定很感激。 "He must feel very grateful for your earnest and sincere help."

- 就不**跟您客气**了。
  跟…客气 (客气 [kèqi] polite, courteous, modest) "Be polite with …." … is usually a pronoun or a noun. For example, 咱们是老朋友, 你别跟我那么客气。 "We've been friends for a long time; please don't be so polite with me."

- 以后我要有**求得着**您的事儿, 您给我帮把手。
  求得着 (求 [qiú] beg; request; 着 [zháo] used as a complement to another verb) One meaning of this expression is "need help from." For example, 我求得着你的时候你没空儿, 现在你才来。 "You didn't have time when I needed your help—you only come now."

- 以后我要有求得着您的事儿, 您给我**帮把手**。

  帮把手 "Give a helping hand." 把 is a measure word in this pattern. For example, 昨天他修自行车的时候, 我给他帮了把手。 "When he was repairing his bicycle yesterday, I helped him somewhat."

- 出国**办事儿**正是用钱的时候。

  办事儿 A colloquial form of "work" or "handle affairs." For example, 他要在那儿办点事儿。 "He is going to do work there."

- **说实话**, 五百块钱也是少了点儿。

  五百块钱也**是少了点儿**。

  是...了点儿 "Yes, it is quite ...." This pattern is often used to show agreement. For example, 这本字典是旧了点儿, 不过还是很有用。 "Yes, this dictionary is quite old, but it's still very useful."

- **没问题,** 您回来以后咱一块儿聚聚。

  没问题 "No problem." This expression is often used to make a promise. For example, "你明天一定能把我的车修好吗?" "没问题!" "Are you sure you can fix my car tomorrow?" "No problem."

———————— ■ ————————

▌ VOCABULARY

大爷	dàye	uncle (a respectful form of address for an elderly man)
县城	xiànchéng	county seat; county town
旅馆	lǚguǎn	hotel
家庭	jiātíng	family
一宿	yìxiǔ	one night

麻烦	máfan	to trouble; bother
介绍	jièshào	recommend
解决	jiějué	solve; resolve; settle; dispose of; finish off
顺	shùn	along
拐	guǎi	turn
皮包	píbāo	leather handbag
派出所	pàichūsuǒ	local police station; police substation
趟	tàng	(measure word, similar to "number of trips")
护照	hùzhào	passport
证件	zhèngjiàn	identification; certificate
拾金不昧	shíjīnbùmèi	not pocket the money one picks up
嘱咐	zhǔfu	enjoin; tell
运气	yùnqi	fortune; luck
既然	jìrán	since; as; now that

———— ▬ ————

EXERCISES

A. Fill in the spaces with the appropriate words or phrases:

要是不嫌弃　不瞒你说　往北拐　亏得　都
那再好不过啦　糊里糊涂　直着急　是吗　这不

1　这么大雨，_____带伞了，要不就回不了家了。

2　我说昨天的足球赛国安队输了。他说："_____?
　那他们连输三场了。"

3 别看我现在壮得像头牛似的, _____, 我以前身体特别不好。

4 你怎么_____的? 不是拿错东西就是说错话。

5 天这么冷, _____, 就先把我这件毛衣穿上, 省得着凉。

6 他想把旧杂志拿去看, 我说: " _____! 我正好没地方放呢。

7 你_____三次没交作业了, 希望你不要有第四次。

8 这个地方不好找, 我又没来过, 所以心里 _____.

9 去加油站得先_____, 再走一条街。

10 你老批评我迟到, 你_____也来晚了吗?

B. Choose the expression from the following list that best corresponds to the underlined words or phrases:

有的是	这会儿	凑合	发毛	
跟你打听	走几步	顺路	不愁	甭

1 您再往前<u>走一点儿</u>就能看见那家饭馆了。

2 那本书买不着就<u>别</u>买了, 我还有本旧的, 你拿去用吧。

3 我昨天没做作业, 今天一上课就心里<u>发慌</u>, 怕老师问。

4 刚才让你去你不去, <u>现在</u>下雨了, 你想去也去不成了。

5 到了中国<u>不用担心</u>找不到会英文的导游。

6 我们家没有多余的床, 你就在客厅的沙发上<u>将就</u>一晚上吧。

7 中国<u>有好多</u>你没见过、没吃过的东西呢。

8 张林, <u>我问你</u>件事, 今天早上是谁第一个来上班的?

9 <u>您沿着这条路</u>往东, 走五分钟就到图书馆了。

C. Fill in the spaces with the appropriate words or phrases:

过意不去　求得着　办事儿　又是　　有得
诚心诚意　小意思　滋味儿　没什么　客气　帮

1 我说这么麻烦他, 真不好意思。他说: "_____, 不麻烦。"

2 今天我进城_____, 午饭不回来吃。

3 他昨天被解雇了, 第一次尝到了失业的_____。

4 他是个好人, 朋友同事有_____的事儿, 他没有不帮忙的。

5 这件礼物是我的一点儿_____, 请你一定收下。

6 我在会上批评小王批评错了, 心里挺_____。

7 我_____给他帮忙, 他反倒嫌我啰嗦。

8 他本来身体就不好, 又得了这么重的病, 这下_____折腾了。

9 我是你爸爸, 你跟我还_____什么!

10 我母亲犯心脏病的时候, 要不是邻居_____了她大忙, 就危险了。

11 咱们坐飞机去行吗? 这_____火车又是轮船的, 太麻烦了。

D. Choose the expression from the following list that best corresponds to the underlined words or phrases:

将心比心 没问题　不过是　专门　哪位　　乱套
贵了点儿 帮把手　费事儿 没事儿人似的　要不是

1　请问<u>谁</u>是这儿的负责人?

2　下这么大雨, 你还<u>特地</u>来给我送伞, 太感谢了。

3　他说怕毕不了业, 我说他那么用功, <u>不会毕不了业</u>。

4　这箱子太沉, 我一个人搬不动, 你来给我<u>帮个忙</u>。

5　那个小国家成立了三个政府, 谁也不听谁的, 怎么能不<u>乱</u>呢?

6　他现在多困难呀, 咱们<u>好好为他</u>想一想, 怎么能不帮他呢?

7　他不但抢了钱, 还把人打伤了, 可是在法庭上还<u>满不在乎的</u>。

8　我停车时, <u>只是</u>超出了停车线一点点, 警察就罚了我好多钱。

9　这个活儿这么干可太<u>麻烦</u>了, 还是想个简单一点儿的办法吧。

10　这个戒指是<u>有点儿贵</u>, 可是贵也得买, 我女朋友就喜欢这个。

11　他这次病得很重, <u>如果不是</u>抢救得及时, 可就危险了。

ANSWER KEY

Exercise A (Dialogue 1)

1 亏得
2 是吗
3 不瞒你说
4 糊里糊涂
5 要是不嫌弃
6 那再好不过啦
7 都（都...了）
8 直着急（直...）
9 往北拐（往...拐）
10 这不（这不...吗）

Exercise B (Dialogue 1)

1 走几步
2 甭（甭...）
3 发毛
4 这会儿
5 不愁（不愁...）
6 凑合
7 有的是
8 跟你打听（跟您打听...）
9 顺路（顺路往...）

Exercise C (Dialogue 2)

1 没什么
2 办事儿
3 滋味儿
4 求得着
5 小意思
6 过意不去
7 诚心诚意
8 有得（有得 ...了）
9 客气（跟...客气）
10 帮（帮了...大忙）
11 又是（又是..., 又是...）

Exercise D (Dialogue 2)

1 哪位
2 专门（专门...）
3 没问题
4 帮把手
5 乱套
6 将心比心
7 没事儿人似的
8 不过是(不过是...)
9 费事儿（费...）
10 贵了点儿（是...了点儿）
11 要不是（要不是..., 可
    就...了）

▌TO VALUE JUSTICE ABOVE MATERIAL GAIN

In China, you often see a group of Chinese fighting to pay the bill in a restaurant. If you offer to pay a friend after living and eating in his home, he might think it's an insult. Chinese have a long tradition of valuing justice above material gain. As the saying goes, "A man of virtue will seek after righteousness. Similarly, the mind of the mean man is conversant with gain." Most Chinese words related to 义 (justice or righteousness) are commendatory terms, while those related to 利 (benefits; interests, advantages, profit) are not. For example:

义举 righteous deed

义士 high-minded or chivalrous person

义愤 moral indignation

义师 or 义军 righteous army

见利忘义 Seeing profit, forgetting the moral principle; Double crossing for money; Honor and profit lie not in one sack; Two dogs over one bone seldom agree

利令智昏 Profit makes wisdom blind; Wealth makes wit waver; Greedy for money

我属虎,就爱鸡鸭鱼肉
出门在外,怎么也得住舒服了

ISSUING ORDERS
•
MAKING A REQUEST

CONVERSATION A:

Simplified

小刘、小石 和老丁三人到北京出差。星期天他们一起去
一家饭馆吃饭。

服务员: 先生们好! 请这边坐,这边儿清静。这是菜单.
今天想吃点儿什么?

小刘: **实话跟您说,**我这个人哪,**最烦看菜单了**,特
别是你们北京的菜单,**净起些花里胡哨的名
字,整**得人晕头转向的。上次我点了个 "蚂蚁
上树",**端出来一看,**您猜怎么着? 就是肉末炒
粉丝! 您说可笑不可笑? 所以啊,今儿我**听您
的**,您说哪个好,我就点哪个。我喜欢清淡的,
您说我该点什么?

鸡蛋里挑骨头 (lit: "try to find bones in an egg.") nitpick (see page 171.)

Liu, Shi, and Ding are going to Beijing on business. They are eating out at a restaurant on Sunday.

Waiter: Good day! Please sit over here; it's less crowded here. Here's the menu, what would you like today?

Liu: To be completely honest, for me, looking at menus is the worst thing in the world. Especially your menus in Beijing, they've got all these absurd names, and you get so puzzled that you're dizzy. Last time I got an "ants up a tree." When they brought it out, what do you think it was? Ground pork stir fried with rice sticks! Is that funny or what? So, today I'll just listen to you; whatever you say, I'll get. I like light food; what do you think I should get?

服务员： 那冷菜就要个素拼盘"大丰收"，热菜来个"海鲜豆腐煲"吧。

小刘： 成。

老丁： 他**属兔**，专啃**青菜箩卜**。我属虎，就爱**鸡鸭鱼肉**，给我来盘"无锡排骨"，再要只"香酥鸡"。

小石： 这两个南方菜好是好，就是 都挺甜，**我说你**还是少吃糖好。

老丁： 甜就甜吧，反正也不是天天吃。

小石： 你有轻度糖尿病，**我这还不是为了你好?**

老丁： 管不了那么多了! **这也不能吃，那也不能吃**，还活不活了!

小石： 好你个老丁，为了嘴**不要命**呀! 小姐，您再给推荐两个鱼吧。

服务员： 我们这儿的"水煮鱼"和"松鼠桂鱼"都不错。

小石： 早就听说你们的"水煮鱼"做得好，可是我嗓子不好，吃不了辣的，不放辣椒成不成?

服务员： 一点儿辣椒不放，就不是"水煮鱼"了。少放些行不行?

小石： **这个"少"是多少根本说不清楚，一个辣椒是它，一把辣椒也是它**。上次点菜，我**紧着**说少放少放，结果炒出来都成红的了，大师傅说，**少得不能再少了**，只抓了一小把。弄得我吃也不是，不吃也不是。就要"松鼠桂鱼"吧。

Waiter: Then for the cold dish get the vegetarian sampler, "Grand Harvest," and for the hot dish order a "Seafood Tofu Stew."

Liu: Sure.

Ding: He was born a rabbit; he likes to munch on lettuce and carrots. I'm a tiger, I only like meat, so give me a "Wuxi Ribs," and give me a "Crispy Chicken."

Shi: These two southern dishes are good; it's just that they're both sweet. I say you should stop eating so much sugar.

Ding: So what if they're sweet; anyway I don't eat sweets every day.

Shi: You've got early diabetes; I'm acting for your own good.

Ding: I can't worry that much! I can't eat this, I can't eat that. Do I go on living or not!

Shi: Really now, Ding, you're going to throw away your life for your mouth! Miss, recommend some fish dishes, please.

Waiter: Our "Water boiled fish" and "Squirrel Style Fish" are both good.

Shi: I've always heard that your "Water boiled fish" was good, but I've got a bad throat and can't eat anything spicy. Can you make it without peppers?

Waiter: Without any peppers it's not "Water boiled fish." How about we go easy on the peppers?

Shi: It's impossible to say how much "go easy" is, one pepper is "easy," a handful is also "easy." Last time I ordered, I kept telling them to go easy, but when it came the dish was red. The chef said, that was the least he could put, only a small handful. And I

小刘: 再要个 "三鲜汤" 怎么样? 三个人, 五菜一汤, 够丰盛的了。

Traditional

小劉、小石 和老丁三人到北京出差。星期天他們一起去一家飯館吃飯。

服務員: 先生們好！請這邊坐,這邊兒清靜。這是菜單。今天想吃點兒什麼?

小劉: **實話跟您說**,我這個人哪,**最煩看菜單了**,特別是你們北京的菜單,**淨起些花裏胡哨的名字**,**整**得人暈頭轉向的。上次我點了個 "螞蟻上樹",**端出來一看**,您猜怎麼著? 就是肉末炒粉絲! 您說可笑不可笑? 所以啊,今兒我**聽您的**,您說哪個好,我就點哪個。我喜歡清淡的,您說我該點什麼?

服務員: 那冷菜就要個素拼盤 "大豐收",熱菜來個 "海鮮豆腐煲" 吧。

小劉: 成。

老丁: 他**屬兔**,專啃**青菜籮蔔**.我屬虎,就愛**雞鴨魚肉**,給我來盤 "無錫排骨",再要隻 "香酥雞"。

小石: 這兩個南方菜好是好,就是都挺甜,**我說你**還是少吃糖好。

老丁: 甜就甜吧,反正也不是天天吃。

couldn't eat it, and I couldn't leave it. Just go with the "Squirrel Style Fish."

Liu: How about we also get a "Three Delicacies Soup?" For three people, five dishes and a soup, it's more than enough.

———◼———

小石：　你有輕度糖尿病，**我這還不是為了你好？**

老丁：　管不了那麼多了！**這也不能吃，那也不能吃，**還活不活了！

小石：　好你個老丁，為了嘴**不要命**呀！小姐，您再給推薦兩個魚吧。

服務員：我們這兒的"水煮魚"和"松鼠桂魚"都不錯.

小石：　早就聽說你們的"水煮魚"做得好，可是我嗓子不好，吃不了辣的，不放辣椒成不成？

服務員：一點兒辣椒不放，就不是"水煮魚"了。少放些行不行？

小石：　**這個"少"是多少根本說不清楚，一個辣椒是它，一把辣椒也是它。**上次點菜，我**緊著**說少放少放，結果炒出來都成紅的了，大師傅說，**少得不能再少了，**只抓了一小把。弄得我吃也不是，不吃也不是。就要"松鼠桂魚"吧。

小劉：　再要個"三鮮湯"怎麼樣？三個人，五菜一湯，夠豐盛的了。

词语注释

- **实话跟您说,** 我这个人啊, 最烦看菜单了
  实话跟您说 (实话 [shíhuà] truth) Also as 实话对你说。 "To tell you the truth." For example, 你以为我没去过北京呀? 实话跟您说, 我在那儿住过一年多呢! "You thought that I hadn't been to Beijing? To tell you the truth, I lived there for over a year." 实话对你说吧, 她绝不会嫁给你的。 "To tell you the truth, she will never marry you."

- 实话跟您说, 我这个人啊, **最烦看菜单了**
  最烦... (烦 [fán] be annoyed; be troubled) This pattern means "hate to …." For example, 她说她最烦学外语, 所以她只会说一种语言。 "She said that she hated to learn foreign languages, so she could only speak one tongue."

- **净起些花里胡哨的名字**
  净... A colloquial form of "only"; "all the time." 净 is an adverb, and … is a verbal phrase. For example, 她净胡说。 "She talks nothing but nonsense."

- **整得人晕头转向的。**
  整 A colloquial form of the verb "make," with a certain degree of negative connotation, depending on the context. For example, 看你, 整得我把要紧事儿都忘了。 "Look, you made me forget something important."

- **端出来一看,** 您猜怎么着? 就是肉末炒粉丝!
  ... 一看 "… and have a look." In this pattern, … often shows an action. … 一看 is followed by an expression of what is seen, and is often used in a narration to reveal a discovery. For example, 我打开礼物一看, 原来是一本书。 "I opened the gift and what did I see? A book." Sometimes, between …一看 and the following expres-

sion, there is a statement or question, like 您猜怎么着, to express the speaker's feeling, such as surprise. For example, 我打开礼物一看, 你猜是什么？原来是一本书。"I opened the gift and had a look, and guess what? I saw a book."

- 所以啊, 今儿我**听您的**

  听...的 "Listen to …." For example, 你看, 我没说错吧？他不听我的。"See, wasn't I right? He won't listen to me."

- 他**属兔**,

  属... (属[shǔ] be born in the year of [one of the twelve animals].) This pattern expresses the meaning, "be born in the year of…" …is one of the twelve Chinese zodiacs. For example, 我属龙, 我弟弟属马。"I was born in the year of the dragon, and my brother the year of the horse."

- 专啃**青菜萝卜**

  青菜萝卜 (青菜[qīngcài] Chinese cabbage; 萝卜[luóbo] radish) Although the surface meaning is "Chinese cabbage and radish," this four character pattern often refers to green vegetables. For example, 她为了减肥, 每天就吃些青菜萝卜。In order to lose weight, she has been eating nothing but vegetables all day every day."

- 就爱**鸡鸭鱼肉**

  鸡鸭鱼肉 Although the literal meaning is "chicken and duck, fish and meat," this pattern refers to meat, fish, or fine dishes. For example, 咱们每天鸡鸭鱼肉的, 对身体不一定好。"We're eating so richly every day, this can't be good for our health."

- **我说你** 还是少吃糖的好。

  我说你 An expression leading to a suggestion or criticism. For example, 我说你, 怎么就记不住带车钥匙呢! "Hey, I say, how could you never remember to bring your car key?"

- **我这**还不是为了你好?
  我这 这 refers to some event or fact that is mentioned. 我 and 这 together serve as the subject of a sentence to put emphasis on what follows. This pattern is often used in an explanation or commentary. For example, 我这也是没办法才这么作的。 "I had no other choice here, and that's why I did this." The more general use of the pattern 我这 is to convey a personal pronoun plus 这. For example, 你这 in 你这可不应该! "You shouldn't have done so!"

- 我这**还不是为了**你好?
  还不是为了... This is a rhetorical question, that expresses the same meaning as 还是为了...,"the reason is ...," with a strong tone. For example, 他不告诉你还不是为了不让你着急? "The reason he didn't tell you is that he didn't want you to worry about it."

- **这也不能吃, 那也不能吃,** 还活不活了!
  这也不..., 那也不... In this pattern, the parallel structure 这也不..., 那也不..., shows that under no circumstances will ... happen. This pattern is often followed by an expression of the speaker's conclusion, comments, or other opinion on the situation. For example, 这也不喜欢, 那也不喜欢, 你今天怎么啦? "You don't like this, you don't like that; what is wrong with you today?"

- 好你个老丁, 为了嘴**不要命**呀!
  不要命 (命 [mìng] life) "Want to die." For example, 你没看见有车过来呀? 不要命啦? "Didn't you see the car coming? Do you want to die?"

- 这个"少"是多少**根本**说不清楚,
  根本 An adverb with the meaning, "simply" or "at all," used in negative expressions. For example, 他根本没来过这里。 "He's never been here at all."

- 这个 "少" 是多少根本说不清楚, 一个辣椒是它, 一把辣椒也是它。

  …, …是它, …也是它. … is often a statement, and the parallel structure contains … and … to provide explanation of …. For example, 作这种练习真费时间, 一个小时是它, 两个小时也是它。 "It's so time-consuming to do exercises like these. It could take an hour, or two hours."

- 我**紧着**说少放少放,

  紧着 A colloquial form for 赶紧, "hurry." For example, 一听说你在这儿, 我就紧着往这儿赶, 想早点儿见着你。 "As soon as I heard that you've been here, I hurried here hoping to see you sooner."

- **少得不能再少了**

  …得不能再…了 This pattern means: "It couldn't be more …." For example, 他那儿乱得不能再乱了, 咱们还是别去他那儿好。 "His place is so messy it couldn't be messier. We'd better not go there."

CONVERSATION B:

Simplified

周正到北京办事, 没来得及事先订旅馆, 所以一到北京就先去找旅馆。

服务员: 先生您好。

周正:　你好。有空房吗?

服务员: 您预订了吗?

周正：　没来得及。怎么,没房啦?

服务员：有房,有房。不过,因为这几天有个大型会议,**房紧得要命**。

周正：　怪不得我连着问了几家饭店都没房,原来是有会。我一个人,好凑合,有间房就行。

服务员：别凑合呀,**出门在外**,**怎么也得住舒服了**。三楼套间怎么样? 里边睡觉,外面会客办公。

周正：　听着不错,可是价钱呢? 多少钱一夜?

服务员：不贵,才一千二。您先上楼看看去就知道有多值了。**猛一看**简直就和总统套间一模一样。

周正：　**我的天! 都一千二了,还 "才" 呢! 咱小老百姓**可住不起。

服务员：这好房您要是不要,可就真得凑合了。一楼楼梯**把角儿**那儿有一间标准间,便宜,二百五一天。您**还真有运气,**会议把一楼都包了,就甩下这一间。

周正：　他们干吗不要这间呢?

服务员：其实也没什么,他们是**鸡蛋里挑骨头,非嫌对面有个厕所不可,说是味儿太冲。要我说**,门关严了,哪儿闻得着什么味儿呀?

周正：　别人都不要的我要,那我真成了**二百五**了。不瞒您说,我这鼻子特**灵**,有点味儿就睡不着,还头晕。麻烦你再给换一间。

服务员: 您看看, 房这么紧, 您还**横挑鼻子竖挑眼**的, 好
的不要, 便宜的也不要。得, 顾客是上帝, 我再
给您找找。嘿, 您的福气真不错, 楼顶上还有
一间二百五的。

周正: 这间有什么毛病没订出去?

服务员: **瞧您这话说的**! 我们这星级旅馆, 哪能靠有毛
病的房赚钱呢! 这房朝西, 稍微有点儿西晒。
关上窗帘儿, 空调一开, 一觉睡到天亮, **保您什**
么都觉不出来。

周正: 就是它了。谢谢您了。

———————■———————

Zhouzheng is in Beijing on an errand, and didn't have time to reserve a
room beforehand, so he looks for a hotel as soon as he arrives.

Receptionist: Hello, sir.

Zhou: Hi. Do you have vacancies?

Receptionist: Have you reserved with us?

Zhou: I didn't have time. What, there's no more rooms?

Receptionist: There are, there are. But, because there are several
               large conferences these next few days, the rooms are
               very tight.

Zhou: So that's why I asked at several hotels and couldn't
               find any rooms. There's a conference. I'm by myself,
               so it's easy to get by, I just need a room.

Receptionist: Don't just get by; when you travel, travel in comfort.
               How about a suite on the third floor? You can sleep
               inside, and meet people and do business outside.

Zhou: That sounds good, but what about the price? How much for a night?

Receptionist: Not much, only 1200. If you go take a look at it now you will know what a value it is. At a glance it looks just like the Presidential suite.

Zhou: My god! It's 1200, and you say "only!" A normal guy like me couldn't possibly afford that.

Receptionist: If you don't want the quality room, we really have to get by. By the corner of the first floor staircase there's a standard room. It's cheap, only 250 a day. You're really lucky; the conference rented the entire first floor, and left only this room.

Zhou: Why didn't they take this room?

Receptionist: It's nothing, really, they were nitpicking, and didn't like the bathroom across the hallway. They said that it was too smelly. If you ask me, if you shut the door, how can you possibly smell anything?

Zhou: If I take something that other people tossed, I'm really going to be a chump. Honestly, my nose is really sensitive. If there's any smell I can't sleep and get dizzy. Please switch me to another one.

Receptionist: See here, with so few rooms left you're still being picky. You didn't want the good room, and you didn't want the cheap one. Well, customers are always right; I'll look again for you. Eh, you truly are lucky, there's another room for 250 on the top floor.

Zhou: What was wrong with this room that it wasn't rented out?

Receptionist: Now look what you said! We are a star-class hotel here, how can we make money on sub-par rooms? This room faces west; it gets a little bit more sun. Close the drapes, turn on the air conditioning, and you'll sleep the whole night. I guarantee you won't feel anything.

Zhou: That's it, then. Thank you.

------◼︎------

Traditional

周正到北京辦事,沒來得及事先訂旅館, 所以一到北京就先去找旅館。

服務員: 先生您好。

周正: 你好。有空房嗎?

服務員: 您預訂了嗎?

周正: 沒來得及。怎麼,沒房啦?

服務員: 有房,有房。不過,因為這幾天有個大型會議,**房緊得要命。**

周正: 怪不得我連著問了幾家飯店都沒房,原來是有會。我一個人,好湊合,有間房就行。

服務員: 別湊合呀,**出門在外,怎麼也得住舒服了。**三樓套間怎麼樣? 裏邊睡覺,外面會客辦公。

周正: 聽著不錯,可是價錢呢? 多少錢一夜?

服務員: 不貴,**纔**一千二。您先上樓看看去就知道有多值了。**猛一看**簡直就和總統套間一模一樣。

周正: **我的天! 都一千二了,還"纔"呢!** 咱**小老百姓**可住不起。

服務員：　這好房您要是不要,可就真得湊合了。一樓樓
梯**把角兒**那兒有一間標準間,便宜,二百五一
天。您**還真有運氣**,會議把一樓都包了,就甩
下這一間。

周正：　　他們幹嗎不要這間呢?

服務員：　其實也沒什麼,他們是**雞蛋裏挑骨頭**,**非嫌對
面有個廁所不可**,**說是味兒太衝**。**要我說**,門
關嚴了,哪兒聞得著什麼味兒呀?

周正：　　別人都不要的我要,那我真成了**二百五**了。不
瞞您說,我這鼻子特**靈**,有點味兒就睡不著,還
頭暈。麻煩你再給換一間。

服務員：　您看看,房這麼緊,您還**橫挑鼻子豎挑眼**的,好
的不要,便宜的也不要。**得**,顧客是上帝,我再
給您找找。嘿,您的福氣真不錯,樓頂上還有
一間二百五的。

周正：　　這間有什麼毛病沒訂出去?

服務員：　**瞧您這話說的!** 我們這星級旅館,哪能靠有
毛病的房賺錢呢! 這房朝西,稍微有點兒西
曬。關上窗簾兒,空調一開,一覺睡到天亮,**保
您什麼都覺不出來**。

周正：　　就是它了。謝謝您了。

———————■———————

词语注释

- 因为这几天有个大型会议, 房**紧得要命**

  ...得要命 With the literal meaning, "drive somebody to his death," 要命 often stands for "extremely." For example, 天冷得要命, 我哪儿都不想去。 "The weather is extremely cold, and I don't want to go anywhere."

- **出门在外**, 怎么也得住舒服了。

  出门在外 "Be away from home." For example, 你出门在外, 要好好照顾自己, 千万别得病。 "When you're away from home, you should take good care of yourself, and make sure you don't fall ill."

- 出门在外, **怎么也得住舒服了**。

  怎么也得... This pattern is used to indicate that one should do ... no matter what. For example, 你忙了一天了, 怎么也得休息休息。 "You've been busy for the whole day, so you need to get some rest no matter what."

- **猛一看**简直就和总统套间一模一样。

  猛一看 (猛 [měng] suddenly, abruptly)

  In the pattern, 猛一看 refers to "at first glance," For example, 这儿真象北京, 这条街猛一看就跟北京的长安街一个样。 "This place looks so much like Beijing, and from first impressions this street looks exactly like Beijing's Changan Street."

- **我的天**! 都一千二了, 还"才"呢!

  我的天 "My God." For example, 我的天, 都是十点了, 你怎么还在这儿? "Oh, my God, it's ten o'clock already; why are you still here?"

- 我的天！ **都一千二了,还 "才" 呢!**

  都... 了,还... "already ..., but still ...." 都...了 is used to focus on the situation ..., and 还 is used to indicate the contrast between the actual situation ... and the expected situation. The subject of the sentence should usually be put either before 都..., or before 还.... For example, 都十一点了, 他还不起床。 "It's already eleven o'clock, but he is still sleeping."

- **咱小老百姓**可住不起。

  小老百姓 老百姓 means "common people." 小老百姓 also refers to common people, but with a negative connotation such as "powerless" or "financially weak." For example, 市长想干这事儿, 我们小老百姓都没兴趣。 "The mayor wants to do this, but we, the common people, are not interested in it."

- 一楼楼梯**把角儿**那儿有一间标准间

  把角 A colloquial expression that is used as a noun, "corner." For example, 我就住在把角的那间屋子里。 "I am living in the corner room."

- 您**还真有运气**

  还真... (运气 [yùnqi] fortune, luck)

  This pattern is used to express the realization or discovery of the fact .... For example, 你是大忙人, 没想到你还真来了。 "I didn't expect that you'd come, as you are such a busy person."

- 他们是**鸡蛋里挑骨头**

  鸡蛋里挑骨头 (挑 [tiāo] choose, select; 骨头 [gútou] bone)

  The literal meaning of the expression is: "to look for a bone in an egg," and the contextual meaning is "to nitpick." For example, 这个电影够好的, 你就别鸡蛋里挑骨头了! "The movie is good enough. Don't be so picky!"

- **非嫌对面有个厕所不可**

  非...不可 "Simply must …," or "have got to …." This pattern can be shortened to 非…. The example 非嫌对面有个厕所 is a shortened version of 非嫌对面有个厕所不可. Another example: 她非要去看电影(不可), 我有什么办法? "She simply wants to watch the movie. What can I do?"

- 非**嫌**对面有个厕所不可

  嫌... (嫌[xián] resentment, dislike) 嫌, "complain of" or "dislike." In this pattern, … represents the reason for complaint or 嫌, "resentment." For example, 你总嫌那家饭馆人太多, 咱们今天就换一家吧。 "You always complain that restaurant is too crowded, so let's go to another one today."

- 说是味儿太**冲**.

  冲 This word often means that the smell of something is "strong." For example, 这是哪儿来的味儿啊? 这么冲。 "Where is the smell coming from? It's so strong."

- **要我说**, 门关严了, 哪儿闻得着什么味儿呀?

  要我说 A colloquial form of "in my view." For example, 要我说, 这事儿好办! "As I see it, this matter is easy to deal with."

- 别人都不要的我要, 那我真成了**二百五**了。

  二百五 "a stupid person." For example, 你以为他是二百五啊? 那你可搞错了! "Do you think that he's stupid? If you do, then you are wrong."

- 我这鼻子特**灵**,

  灵 (灵[ling] quick, sharp, keen) 灵 In this context, the word is used to describe a keen sense of smell. It can also be employed to refer to sharp hearing. For example, 你耳朵怎么这么灵? "How could your hearing be so sharp?"

- 您还**横挑鼻子竖挑眼**的,
  横挑鼻子竖挑眼 (横 [héng] horizontal; 挑 [tiāo] choose, select; 竖 [shù] vertical) This is an idiom with the meaning: "pick faults right and left" or "nitpick." For example, 你就别横挑鼻子竖挑眼的了好不好? "Don't be so picky, OK?"

- **瞧您这话说的!**
  瞧你...的 This pattern is often used in an exclamation to express a comment, blame, or even rebuke. This pattern is often followed by a further comment. For example, 瞧你写的! 那么乱! "Look at what you wrote! What a mess!"

- **保您什么都觉不出来**。
  保你... 保 is a colloquial form of 保证, "guarantee." This pattern means: "Ensure that you ...." For example, 我的礼物, 保你喜欢. "I am sure that you'll love my gift."

- 保您什么都**觉不出来**.
  觉出来 (觉 [jué] sense, feel) The expression means "sensed something." For example, 她挺不高兴, 你觉出来了吗? "Have you noticed that she was unhappy?"

———■———

| VOCABULARY

出差	chūchāi	be on a business trip
清静	qīngjìng	quiet
菜单	càidān	menu
花里胡哨	huālihúshào	gaudy; garish; showy
晕头转向	yūntóuzhuànxiàng	confused and disoriented

蚂蚁	mǎyǐ	ant
猜	cāi	guess
肉末	ròumò	ground meat; minced meat
粉丝	fěnsī	vermicelli made from bean starch, etc.
清淡	qīngdàn	light; not greasy or strongly flavored
素	sù	vegetable
拼盘	pīnpán	assorted cold dishes
大丰收	dàfēngshōu	name of the dish "bumper harvest"
海鲜	hǎixiān	seafood
豆腐煲	dòufubāo	bean curd pot or saucepan
无锡	Wúxí	Place Name
排骨	páigǔ	spareribs
香酥鸡	xiāngsūjī	crisp fried chicken
糖	táng	sugar
轻度	qīngdù	mild
糖尿病	tángniàobìng	diabetes
推荐	tuījiàn	recommend
煮	zhǔ	boil; cook
松鼠	sōngshǔ	squirrel
桂鱼	guìyú	Mandarin fish
嗓子	sǎngzi	throat
辣椒	làjiāo	hot pepper
炒	chǎo	stir-fry
大师傅	dàshīfu	cook; chef
丰盛	fēngshèng	rich; sumptuous

抓	zhuā	grab
汤	tāng	soup
来得及	láidejí	be able to do something in time
事先	shìxiān	in advance; beforehand
预订	yùdìng	book; place an order
大型	dàxíng	large-scale; large
会议	huìyì	meeting; conference
套间	tàojiān	a suite of rooms
会客	huìkè	receive a visitor
简直	jiǎnzhí	simply; at all
总统	zǒngtǒng	president
一模一样	yīmúyīyàng	exactly alike
楼梯	lóutī	stairs; staircase
标准间	biāozhǔnjiān	a hotel room up to the standard
甩	shuǎi	throw off
严	yán	tight
特灵	tèlíng	very sensitive
头晕	tóuyūn	dizzy; giddy
顾客	gùkè	customer
福气	fúqi	happy lot; good fortune
毛病	máobing	defect; shortcoming
星级旅馆	xīngjílǚguǎn	luxury hotel
赚钱	zhuànqián	make money
西晒	xīshài	(of a room) with a western exposure or facing west (hot on summer afternoons)
窗帘	chuānglián	(window) curtain
空调	kōngtiáo	air conditioner

天亮   tiānliàng   daybreak; dawn
保   bǎo   guarantee; ensure

EXERCISES

A. Fill in the spaces with the appropriate words or phrases:

> 鸡鸭鱼肉   我说你   紧着   一看
> 实话跟您说   青菜萝卜 我这   根本   属

1 他说他跟我是朋友, 可是我_____不认识他。

2 _____全是为她好, 可是她一点儿都不明白, 还生我的气。

3 每天早上一到六点钟, 我妈就_____催我快起床.

4 云云, _____快点儿行不行? 咱们快迟到了。

5 你光吃_____怎么行? 我可每天都得吃大鱼大肉.

6 他以前一上饭馆就点_____, 现在只敢吃些青菜萝卜了。

7 你以为我不会打篮球呀? _____, 我以前是篮球队的。

8 他比我小一岁, 应该是_____的。

9 那么多人围着, 我过去_____, 原来是个卖水果的。

B. Choose the expression from the following list that best corresponds to the underlined words or phrases:

　　　咸得不能再咸了　　　整　　　净　　　听他的
　　　这也不买, 那也不买　　　　最烦　　还不是
　　　干完了是它, 干不完也是它　　不要命

1　你别只跟我说些没关系的话, 快点儿回答我的问题.

2　我最不爱听她叨唠了, 她一叨唠上就没完没了。

3　你不想活啦? 也不看看有没有车就过马路。

4　你干什么这么着急? 丢得她连话都不敢说了。

5　他是你老板, 上班的时候, 你得做他要你做的事。

6　他这么做就是为了让你高兴!

7　你既然什么都不买, 那咱们就回家吧。

8　你干一个小时就行了, 反正干得完干不完都是一小时.

9　这个菜是谁做的? 也太咸了!

C. Fill in the spaces with the appropriate words or phrases:

　　　保你满意　　　小老百姓　　觉出来　　把角　　冲
　　　鸡蛋里挑骨头　出门在外　猛一看　说是　嫌

1　这种酒的味儿_____极了, 你闻闻看。

2　你上了二楼往前走, _____的那间屋子就是我的办公室。

3　这件事市长办得不错, 这是我们_____最关心的事。

4　她今天好像有什么事, 你_____了吗?

5 你_____,要注意安全,好好照顾自己。

6 他们俩长得真象,_____简直分不出谁是谁。

7 他总_____我下了班不马上回家,我今天得早点回去。

8 她今天没来,_____有别的事儿,来不了。

9 这么一点小毛病算什么,你真是_____。

10 这件衣服大小正好,你穿穿看,_____。

D. Choose the expression from the following list that best corresponds to the underlined words or phrases:

> 二百五　　还真　　灵　我的天　　要我说
> 瞧你这事办的　　　非去不可　　天都黑了
> 横挑鼻子竖挑眼　　怎么也得　　贵得要命

1 天哪! 你怎么病得这么厉害了才去看医生?

2 你别看她都快九十岁了,耳朵还可好呢。

3 我看哪,你们谁也不用着急,他是逗你们玩儿的。

4 你还叫他笨蛋呢,你看他这事儿办得多聪明。

5 我以为你是说着玩儿的,没想到你真的要这么干。

6 你今天对什么都看不顺眼,你是怎么啦?

7 她一定要去,我就只好让她去了。

8 现在汽油太贵了,咱们俩人开一辆车上班吧。

9 我这车有毛病了,今天一定得请假去修车。

10 看你怎么这么办事, 下回可不能这样了。

11 天已经黑了,这孩子怎么还不回来呢?

ANSWER KEY

Exercise A (Dialogue 1)

1 根本
2 我这
3 紧着
4 我说你
5 青菜萝卜
6 鸡鸭鱼肉
7 实话跟您说
8 属牛（属…）
9 一看（…一看）

Exercise B (Dialogue 1)

1 净（净…）
2 最烦
3 不要命
4 整
5 听他的（听…的）
6 还不是（还不是为了…）
7 这也不买，那也不买（这
   也不…，那也不…）
8 干完了是它,干不完也是它
   （…，…是它，…也是它）
9 咸得不能再咸了（…得不
   能再…了）

Exercise C (Dialogue 2)

1 冲
2 把角
3 小老百姓
4 觉出来
5 出门在外
6 猛一看（猛一看…）
7 嫌（嫌…）
8 说是
9 鸡蛋里挑骨头
10 保你满意（保你…）

Exercise D (Dialogue 2)

1 我的天
2 灵
3 要我说
4 二百五
5 还真（还真…）
6 横挑鼻子竖挑眼
7 非去不可（非…不可）
8 贵得要命（…得要命）
9 怎么也得（怎么也得…）
10 瞧你这事办的（瞧
    你…的）
11 天都黑了（都…了，还…）

WHY DOES "二百五" MEAN "HALFWIT" OR "STUPID?"

There are quite a few stories to answer this question. Here is one. In ancient times, China used a copper coin with a square hole through the middle; a string of 1,000 copper coins was called "A String," 一贯 [yí guàn] or 一吊 [yí diào]. One half of the string, 500 copper coins, was called "Half String" "半贯" or "半吊." So people used "半吊子" to describe a uninformed, unskilled, tactless, impulsive, lackadaisical, or irresolute person. "二百五.", 250 copper coins, was only one half of the half string; and so this concept became a metaphor for a person who is a halfwit or stupid.

Similar slang:

半瓶醋 [bàn píng cù] dabbler or smatterer

半半拉拉 [bàn bàn lā lā] incomplete; unfinished

二五眼 [èr wǔ yǎn] incompetent or mediocre (person); or low quality (thing)

十三点 [shí sān diǎn] nitwit; dunce; person who is muddle-headed or unreasonable

三八 [sān bā] airhead, braggart, slut. Mainly used in Taiwan to insult women. One derivation claims that at one point in the Qing dynasty, foreigners were only permitted to circulate on the eighth, eighteenth, and twenty-eighth of each month, and the Chinese deprecated these aliens by calling them 三八 (three eight). Others claim the expression refers to March 8th: International Women's Day.

宰我?没门儿!
一开口就给我打了九折

BARGAINING
·
COMPLACENCY

▌CONVERSATION A:

Simplified

张常立和刘贵元在他们单位食堂里一边吃饭一边聊天。

张常立: 昨儿我买皮夹克**拣了个便宜**。

刘贵元: 这年头儿买东西, 不**挨宰**就是拣着便宜了。

张常立: 宰我?**没门儿**! 我买东西**货比三家**不说, 还**特能砍价**。

刘贵元: **一分钱一分货**, 便宜没好货。 买的再精也精不过卖的。 我倒要听听你拣了什么便宜了。

张常立: 我早就看准了一件皮夹克, 一样的货, 别处卖一千, 那儿卖八百五。 **买卖人都图开门红**, 头笔生意舍不得丢, 所以昨儿一大早我就赶着去了。

跳楼价 (lit: "Suicidal Prices.") Fire sale; very low prices (see page 188.)

Zhang and Liu are chatting over lunch in their office cafeteria.

Zhang:	Yesterday I got a good deal on a leather jacket.
Liu:	Buying things in this day and age and not getting ripped off is a good deal already.
Zhang:	Rip me off? No way! I don't buy anything without getting a third opinion, and I'm really good at haggling.
Liu:	You buy what you pay for; nothing good comes cheaply. And no matter how good you get, you can't get better than the seller. Let's hear what you bought that's so cheap.
Zhang:	I've been looking at a leather jacket for a long time, and for the same jacket, it's a thousand at other places, but only 850 where I went. Store owners all want a good start; they never want to lose the first deal, so early yesterday morning I hurried over.

刘贵元: 这么勤快呀, 你?

张常立: 他那儿门口贴着"名牌大甩卖"、"跳楼价"。
里边儿还挂着牌子, 说是货真价实,还价免谈。
我才不理那套**花样**呢, 都是我**玩儿剩下的**。

刘贵元: 你出多少钱?

张常立: 我**一上来**就告诉老板: "我**看上**这件皮夹克
了。你别玩**猫匿**,给我说个最低价吧。"

刘贵元: 人家说"还价免谈", 那就是**一口价**, 不能再还
了。（待续）

———————■———————

Traditional

張常立和劉貴元在他們單位食堂裏一邊吃飯一邊聊天。

張常立: 昨兒我買皮夾克**揀了個便宜**。

劉貴元: 這年頭兒買東西,不**挨宰**就是揀著便宜了。

張常立: 宰我?**沒門兒**! 我買東西**貨比三家**不說,還**特
能砍價**。

劉貴元: **一分錢一分貨**, 便宜沒好貨。買的再精也精不
過賣的。我倒要聽聽你揀了什麼便宜了。

張常立: 我早就看準了一件皮夾克,一樣的貨,別處賣
一千,那兒賣八百五。**買賣人**都**圖開門紅**,頭筆
生意捨不得丟,所以昨兒**一大早**我就趕著去了.

劉貴元: 這麼勤快呀, 你?

Liu: You're that hard working?

Zhang: Outside he's got signs saying "Designer Blowout,"
            "Suicidal Prices." Inside there's "Real Products Real
            Value" and "All Prices Are Final." Like I care for
            those tricks; I've been there, done that.

Liu: How much did you pay?

Zhang: The first thing I told the owner was: "I like that
            leather jacket. Now don't play games with me, and
            give me the lowest price."

Liu: They said, "All prices are final." they go by the
            sticker price, and you can't bargain.

———————————————

張常立:　他那兒門口貼著"名牌大拍賣"、"跳樓價"。
　　　　裏邊兒還掛著牌子, 說是貨真價實, 還價免談。
　　　　我才不理那套**花樣**呢, 都是我**玩兒剩下的**。

劉貴元:　你出多少錢?

張常立:　我**一上來**就告訴老闆: "我**看上**這件皮夾克
　　　　了。你別玩**貓匿**, 給我說個最低價吧。"

劉貴元:　人家說"還價免談", 那就是**一口價**, 不能再還
　　　　了。（待續）

———————————————

词语注释

- 昨儿我买皮夹克**拣了个便宜**。
  拣便宜 "Get a bargain"; "gain a small advantage." For example, 昨天我家门口那个商店关门大甩卖, 很多人去拣便宜。"Yesterday, the store close to my home had a closing sale. Quite a few people went there to get a bargain."

- 这年头儿买东西, 不**挨宰**就是拣着便宜了。
  挨宰 (挨 [āi] suffer; endure; 宰 [zǎi] overcharge, soak, fleece) A colloquial word to express "to be overcharged." For example, 那个饭馆儿老板可黑心了, 去那儿吃饭的没有不挨宰的。"The owner of that restaurant is very greedy; everybody eating there got overcharged."

- 宰我?**没门儿**!
  没门儿 ""No way"; "no go"; "nothing doing." For example, 你甭想骗我。没门儿! "You can't fool me. No way!"

- 我买东西**货比三家**不说, 还特能砍价。
  货比三家 "Shop around." For example, 我妈妈总是对我说, 买东西一定要货比三家, 才能不吃亏。"My mom always tells me, when buying something always shop around, so you don't get ripped off."

- 我买东西货比三家不说, 还**特**能砍价。
  特 A shortened and colloquial form of 特别, "very" or "especially." For example, 今天特热。"It's extremely hot today." 她特会买东西。She is especially good at buying things." 这个老师讲课特好。"That teacher lectures very well."

- 我买东西货比三家不说, 还特能**砍价**。
  砍价 Literally "cut price," a colloquial expression for "bargain." For

example, 去农贸市场买东西, 先得学会砍价。 "You have to learn how to haggle before going to a farmer's market."

- **一分钱一分货**, 便宜没好货。
  一分钱一分货 "You get what you pay for." For example, 我图便宜买的夹克才一个月扣子就都掉了, 真是一分钱一分货。 "The jacket I bought at a discount lost all its buttons in a month. You really get what you pay for."

- **买买人**都图开门红, 头笔生意舍不得丢。
  买买人 A colloquial form for "businessman" or "trader." For example, 他这么懒, 哪儿能当买卖人? "He is so lazy, how could he ever become a businessman?"

- 买买人都**图开门红**, 头笔生意舍不得丢。
  图... "Pursue ...";"seek ...." For example, 你这么拼命地工作, 连周末也不休息, 图什么呀? "You work so hard that you don't even take your weekends off. What are you after?"

- 买买人都图**开门红**, 头笔生意舍不得丢。
  开门红 "Get off to a good start." For example, 希望你们新公司开门红。 "I hope that your new company gets off to a good start."

- 所以昨儿**一大早**我就赶着去了。
  一大早 A colloquial expression for "early in the morning." For example, 他今天一大早就去学校了。 "He went to school early in the morning today."

- 我才不理那套**花样**呢,
  花样 "Trick." For example, 你又在玩儿什么花样? What tricks are you playing this time? 他玩儿的花样没一样能骗得了我。 "I was never fooled by any trick he played."

- 都是我**玩儿剩下的**。
  玩儿剩下的 Literally, "the leftover of what somebody played";
  "something that somebody already disdains to do." For example, 别
  再跟我来这一套了，这都是我玩儿剩下的了。Don't try
  that stuff on me; those are leftovers from the fun I used to have."

- 我**一上来**就告诉老板
  一上来 Also as 上来, a colloquial expression for "as soon as" or
  "immediately." For example, 他一上来就说我错了，我当然生
  气啦。"He blamed me right off the bat, so of course I got angry."

- 我**看上**这件皮夹克了。
  看上 "Take a fancy to"; "settle on." For example, 他看上了一个
  漂亮的姑娘。"He's taken a fancy to a pretty girl."

- 你别玩**猫匿**，给我说个最低价。
  猫匿 (匿 [nì] hide; conceal) A colloquial expression usually meaning "tricks"; "underhanded activity"; "hanky-panky"; "goings-on."
  For example, 买旧车的时候，你可得小心，里面有不少猫
  匿。"You have to be very careful when you buy a used car, because
  there's a lot of dirty tricks being played."

- 那就是**一口价**，不能再还了。
  一口价 "A firm price (which is not negotiable)"; 一口 means "to
  say something flatly or with certainty." For example, 王师傅仗着自
  己技术好，给人修车从来是一口价，你要是还价他就不
  给你修了。"Relying on his good skill, Master Wang never negotiates
  his price when repairing cars. If you try to bargain he'll refuse to do it."

CONVERSATION B:

Simplified

张常立和刘贵元在他们单位食堂里一边吃饭一边聊天。（续）

张常立： 看看，你**傻冒**了吧?这年头儿买东西，二百五才信一口价呢。老板**一开口**就给我**打了九折**。

刘贵元： **真有你的**，一句话就省了八十五块!

张常立： 才**杀**一折还算**能耐**?我假装扭头就走，扔给他一句话:"要是找不到比这便宜的我再回 来。"

刘贵元： 那他不会让你走。

张常立： **没错儿**。他连忙追了上来，**硬要我自己出个价**。说是为做成头一笔买卖，**放血**也**认了**。

刘贵元： 那你还了多少?

张常立： 我一看**有戏**，就说:"图个吉利，五百八十八吧。两个'发'，你我都发。这也是一口价，不成**拉倒**。"

刘贵元： 这可连七折都不到啦，人家干吗?

张常立： 这是"漫天要价，就地还钱。" 我早就**吃准**了:那儿的货起码打八折。

刘贵元： 他怎么说?

张常立： 那还有什么说的?他直嘟囔: "开门生意，**认赔了，认栽了**。" 可是我一给钱，他又**乐**了。

刘贵元： 这五百多可是猪皮夹克的价儿，你别是买的假冒伪劣吧?

张常立: 哟, 我还真**没留神儿**是什么皮的。 我**这就**回
去拿来, 你给看看。

———————■———————

Zhang and Liu are chatting as they have lunch in their office cafeteria.

(continuation of Conversation A)

Zhang: See, are you a chump or what? These days, only idiots pay sticker price. The owner cut the price by ten percent right there.

Liu: Good job, one sentence and you got eighty-five bucks off!

Zhang: Ten percent and you call that good? I turned around and pretended to leave, and threw him: "I'll come back if I can't find a cheaper one."

Liu: Then he's not going to let you go.

Zhang: That's right. He came right up behind me, and made me give my own price. He said that for the first deal of the day, he'll do it even if he had to lose money.

Liu: So how much did you name?

Zhang: I saw that there's still hope, so I said: "Why don't we try for luck, and do five eighty-eight. Two eights, that's a lucky number, one for you and one for me. This is his final asking price, too, take it or leave it.

Liu: That's not even 70%, is he going to agree?

Zhang: This is called "asking sky high, bidding dirt cheap." I knew it from the start: stuff over there goes for at least a 20% discount.

Liu: What did he say?

Zhang:	What could he say? He kept grumbling: "First deal of the day, I'll take the loss, it's just my luck." But when I paid, he smiled.
Liu:	Five hundred is the price for a pigskin jacket; you didn't buy a fake, did you?
Zhang:	Oh, I really didn't pay attention to what kind of leather it is. I'll go back and get it right now. Check it for me.

———————————

Traditional

張常立和劉貴元在他們單位食堂裏一邊吃飯一邊聊天。
（續）

張常立: 看看, 你**傻冒**了吧?這年頭兒買東西, 二百五才信一口價呢。 老闆**一開口**就給我**打了九折**。

劉貴元: **真有你的**, 一句話就省了八十五塊!

張常立: 才**殺**一折還算**能耐**?我假裝扭頭就走, 扔給他一句話:"要是找不到比這便宜的我再回 來。"

劉貴元: 那他不會讓你走。

張常立: **沒錯兒**。他連忙追了上來, **硬要我自己出個價**。說是為做成頭一筆買賣, **放血**也**認了**。

劉貴元: 那你還了多少?

張常立: 我一看**有戲**,就說: "圖個吉利, 五百八十八吧。兩個 '發', 你我都發。這也是一口價, 不成**拉倒**。"

劉貴元: 這可連七折都不到啦, 人家幹嗎?

張常立: 這是"漫天要價, 就地還錢。" 我早就**吃准**了: 那兒的貨起碼打八折。

劉貴元: 他怎麼說?

張常立: 那還有什麼說的?他直嘟囔: "開門生意, **認賠**了, **認栽**了。" 可是我一給錢, 他又**樂**了。

劉貴元: 這五百多可是豬皮夾克的價兒, 你別是買的假冒偽劣吧?

張常立: 喲, 我還真**沒留神兒**是什麼皮的。我**這就**回去拿來, 你給看看。

----■----

词语注释

* 看看, 你**傻冒**了吧?
  傻冒 (傻冒 [shǎ mào] fool; blockhead; foolish or stupid)
  This is a colloquial word. For example, 昨天在地摊儿买钱包时我真傻冒, 他要十块我就给了十块。其实旁边不远的那个摊儿才卖五块。"I acted like an idiot when I bought the wallet at the street stall yesterday. He asked for ten and I gave him ten. Actually another stall not far away charged only five."

* 老板**一开口**就给我打了九折。
  一开口 The first thing out of one's mouth. For example, 他根本不听我的解释, 一开口就说我错了。"He did not listen to me at all, and the first thing out of his mouth was that I was wrong."

- 老板一开口就给我**打了九折**。

  打…折 打折,"give discount" or "sell at a discount." For example, 逢年过节的时候, 商店都喜欢打折促销。"On New Year's Day and during other festivals, stores like to give discounts in order to boost sales." When a price is reduced to … percentage in transaction, it is called 打…折, "a … percent discount." e.g., if the price is ten Yuan (Chinese dollar) and then reduced to 9 Yuan, it is called 打九折,"a ninety percent sale." If the price is reduced to 7.5 Yuan, it is called 打七五折. For example, 这些东西今天都打八折。 "Today these items are all selling at eighty percent."

- **真有你的**, 一句话就省了八十五块!

  真有你的 A colloquial expression when praising or blaming somebody to add emphasis. For example, 上次考试全班都不及格, 你倒得了一百分, 真有你的! "The whole class failed the last test but you got a perfect score. You're really something." 真有你的! 看见那个老头快摔倒了都不扶一把。"How could you not lend your hand, seeing the old man was going to have a fall?"

- 才**杀**一折还算能耐?

  杀 A short form of 杀价,"beat the seller down";"knock down the price." For example, 碰上漫天要价的车商, 你要是不杀价肯定吃亏。"When you encounter a car dealer who demands an exorbitant price, you'll definitely get ripped off unless you cut the price down."

- 才杀一折还算**能耐**?

  能耐 "Ability" or "aptitude," used in colloquial expressions. For example, 那个孩子的能耐真不小, 才十岁就会开车了。"That kid is really capable. He is only ten years old and he can drive already."

- **没错儿**。他连忙追了上来, 硬要我自己出个价。

  没错儿 A colloquial expression to show agreement:"You are

right"; "I'm quite sure." For example, "咱们的会是在下午一点开始吗?" "没错儿。" "Does our meeting start at one p.m. ?" "Yes, that's right." 没错儿, 一定是他干的。 "I'm quite sure that he is the one who did it."

- 他连忙追了上来, **硬要我自己出个价**。
  硬... (硬 [yìng] obstinately) "Stubbornly insist ….." In this pattern, 硬 means: "obstinate"; and … should be a verb. For example, 要是她不愿意去那儿, 别硬叫她去。 "Don't make her go if she doesn't want to go."

- 说是为做成头一笔买卖, **放血**也认了。
  放血 The literal meaning is: "to purposely make somebody bleed profusely, even to death." As a slang expression, people use it to mean: "lose or pay money." For example, 咱们在饭馆儿一块儿吃饭你从来没掏过钱, 今天该你放点儿血了。 "You never paid when we ate out. It's your turn to bleed today."

- 说是为做成头一笔买卖, 放血也**认了**。
  认了 "Accept as unavoidable"; "so be it." For example, 这件衣服我太喜欢了, 贵点儿我也认了。 "I love this dress so much, if I get overcharged a little then so be it."

- 我一看**有戏**, 就说...
  有戏 (戏 [xì] drama; play; show) This is a colloquial expression for "hopeful." The opposite expression is 没戏, "hopeless." For example, 我看这事还有戏。 "I think that there is still hope." 他想和她结婚, 我看没戏。 "I think there is no hope for him to marry her."

- 这也是一口价, 不成**拉倒**。
  拉倒 A colloquial expression: "forget about it"; "leave it at that"; or "drop it." For example, 这件事你不愿意就拉倒。 "If you don't want to, then forget about it."

- 我早就**吃准**了：那儿的货起码打八折
  吃准 A colloquial form for "firmly believe." For example, 他就吃准你不会来, 所以才这么作。 "He knew that you wouldn't come, that's why he acted like that."

- 开门生意, 认赔了, 认栽了。
  认… "Admit to …";"resign oneself to taking…." … is often 赔 ([péi] "lose money in business") or 栽 ([zāi] short form for 栽跟头, "come a cropper"). For example, 作生意赔了应当认赔。 "If you lose money at business you should admit it to yourself." 他栽了跟头从来不认栽。 "When bad things happen to him he never admits it."

- 可是我一给钱, 他又**乐**了。
  乐 "Happy";"cheerful";"joyful." For example, 什么事儿乐成这样呀? "What makes you so happy?"

- 哟, 我还真**没留神儿**是什么皮的。
  没留神 (留神 [liú shén] be careful; take care)
  "Did not pay attention to." For example, 昨天我没留神摔了一交。 "Yesterday I was not careful and fell down."

- 我**这就**回去拿来, 你给看看。
  这就 A colloquial form for 现在就 or 马上就, "right now." For example, 别着急, 我这就给你办。 "Don't worry. I'll do it for you right now."

VOCABULARY

食堂	shítáng	dining room; mess hall
皮夹克	píjiákè	leather jacket

精	jīng	smart; sharp; clever
开门红	kāiménhóng	make a good beginning
头	tóu	first
笔	bǐ	(measure word, similar to "number of deals")
舍不得	shěbude	hate to part with or use; grudge
勤快	qínkai	diligent, hardworking
名牌	míngpái	famous brand
甩卖	shuǎimài	disposal of goods at reduced prices
牌子	páizi	brand; trademark
货真价实	huòzhēnjiàshí	genuine goods at a fair price
还价	huánjià	counteroffer; counterbid
免	miǎn	not allowed
杀	shā	reduce; abate; take off
扭头	niǔtóu	turn around
扔	rēng	throw; cast
图	tú	pursue; seek; intent
吉利	jílì	luckiness; auspiciousness
漫天要价, 就地还钱	màntiānyàojià jiùdìhuánqián	The seller can ask a sky-high price; the buyer can make a down-to-earth offer.
吃准了	chīzhǔnle	for sure
起码	qǐmǎ	at least
嘟囔	dūnang	mutter to oneself; mumble
赔	péi	lose money in business
栽	zāi	suffer a setback

| 假冒 | jiǎmào | fake commodities; counterfeit goods |
| 伪劣 | wěiliè | fake and poor products |

———— ■ ————

EXERCISES

A. Fill in the spaces with the appropriate words or phrases:

货比三家　　一口价　　看上　花样　挨宰
玩儿剩下的　一分钱一分货　便宜　猫匿

1　他昨天在路边小摊买东西, 又＿＿＿＿＿＿了。

2　这一定是他搞的＿＿＿＿＿, 又想骗人。

3　兰兰, 你们班有那么多好小伙子, 你＿＿＿＿＿哪一个了?

4　跟他作买卖可要小心点, 他最会玩＿＿＿＿＿了。

5　他把我＿＿＿＿＿拿来骗我, 哪能骗得了我呢?

6　在农贸市场, 有些摊贩要＿＿＿＿＿, 不让人家讨价还价。

7　买东西的时候＿＿＿＿＿是好办法, 就是太费时间。

8　这双鞋虽然贵, 可是穿起来特别舒服, 真是＿＿＿＿＿。

9　她今天买了一双半价的皮鞋, 觉得是拣了＿＿＿＿＿了。

B. Choose the expression from the following list that best corresponds to the underlined words or phrases:

> 开门红　　一上来　　砍价　　　特
> 没门儿　　一大早　　买卖人　　图

1 北京人说话的时候<u>很爱说"特"</u>怎么样。

2 老王买什么都跟人家<u>讨价还价</u>,连上饭馆吃饭也这样。

3 那个会开得不错,老李<u>一开始</u>就想出个新办法,大家都说好。

4 有的<u>商人</u>喜欢骗人,买东西的时候要小心,别受骗。

5 上大学以后的第一次考试,我就考了个<u>好成绩</u>。

6 你想不用功就考一百分?<u>不可能</u>!

7 他买了张便宜机票,时间不好,明天<u>天刚亮</u>就得往机场赶。

8 她这么用功,不是只<u>想</u>得个好分,她是想学点真本事.

C. Fill in the spaces with the appropriate words or phrases:

> 吃准　　有戏　　放血　　杀　　乐
> 认栽　　拉倒　　认赔　　认了

1 这次工厂要招好多人,他条件挺好,所以可能_____。

2 这次亏钱是因为咱们没作好市场调查,只好_____了。

3 这事既然大家都不太想作,那就_____算了。

4 一拿到大学录取通知书,他就_____得跳了起来。

5 在农贸市场买东西哪有不还价的?最少也
   得_____两折。

6 我_____了你会忘记带伞,所以给你带了一把来.

7 他这次失败完全是他自己造成的,所以他只
   好_____。

8 老王太小气了,从来不出钱,今天可该他_____了。

9 这件事我一定要作,就是让老板解雇也_____。

D. Choose the expression from the following list that best corresponds
   to the underlined words or phrases:

   没留神   一开口   这就   能耐
   真有你的   没错儿   打五折   傻冒   硬

1 这件事, 我看你<u>马上</u>作吧, 别拖到明天去了。

2 刚才咱们碰见的那个男的, <u>一说话</u>我就知道他不是
   好人。

3 这个人挺有<u>本事</u>, 才二十几岁就当上校长了。

4 你怎么去那种地方买东西啊?真是<u>傻瓜</u>!

5 咱们猜得<u>挺对</u>, 他真是考上哈佛大学了。

6 在公共汽车上, 我<u>一不小心</u>让小偷把我的钱包偷走
   了。

7 居然敢跟老板吵架! <u>你可真行</u>!

8 你女朋友不愿意去, 你<u>一定</u>要她跟你去, 她当然不高
   兴啦。

9 那家商店就要关门了, 所有的东西都<u>卖半价</u>。

ANSWER KEY

Exercise A (Dialogue 1)

1 挨宰
2 花样
3 看上
4 猫匿
5 玩儿剩下的
6 一口价
7 货比三家
8 一分钱一分货
9 便宜（拣便宜）

Exercise B (Dialogue 1)

1 特
2 砍价
3 一上来
4 买卖人
5 开门红
6 没门儿
7 一大早
8 图（图...）

Exercise C (Dialogue 2)

1 有戏
2 认赔（认...）
3 拉倒
4 乐
5 杀
6 吃准
7 认栽（认...）
8 放血
9 认了

Exercise D (Dialogue 2)

1 这就
2 一开口
3 能耐
4 傻冒
5 没错儿
6 没留神
7 真有你的
8 硬（硬...）
9 打五折（打...折）

▌ WHY IS 4 BAD BUT 8 GOOD?

Just like some Western people do not like the number 13, some Chinese do not like the number 4. For example, you cannot find the 4th floor or room or bed number 4 in hospitals and hotels in some areas in China. This is because "4 [sì] four" is a homophone of "死 [sǐ] die, be dead, death." The two words have the same pronunciation in some dialects. Some people think unlucky words could bring them bad luck, so they avoid using either "死 die" or "4 four." Some people even do not like other numbers with 4 in them. For example, "47 [sì qī]" sounds like "死期 [sǐ qī] date of death;" "14 [shí sì]" sounds like "失事 [shī shì] have an accident." On the other hand, some Chinese like number "8 [bā]" very much, since its pronunciation is similar to "发 [fā] flourish through obtaining a great deal of wealth." The car plates or telephone numbers with "8888" can be sold for thousands of dollars at auction.

However, when talking about "Chinese culture," it should be noticed that China is so large and has so many nationalities that no custom or habit is the same for all Chinese. You can always find some differences or even contradictions among different ethnic groups or areas or among different time periods. For example, generally speaking, 4 has been a good number for most Chinese since ancient times. In Chinese, a lot of words or phrases related to 4 are good, and about ninety-five percent of Chinese idioms are four characters. On the other hand, some Chinese in some areas think 8 is a bad number because the two strokes of the Chinese character 八 are separate and go two directions. So they avoid going out on the 8th, 18th, and 28th day of the month, believing these dates would bring them bad luck and separation from their families.

好, 赌就赌!
你可不是我的对手!

BETTING
·
ARGUING
·
BOASTING
·
BRAGGING

CONVERSATION A:

Simplified

王军生和赵庆春是邻居, 两人在聊世界杯足球赛。

王军生: 这几天世界杯看得真**来劲**。今天我**连班儿都没上**, 请了一天假。

赵庆春: **看把你迷得, 值当的吗?**

王军生: **我这人**就爱看足球。甭说世界杯了, 就是学校足球赛, 我都觉着挺好看。

赵庆春: 哪有像你这么**着迷**的? 再怎么也得上班呀!

王军生: 不知怎么的, 自打世界杯一开赛, 我除了看球,

吹牛 (lit: "to blow up a cow") to brag (see page 214.)

Junsheng Wang and Qingchun Zhao are neighbors. They are talking about the World Cup.

Wang:	It was awesome watching the World Cup these past few days. Today I didn't even go to work—took the time off.
Zhao:	Look at you, you're hooked. Is it worth it?
Wang:	What can I say, I love watching soccer. Forget the World Cup, even if it was just a school game, I'd enjoy it.
Zhao:	Aren't you taking the addiction too far? You have to go to work!

干什么也**提不起精神来**。电视上只要有球赛,
我是非看不可,**要不就吃也吃不下**,**睡也睡不
着**,哪儿还能上班?

赵庆春: 那你说今儿晚上巴西和法国踢,谁赢啊?

王军生: 那还用说? 当然是巴西赢啦! 跟巴西踢,法国
不是个儿。

赵庆春: 到今天为止,法国可一场还没输过呢! 我看这
回法国挺厉害。

王军生: 巴西哪会**败在法国手下**! **不管怎么说**,法国都
甭想赢巴西。

赵庆春: **不见得**吧?

王军生: 要不咱打赌? 甭说法国队赢巴西队,就是踢平
了,都算我输。输了我请你**撮一顿**,怎么样?

赵庆春: 什么赌不赌的,我可没这么大瘾。巴西踢得好
也输了不止一场了吧? 人家法国一场还没输
过呢!

王军生: 你这人,**到底**敢不敢赌一把?

赵庆春: 好,赌就赌! 法国队要是输了,我请你一顿!

———◼———

Wang:	I don't know why—ever since the World Cup started, besides watching soccer, I couldn't put my heart into doing anything. As long as there's soccer on TV, I have to watch, otherwise I can't eat and I can't sleep, and you want me to go to work?
Zhao:	In that case, who's going to win when Brazil plays France tonight?
Wang:	Isn't that obvious? Brazil, of course! Going against Brazil, France is out of its league.
Zhao:	Up till now, France hasn't lost one game! I think France is pretty strong this time around. .
Wang:	How is it even possible for Brazil to lose to France? Whatever you say, France has no chance of beating Brazil.
Zhao:	I doubt it.
Wang:	You wanna bet? Forget France beating Brazil. Even if they tie, it'll count as me losing. If I lose, lunch's on me, how 'bout it?
Zhao:	What's this with the bets? I'm not as hooked as you are. I don't care how good Brazil is; they've lost more than once, haven't they? France is undefeated!
Wang:	Now you listen to me, are you going to bet or are you going to chicken out?
Zhao:	Fine, I'll bet! If France loses, I'll invite you out!

———— ■ ————

Traditional

王軍生和趙慶春是鄰居, 兩人在聊世界盃足球賽。

王軍生: 這幾天世界盃看得真**來勁**。今天我**連班兒都沒上**, 請了一天假。

趙慶春: **看把你迷得, 值當的嗎**?

王軍生: **我這人**就愛看足球. 甭說世界盃了, 就是學校足球賽, 我都覺著挺好看.

趙慶春: 哪有像你這麼**著迷**的? 再怎麼也得上班呀!

王軍生: 不知怎麼的, 自打世界盃一開賽, 我除了看球, 幹什麼也**提不起精神來**. 電視上只要有球賽, 我是非看不可, **要不就吃也吃不下**, **睡也睡不著**, 哪兒還能上班?

趙慶春: 那你說今兒晚上巴西和法國踢, 誰贏啊?

王軍生: 那還用說? 當然是巴西贏啦! 跟巴西踢, 法國**不是個兒**.

趙慶春: 到今天為止, 法國可一場還沒輸過呢! 我看這回法國挺厲害.

王軍生: 巴西哪會**敗在法國手下**! **不管怎麼說**, 法國都甭想贏巴西.

趙慶春: **不見得**吧?

王軍生: 要不咱打賭? 甭說法國隊贏巴西隊, 就是踢平了, 都算我輸. 輸了我請你**撮一頓**, 怎麼樣?

趙慶春: 什麼賭不賭的, 我可沒這麼大癮. 巴西踢得好也輸了不止一場了吧? 人家法國一場還沒輸過呢!

王軍生: 你這人, **到底**敢不敢賭一把?

趙慶春: 好, 賭就賭! 法國隊要是輸了, 我請你一頓!

———■———

词语注释

- 这几天世界杯看得真**来劲**。

  来劲 Colloquial form for "exciting"; "exhilarating"; "thrilling." 真来劲. "It's really exciting." For example, 昨天不上课, 我玩儿了一天的电子游戏, 真来劲! "There was no class yesterday, so I played video games for a whole day. It was really exciting."

- 今儿我**连班儿都没上**

  连...都没... "Didn't even ..." When 连 is used correlatively with 也 or 都, it means "even." The first "..." is a verb, and the second "..." is often used as it's object. The objective comes first and is emphasized in meaning. For example, 我连饭也没吃, "I didn't even eat anything." 他连报也看不懂。"He can't even read a newspaper."

- **看把你迷得**, 值当的吗?

  看把... 得 A colloquial sentence pattern: "Look how ... ... is." The first "..." is usually a noun or pronoun, and the second "..." expresses a verbal mood. For example, 你看把老头乐的。"Look how joyful the old man is." 你看把他们醉得。"Look how drunk they are." 看把你迷得。"Look how fascinated you are."

- 看把你迷得, **值当的吗**?

  值当的吗 (值当 [zhí dàng] be worthwhile; be to one's advantage) "Is it worth it?" A colloquial expression usually used in a negative sentence or rhetorical question. For example, 为这事儿生那么大气, 值当的吗? "Getting so angry over this—is it worth it?"

- **我这人**就爱看足球

  我这人 This phrase literally means: "I, this person." It is an appositive phrase, which is a combination of two words that refer to the same person or thing from different aspects. For example, 我这人

最喜欢交朋友。"I really like to make friends." Appositive phrases are frequently used in Chinese. For example, 他自己, "he himself." 我们年轻人, "we, the youth." 你们三个人, "the three of you." 中国首都北京, "the capital of China, Beijing."

- 哪有像你这么**着迷**的?
  着迷 ([zháomí]) "Be fascinated"; "be captivated." For example, 你怎么会对这个电影这么着迷? "How could you be so fascinated by this movie?"

- 干什么也**提不起精神来**
  提起精神来 (精神 [jīngshén] spirit) "Raise one's spirits," "brace oneself up." The negative form is 提不起精神来, "down in the dumps." For example, 大家提起精神来, 把这点儿工作做完. "Everybody, perk up and finish up the work."

- **要不**就吃也吃不下, 睡也睡不着
  要不 "Otherwise"; "or." For example, 我今天一定把作业做完, 要不就不睡觉。"I have to finish my homework today; otherwise I won't go to bed."

- 要不就**吃也吃不下**, **睡也睡不着**
  …也…不…, 也…不… This is a colloquial pattern to express "can do neither … nor …." In each… **也…不…**of the parallel structure, the "…" before or after **不** is the same verb, and the last "…" is its complement. For example, 这事儿真难办呀, 我走也走不了, 留也留不下。 "This matter is really hard to handle; I can neither go nor stay."

- 跟巴西踢, 法国**不是个儿**。
  不是个儿 A colloquial expression for "somebody is not an adversary or match." For example, 和我比游泳, 你不是个儿。"You're no match swimming against me."

- 巴西哪儿会**败在法国手下**

  败在...手下 (败 [bài] be defeated; lose; fail) "Be defeated by ...."
  For example, 这次比赛中国乒乓球队败在了瑞典队手
  下。"In this tournament the Chinese Ping-Pong team was defeated
  by the Swedish team."

- **不管怎么说**, 法国都甭想赢巴西。

  不管怎么说 "No matter what" or "in any case." This is a colloquial expression that is usually used in an argument or discussion.
  For example, 不管怎么说, 他也没有这么坏。"No matter
  what, he's not that bad."

- **不见得**吧

  不见得 A colloquial form for "not necessarily" or "not likely." For
  example, 他今晚不见得会来。"He might not come tonight."

- 输了我请你**撮一顿**

  撮一顿 (撮 [cuō] gather; bring together) A colloquial expression
  meaning "to have a meal." For example, 老王, 周末咱们一块儿撮
  一顿怎么样? "Lao Wang, how about we eat together this weekend?"
  When used in 请...撮一顿, "treat...to dinner." For example, 上次
  你请我, 这此该我请你撮一顿了。"You treated me last time.
  It's my turn to treat you to dinner this time."

- **到底**敢不敢赌一把?

  到底 Literally, "to the bottom." It is often used for emphasis in a
  question. For example, 到底发生了什么事? "What on earth is
  the matter?" 他到底在哪儿? "Where in the world can he be?"

CONVERSATION B:

Simplified

星期天晚上, 钱学东和高中同学林小鹏在一家饭馆喝酒。
钱学东还在上大学, 林小鹏已经工作了三年多了。

钱学东： 瞧你又把杯子碰倒了, 醉了吧?

林小鹏： 说谁呢? 我醉了? 没的事儿! 甭说这几瓶酒,
就是喝到天亮, **哥们儿**也醉不了。我**打十六岁
起**, 喝白酒就跟喝白水一样。**这辈子**还**没尝过
醉的滋味儿**呢!

钱学东： 吹牛也得有个**边儿**。你舌头都**不听使唤**了, 还
说没醉呢! 来, 先喝口茶, **醒醒神儿**。我把这半
瓶**干**了, 咱就回家。

林小鹏： 想回家啦? 是你不行了吧? 你可**不是我的对
手**! **有本事**咱接着干, 这就**见个高低**。对了, 你
说你们明天有考试, 今儿晚上是要**开夜车**吧?
你怕再**考砸了**是不是?

钱学东： 考试还不是**小菜儿一碟**? 打上小学起, 我考试
就没考砸过, 还回回得第一呢。我是说, 咱都
别喝了, 再喝你**该**开不了车了。

林小鹏： **哪儿的话**! 你只管放心, 我这人的特点是喝酒
越多, 开车越稳。上回我干完两瓶二锅头就开
车, 还不是**照样儿**在高速上跑120多公里!

————■————

It is Sunday night and Xuedong Qian and high school friend Xiaopeng Lin are drinking together at a restaurant. Qian is still in college, while Lin has been working for over three years.

Qian:	See, you knocked over the cup again. You're drunk, aren't you?
Lin:	Who are you talking about? Me, drunk? Impossible! Forget these couple of bottles, even if I went till tomorrow morning I'm not going to get drunk. Since I was sixteen I have been drinking wine like I drink water. I haven't felt drunk since I was born!
Qian:	There's a limit to what you can brag about. You lose control of your tongue, and say you're not drunk! Here, drink some tea, and clear your head. Here, I'll drink this half bottle, and then we'll go home.
Lin:	You want to go home? Can't go on, can you? You're no match against me! If you got the goods we can go on, decide it right here, right now. Oh, you said you have a test tomorrow. Are you pulling an all nighter? You're afraid you'll fail that test, right?
Qian:	Tests are no big deal at all, you know? Ever since elementary, I've never failed a test, and have got first place. But I say, let's stop drinking. Any more and you won't be able to drive.
Lin:	What are you talking about! Don't worry; I'm special in that the more I drink, the better I drive. Last time I started driving right after I chugged two bottles of Erguotuo (vodka), and I went 120 kilometers on the freeway, just like always!

Traditional

星期天晚上,錢學東和高中同學林小鵬在一家飯館喝酒。
錢學東還在上大學,林小鵬已經工作了三年多了。

錢學東： 瞧你又把杯子碰倒了,醉了吧?

林小鵬： 說誰呢? 我醉了? 沒的事兒! 甭說這幾瓶酒,
就是喝到天亮,**哥們兒**也醉不了。我**打十六歲
起**,喝白酒就跟喝白水一樣。**這輩子還沒嘗過
醉的滋味兒**呢!

錢學東： 吹牛也得有個**邊兒**。你舌頭都**不聽使喚**了,還
說沒醉呢! 來,先喝口茶,**醒醒神兒**。我把這半
瓶**幹**了,咱就回家。

林小鵬： 想回家啦? 是你不行了吧? 你可**不是我的對
手**! **有本事**咱接著幹,這就**見個高低**。對了,你
說你們明天有考試,今兒晚上是要**開夜車**吧?
你怕再**考砸了**是不是?

錢學東： 考試還不是**小菜兒一碟**? 打上小學起,我考試
就沒考砸過,還回回得第一呢。我是說,咱都
別喝了,再喝你**該**開不了車了。

林小鵬： **哪兒的話**! 你只管放心,我這人的特點是喝酒
越多,開車越穩。上回我幹完兩瓶二鍋頭就開
車,還不是**照樣兒**在高速上跑120多公里!

词语注释

- 就是喝到天亮, **哥们儿** 也醉不了。

  哥们儿 A colloquial form for "buddies" or "pals." Sometimes it is used to denote the speaker himself. For example, 他掏出一把抢来想吓唬我, 哥们儿才不怕呢! "He took out a gun to scare me. I, your buddy, wasn't scared at all!"

- 我**打十六岁起**, 喝白酒就跟喝白水一样。

  打…起 A colloquial form for "starting from …," similar to 从…开始. For example, 你刷碗刷了二十几天了, 打今天起, 吃完晚饭我刷碗。 "You have been washing dishes these last twenty days. Starting from today, I will wash dishes after dinner."

- **这辈子**还没尝过醉的滋味儿呢!

  这辈子 (辈 [bèi] generation) "All one's life." For example, 今天是我这辈子最痛快的一天。 "Today is the happiest day in my life."

- 这辈子还**没尝过醉的滋味儿**呢!

  没尝过…的滋味儿 (尝 [cháng] to taste; to try the flavor of; 滋味儿 [zīwèir] taste; flavor) "Have not tasted the flavor of …." For example, 他从来没尝过艰苦生活的滋味儿。 "He's never had a taste of a hard life."

- 吹牛也得有个**边儿**。

  边儿 A colloquial expression for "a limitation." For example, 你这话可说得太没边了。 "What you said is just absurd." Literally: "What your said is boundless."

- 你舌头都**不听使唤**了, 还说没醉呢!

  不听使唤 (使唤 [shǐhuan] use; handle) A colloquial form for "won't obey." For example, 这匹马不听生人使唤。 "This horse won't obey a stranger." The opposite expression to 不听使唤 is 容

易使唤, "easy to handle." For example, 这种牌子的工具容易使唤。 "This brand of tools is easy to use."

- 来, 先喝口茶, **醒醒神儿**。
  醒醒神 (醒 [xǐng] sober up; 神 [shén] mind; consciousness.) "To sober up"; "to clear one's head." This expression is usually used in the imperative mood, asking somebody to sober up. For example, 你喝醉了, 快喝杯浓茶醒醒神吧。 "You are drunk. Drink a cup of strong tea to sober yourself up."

- 我把这半瓶干了, 咱就回家。
  干 "Empty," "drink up (wine or liquor)." For example, 才两天你就把一大瓶酒喝干了! "You drank up a bottle of liquor in two days!" 干杯, "drink a toast." 为我们的合作成功干一杯! "Let's drink a toast to the success of our cooperative effort!"

- 你可**不是我的对手**
  不是...的对手 "No match for ...." 对手 means "match" or "equal." For example, 他不是你的对手。 "He is no match for you."

- **有本事**咱接着干, 这就见个高低。
  有本事 A colloquial form of "be capable." 本事 means "capability," "ability," or "skill." For example, 他要是有本事, 早就成百万富翁了。 "He would have been a millionaire a long time ago if he were capable enough."

- 有本事咱接着干, 这就**见个高低**。
  见个高低 "see who is better." 高低 means relative superiority or interiority. For example, 你总说你摔跤比我好, 今天咱们见个高低。 "You have been saying that you are a better wrestler. Let's see who is better today."

- 今儿晚上是要**开夜车**吧?

  开夜车 夜车 means "night train." 开夜车 is a colloquial expression for "work late into the night"; "put in extra time at night"; or "burn the midnight oil." For example, 今天的作业太多了,就是开夜车也赶不完。"Today's homework is too much. We could not finish it even if we work all night."

- 你怕再**考砸了**是不是?

  ...砸了 (砸 [zá] fail; fail through; or be bungled) Colloquial expression for "fail." ... is usually a verb. For example, 我考砸了。"I failed the test." 事儿办砸了。"The job was bungled." 戏演砸了。"The performance was a fiasco."

- 考试还不是**小菜儿一碟**?

  小菜一碟 "A piece of cake." 小菜, "common dishes," is used as a colloquial expression for something extremely easy to do or manage. For example, 这件事对咱们来说是个难题,对他只是小菜儿一碟。"This is a difficult problem to us but a piece of cake for him.

- 再喝你**该**开不了车了

  该 A colloquial form for 会, "will." For example, 快点儿吧,要不咱就该迟到了。"Hurry up! Otherwise we'll be late."

- **哪儿的话**

  "What are you saying?" "You shouldn't say that." This is a colloquial expression often used for politeness. For example, "太麻烦你了。" "哪儿的话。" "Sorry to have caused you so much trouble." "You shouldn't say that."

- 还不是**照样儿**在高速上跑120多公里!

  照样 "As usual." For example, 为什么我打了感冒针以后还照样儿感冒? "Why did I catch the flu as before, even after I had the flu vaccine?"

VOCABULARY

世界杯	shìjièbēi	World Cup
迷	mí	be fascinated by; be crazy about; fan
请假	qǐngjià	ask for leave
赢	yíng	win; beat
踢	tī	kick; play (football)
输	shū	lose; be beaten
打赌	dǎdǔ	bet; wager
瘾	yǐn	addiction; strong interest (in a sport or pastime)
为止	wéizhǐ	up to; till
场	chǎng	(measure word, similar to "number of games")
平	píng	(sports) make the same score; tie; draw
敢	gǎn	dare; brave
顿	dùn	(measure word, similar to "number of meals")
醉	zuì	intoxicated
吹牛	chuīniú	boast; brag; talk big
舌头	shétou	tongue
砸	zá	fail; fall through; be bungled
回	huí	(measure word, similar to "number of times")
放心	fàngxīn	set one's mind at rest; feel relieved
特点	tèdiǎn	characteristic; distinguishing feature

瓶	píng	(measure word, similar to "number of bottles")
稳	wěn	reliable; secure; safe
二锅头	èrguōtóu	a strong spirit made from sorghum

EXERCISES

A. Fill in the spaces with the appropriate words or phrases:

| 提起精神来 | 我这人 | 到底 | 要不 |
| 不管怎么说 | 看不见 | 没睡 | 气得 |

1　那个电影儿我还是没看明白,结果_____是怎么回事?

2　_____没有什么特别的爱好,就是喜欢看看电视.

3　周末咱一块儿去爬山怎么样? _____,看电影也行.

4　_____,咱们也得打赢这场比赛。

5　明天就要考试了,你今天可得_____好好准备一下。

6　昨天夜里这些孩子玩得连觉都_____。

7　小刚这次考试又不及格,看把他爸爸_____。

8　空气是无色无味的,所以看也_____,闻也闻不到。

B. Choose the expression from the following list that best corresponds to the underlined words or phrases:

| 值当的吗 | 撮 | 来劲 | 不见得 |

败在他们手下　　着迷　　　不是个儿

1　你们在聊什么呀? 聊得这么<u>高兴</u>。

2　花这么多时间玩游戏机, <u>不可惜呀</u>?

3　你看你, 对上网玩游戏也太<u>上瘾</u>了。

4　跟他们赛长跑, 你可<u>赛不过他们</u>。

5　我看他<u>不一定</u>明白你的意思, 你最好跟他说清楚点儿.

6　明儿咱一块儿到那家新开的饭馆儿去<u>吃</u>一顿怎么样?

7　咱们一定要赢这场球, 咱们可不能<u>输给他们</u>。

C. Fill in the spaces with the appropriate words or phrases:

哪儿的话　　开夜车　　　对手　　　这辈子　　　　边儿

小菜一碟　　滋味儿　　　照样　　　见个高低

1　我_____还没离开过美国呢, 这可是第一次。

2　他说我们这回肯定赢不了, 可我们_____赢了。

3　哪有这种事儿? 他说话也说得太没_____了。

4　你这样天天_____, 对身体可太不好了。

5　打比赛对他来说是_____, 你不用为他担心。

6　小张说小李帮了大忙, 小李说: "_____,就作了点小事儿。"

7　他们俩在赛乒乓球呢, 说是一定要_____。

8　要说比喝酒, 你可不是他的_____。

9　我还没尝过考试不及格的_____呢, 希望永远都别不及格。

D. Choose the expression from the following list that best corresponds
   to the underlined words or phrases:

考砸了　哥们儿　　该　打　干
醒醒神　有本事　　不听使唤

1 你这次考试就是<u>成绩不好</u>也没关系,以后努力就行了.

2 来,把这杯酒<u>喝了</u>,我祝你生日快乐!

3 哎,快<u>别睡啦</u>! 就要上课了,你怎么还睡?

4 别着急,慢慢儿写,要不就<u>会写错了</u>.

5 你要是<u>真行</u>,今天就把这车给我修好.

6 我跟他是<u>朋友</u>,要他帮这么点儿忙没问题.

7 <u>从</u>明天起,吃完晚饭我管洗碗.

8 今天这笔怎么这么<u>不好用</u>? 写出来的字都变样子了.

———■———

ANSWER KEY

Exercise A (Dialogue 1)

1 到底
2 我这人
3 要不
4 不管怎么说
5 提起精神来
6 没睡 (连…都没…)
7 气得 (看把… (B)得)
8 看不见 (…也…不…,
  …也…不…)

Exercise B (Dialogue 1)

1 来劲
2 值当的吗
3 着迷
4 不是个儿
5 不见得
6 撮 (撮一顿)
7 败在他们手下 (败在…手
  下)

Exercise C (Dialogue 2)

1 这辈子
2 照样
3 边儿
4 开夜车
5 小菜一碟
6 哪儿的话
7 见个高低
8 对手（不是…的对手）
9 滋味儿（没尝过…的滋味儿）

Exercise D (Dialogue 2)

1 考砸了
2 干
3 醒醒神
4 该
5 有本事
6 哥们儿
7 打（打…起）
8 不听使唤

―――――■―――――

CULTURE NOTES

If you want to translate English expressions that contain the word "fan," "enchant," or "fascinate" into Chinese, you would often need to use the Chinese word 迷, which often means "be fascinated by," "be crazy about," "fan," "enthusiast," or "fascinate." Please see the following examples:

迷恋   be fascinated with; madly cling to
着迷   be fascinated; be captivated
入迷   fascinated; enchanted
财迷   money grubber; miser
棋迷   chess fan; chess enthusiast
球迷   (ball game) fan
戏迷   theatre fan
足球迷 football fan

In fact, the basic meaning of 迷 is "be confused," "be lost," "fiend," "confuse," or "perplex." The following are words or expressions that contain 迷 with these different meanings.

迷惑	puzzle; confuse; perplex; baffle
迷糊	misted; blurred; dimmed; dazed; confused; muddled
迷路	lose one's way; get lost
迷失	lose one's way; get lost
迷雾	dense fog; anything that misleads people
迷信	superstition; superstitious; belief; blind faith; blind worship; have blind faith in; make a fetish of
昏迷	stupor; coma
哑迷	puzzling remark; enigma; riddle
迷宫	labyrinth; maze
迷人	fascinating; enchanting; charming; tempting
迷魂汤	sth. intended to turn sb.'s head; magic potion
捉迷藏	hide-and-seek; blindman's buff; be tricky and evasive; play hide-and-seek
纸醉金迷	(a life of) luxury and dissipation
鬼迷心窍	be possessed; be obsessed
当局者迷,旁观者清	the spectators see the chess game better than the players; the onlooker sees most of the game.

要不咱去郊区山里转转
这个客请也得请，
不请也得请

TAKING A TRIP
•
THROWING A PARTY

CONVERSATION A:

Simplified

小朋和太太兰兰在商量五一长周末应该一起去什么地方旅行。

小朋：   咱有七天假呢, 光在家**呆着没劲**, 出去玩儿玩儿吧。

兰兰：   行啊, 我也正**琢磨**这几天怎么过呢。你说去哪儿好?

小朋：   去黄山怎么样? "黄山归来不看山" 嘛。

226

惹一肚子气   (lit: "to get a stomach full of anger") to get angry (see page 228.)

Xiao Peng and his wife, Lan Lan, are talking about where they should go for the May Day long weekend.

Peng:	We have seven days off. It's boring staying at home, let's go somewhere.
Lan:	Sure, I've been thinking about what to do with the time, also. Where do you say we go?
Peng:	How about going to Mt. Huang? They say after returning from Mt. Huang, one does not need to see any more mountains.

兰兰：　黄山**除了山还是山**,咱去个**有山有水**的地方
　　　　多好!

小朋：　"桂林山水甲天下",想不想去桂林?

兰兰：　桂林好是好,就是离北京**远了点儿**。**再说**,长
　　　　周末那儿肯定**满眼都是人**。咱还是别上那儿
　　　　去扎堆儿好。

小朋：　倒也是。那要是去泰山和白洋淀呢? 山水倒
　　　　是都有了,可是得跑两个地方。

兰兰：　没错儿。泰山在山东,白洋淀在河北。跑完山
　　　　东跑河北,**还不够路上折腾呢**!

小朋：　**说来说去**,**哪儿都有毛病**,这地方还挺难定的
　　　　呢!

兰兰：　**你想想**,长周末出远门旅游哪儿都挤,什么都
　　　　不方便不说,还到处都猛涨价、狠宰人。节
　　　　过完了,**惹一肚子气**,值得吗?

小朋：　不管怎么说,咱们也不能在家**猫**七天不出门
　　　　吧?

兰兰：　要不,咱去郊区山里**转转**?

小朋：　郊区的山要名没名,要景没景,**有什么转头**?

兰兰：　这你就不知道了,北京郊区有的是好地方,要
　　　　山有山,要水有水。我来给你介绍几个地方,
　　　　保你玩儿得过瘾。

Lan:	On Mt. Huang, there are nothing but mountains. It'd be better if we could go somewhere with both mountains and water!
Peng:	Guilin calls its scenery best in the world; do you want to go there?
Lan:	Guilin is nice, it's just a little far away from Beijing. Besides, over the long weekend I bet there's going to be people everywhere. Let's not fight the crowds there.
Peng:	That makes sense. How about Mt. Tai and Baiyang Lake? There are mountains and there's water, but we have to go to two places.
Lan:	No kidding. Mt. Tai is in Shandong; Baiyang Lake is in Hebei. Going to Shandong then going to Hebei, we'll have too many problems just on the road!
Peng:	Well, no matter how you look at it, nowhere is perfect. It's hard to decide on a place!
Lan:	If you think about it, no matter where you go on a long weekend, it'll be crowded. Besides the inconvenience, everyone's raising their prices and ripping people off. The holiday's going to end and we'll be all stressed out—is it worth it?
Peng:	Well, we can't stay at home for seven days, can we?
Lan:	Why don't we go see the mountains outside the city?
Peng:	Those mountains are neither famous nor scenic. What is there to see up there?
Lan:	You've got it wrong, there are plenty of good places to go outside of Beijing—there are mountains and there's water. I'll introduce you to a few places; I guarantee you'll have a good time.

Traditional

小朋和太太蘭蘭在商量五一長週末應該一起去什麼地方旅行。

小朋：　咱有七天假呢，光在家**呆著沒勁**，出去玩兒玩兒吧。

蘭蘭：　行啊，我也正**琢磨**這幾天怎麼過呢。你說去哪兒好？

小朋：　去黃山怎麼樣？"黃山歸來不看山"嘛。

蘭蘭：　黃山**除了山還是山**，咱去個**有山有水**的地方**多好**！

小朋：　"桂林山水甲天下"，想不想去桂林？

蘭蘭：　桂林好是好，就是離北京**遠了點兒**。**再說**，長週末那兒肯定**滿眼都是人**。咱還是別上那兒**去湊堆兒**好。

小朋：　倒也是。那要是去泰山和白洋澱呢？山水倒是都有了，可是得跑兩個地方。

蘭蘭：　沒錯兒。泰山在山東，白洋澱在河北。跑完山東跑河北，**還不夠路上折騰呢**！

小朋：　**說來說去，哪兒都有毛病**，這地方還挺難定的呢！

蘭蘭：　**你想想**，長週末出遠門旅遊哪兒都擠，什麼都不方便不說，還到處都猛漲價、狠宰人。節過完了，**惹一肚子氣**，值得嗎？

小朋：　不管怎麼說，咱們也不能在家**貓**七天不出門吧？

蘭蘭:　　要不, 咱去郊區山裏**轉轉**?

小朋:　　郊區的山要名沒名, 要景沒景, **有什麼轉頭**?

蘭蘭:　　這你就不知道了, 北京郊區有的是好地方, 要
　　　　山有山, 要水有水。我來給你介紹幾個地方,
　　　　保你玩兒得過癮。

———◼———

词语注释

- 光在家**呆着**没劲
  呆着 (呆 [dāi] stay) This is a colloquial form of "stay." For example, 你在这儿呆着别动, 我马上就回来。"You stay here, I'll be back in a minute."

- 光在家呆着**没劲**
  没劲 (劲 [jìn] interest) This expression is a colloquial form for "not interesting"; or "boring." For example, 这个电影没劲, 我不想看。"This movie is no fun; I don't want to watch it."

- 我也正**琢磨**这几天怎么过呢
  琢磨 ([zuómo] turn something over in one's mind) A colloquial form for "ponder." For example, 这事儿我琢磨好几天了, 还是没办法。"This has been turning over in my mind for several days, but I still haven't found a way out."

- 黄山**除了山还是山**
  除了...还是... (除了 [chúle] except, besides, in addition to...) "Nothing else except ..." For example, 你每天除了上班还是上班, 不觉得烦呀。"You do nothing else except go to work, don't you feel bored?"

- 咱去个**有山有水**的地方多好
  有山有水 "Has mountains and rivers." This expression is used to describe a place with a positive connotation, similar to "with good scenery." For example, 我老家有山有水, 风景可好了。 "My hometown has many mountains and rivers; the scenery is wonderful."

- 咱去个有山有水的地方**多好**
  多好 Here 多 serves as an adverb, and means "to a high degree." 多好 often means "very good," but when it follows a phrase, it often expresses the meaning: "It would be good if ..." For example, 别去看电影了, 咱玩儿电子游戏多好。 "Don't go to the movie. Better to play video games."

- 桂林好是好, 就是离北京**远了点儿**
  ...了点儿 "A little too ...." ... is usually an adjective or a psychological verb. For example, 这件衣服大了点儿, 你试试小一些的吧。 "These clothes are a little too big; why don't you try something smaller?"

- **再说,** 长周末那儿肯定满眼都是人
  再说 This expression is used to express reasons: "besides"; "what's more." For example, 还是别去叫他好。 他不一定有时间来, 再说现在也太晚了。 "Let's not call him. He might not have time to come; besides, it's too late now."

- 再说, 长周末那儿肯定**满眼都是人**
  满眼都是... "... meets the eyes on every side." For example, 那地方有什么好? 满眼都是石头。 "What's so good about that place? It's full of rocks."

- 咱还是别上那儿去**扎堆儿**好
  扎堆儿 (扎 [zā] bind; 堆 [duī] stack) This is a colloquial expres-

sion with the meaning "gather around." For example, 他就爱跟那些人扎堆儿。 "He just likes to hang around with those people."

- 跑完山东跑河北, **还不够路上折腾呢**!

  还不够…呢! This pattern is used to express a comment with a strong tone. The meaning is similar to **够…的**! "It's very …!" … is often a verbal phrase with negative meaning. For example, 你看着他作这些事儿, 还不够替他着急呢。 "When you watch him do things, it's all you can do not to worry about him."

- **说来说去, 哪儿都有毛病**

  说来说去, … "When all is said, the fact remains that …." In this pattern, 说来说去 means "after repeatedly talking about something"; and … means that the fact is still …. For example, 说来说去, 哪儿都没咱们老家好。 "After everything is said and done, there's still no place as good as our hometown."

- **你想想**, 长周末出远门旅游哪儿都挤, …

  你想想 "Just think." This expression is often used to persuade people. It can stand by itself or introduce an opinion. For example, 你想想, 这么好的天气不出去玩儿多可惜. "Just think, what a waste it would be if we didn't go somewhere when the weather's this good."

- 节过完了, **惹一肚子气**, 值得吗?

  惹一肚子气 (惹 [rě] invite or ask for something undesirable; provoke; cause) 惹气 is a phrase with the meaning "get angry." There are often words inserted between 惹 and 气. 惹一肚子气 is one example, also a relatively fixed pattern, which means "get very angry." For example, 我昨天又为这事儿惹了一肚子气。 "I got very angry over this again yesterday."

- 不管怎么说, 咱们也不能在家**猫**七天不出门吧

  猫 As a colloquial expression, 猫 serves as a verb and means: "hide oneself." For example, 你在哪儿猫着呢? 这么多人找你都找不到。 "Where did you hide yourself? So many people looked for you but couldn't find you."

- 要不, 咱去郊区山里**转转**?
  转转 (转 [zhuǎn] turn, shift) A colloquial form for "take a short walk" or "take a trip." For example, 上个周末我们去北海公园转了转。 "Last weekend we took a trip to Beihai Park."

- 郊区的山要名没名, 要景没景, **有什么转头**?
  有什么…头 This is a rhetorical question that means: "Why do …." In this expression, … is a verb, 头 is a suffix added to the verb, and …头 refers to something worth doing. For example, 这种菜有什么吃头? "What's so good about this dish?"

———— ■ ————

CONVERSATION B:

Simplified

林森和丽萍夫妇俩正在讨论要不要请客为林森过三十岁生日的事。

丽萍: 下星期天是你的三十岁生日, 你说咱们怎么个过法?

林森: 嗨, 生日**有什么好过的**? 煮锅面条不就行了? 又省钱又省事儿。

丽萍: 这生日可说什么也得过. 现在人人都兴过生日, 咱**不过不过也得过一回**。你们同事过生日请客哪次都没把你落下, **就算你过不过都无所谓, 也该趁这个机会请请客、还还人情了吧?**

林森：　咱现在是要钱没钱，要时间没时间，每天**穷忙**，哪儿请得起客呀！

丽萍：　我说你怎么就会哭穷呢？咱不是刚拿到年终奖金吗？**存着也是存着，不如拿它过生日**，省得老欠着人家。

林森：　**我把你这个人哪**，一点儿办法也没有。手里刚有几个奖金，就**烧得坐不住了**。请客吃饭这种事儿，**钱花少了吧，怕人笑话；钱花多了吧，根本就没个边儿**，几百块是它，几千块也是它。

丽萍：　你怎么那么**抠门儿**？吃别人的时候挺高兴，轮到自己放血就舍不得了。

林森：　看你说到哪儿去了！什么抠门儿不抠门儿的？我是说，多出钱吧，咱没那个实力；少出钱吧，要让人家笑话。这种客，没什么请头。

丽萍：　同事、朋友都知道哪天是你的三十大寿，要是**不声不响**地过去，怎么**好意思**见人？**我看呀**，这个客**请也得请，不请也得请**。甭说咱还有几个钱，就是没钱，借钱咱也得请。

林森：　唉，请也不是，不请也不是。这主意可真难拿呀！

丽萍：　这有什么难的？咱量力而行，**出得起多少出多少**，没什么可丢人的。

林森：　话是这么说，可真的请起来，没个几千块根本**下不来**。不过，话又说回来，人情欠着不还比欠人钱还难受。得，就**依着**你吧。

Lin Sen and his wife, Li Ping, are discussing whether to invite guests
for Lin's thirtieth birthday.

Li Ping: Next Sunday is your thirtieth birthday; what do you
                say we do to celebrate?

Lin Sen: Hai, what's there to celebrate about a birthday?
                Just make some noodles and it'll be enough. Saves
                money and saves time.

Li Ping: Whatever you say, we're celebrating your birthday
                this time. Everyone's celebrating birthdays these days;
                we're going to do it no matter what. Your coworkers
                never left you out when inviting people for their
                birthdays, so it doesn't matter if you want to or not.
                Shouldn't you use the chance to invite them out,
                and pay them back?

Lin Sen: Right now we've got no money, no time, and we're
                busy every day doing God knows what, so how can
                we afford to invite people!

Li Peng: Now how'd you get so good at crying poor? Didn't
                we just get our year-end bonus? If we save it it'll
                just sit there. I'd rather spend it on your birthday,
                and then we don't have to owe people anymore.

Lin Sen: What am I going to do with you, I've got no clue.
                We just got a bonus, and it's burning a hole in your
                pocket. The thing with inviting people out is, if
                you don't spend that much, you're afraid of getting
                laughed at; if you do spend a lot, there's no limit at
                all to how much—a few hundred, a few thousand.

Li Ping: Why are you so stingy? You were perfectly happy
                eating theirs, but now that it's your turn to bleed
                you can't do it.

Lin Sen: What are you talking about! This stingy or not stingy? I'm saying, if we spend, we don't have the money; if we don't, people will laugh at us. There's no point in inviting people when it is like this.

Li Ping: Your coworkers and friends all know it's your thirtieth. If you just let it pass, how are you going to face them? As I see it, you have to throw a party no matter if you want to or not. Forget us having some money right now; even if we didn't, we'd have to borrow some and do it anyways.

Lin Sen: Man, it's no good inviting people out, and no good not doing it. What a hard choice!

Li Ping: What's hard about it? We do what we can, and spend whatever we can afford. Nothing to be ashamed of.

Lin Sen: That all sounds good, but what if we really go ahead and invite people out—it's impossible without at least a few thousand. But, on the other hand, it's worse to owe people a favor than to owe people money. Fine, let's do it your way.

——————————■——————————

Traditional

林森和麗萍夫婦倆正在討論要不要請客為林森過三十歲生日的事。

麗萍：　下星期天是你的三十歲生日，你說咱們怎麼個過法？

林森：　嗨，生日**有什麼好過的**？煮鍋麵條不就行了？又省錢又省事兒。

麗萍：　這生日可說什麼也得過。現在人人都興過生日，咱**不過不過也得過一回**。你們同事過生日請客哪次都沒把你落下，**就算你過不過都無所謂，也該趁這個機會請請客、還還人情了吧？**

林森：　咱現在是要錢沒錢，要時間沒時間，每天**窮忙**，哪兒請得起客呀！

麗萍：　我說你怎麼就會哭窮呢？咱不是剛拿到年終獎金嗎？**存著也是存著，不如拿它過生日**，省得老欠著人家。

林森：　**我把你這個人哪**，一點兒辦法也沒有。手裏剛有幾個獎金，就**燒得坐不住了**。請客吃飯這種事兒，**錢花少了吧，怕人笑話；錢花多了吧，根本就沒個邊兒**，幾百塊是它，幾千塊也是它。

麗萍：　你怎麼那麼**摳門兒**？吃別人的時候挺高興，輪到自己放血就捨不得了。

林森：　看你說到哪兒去了！什麼摳門兒不摳門兒的？我是說，多出錢吧，咱沒那個實力；少出錢吧，要讓人家笑話。這種客，沒什麼請頭。

麗萍：　同事、朋友都知道哪天是你的三十大壽，要是**不聲不響**地過去，怎麼**好意思**見人？**我看呀，這個客請也得請，不請也得請**。甭說咱還有幾個錢，就是沒錢，借錢咱也得請。　林森：唉，請也不是，不請也不是。這主意可真難拿呀！

麗萍:　這有什麼難的? 咱量力而行, **出得起多少出多少**, 沒什麼可丟人的。

林森:　話是這麼說, 可真的請起來, 沒個幾千塊根本**下不來**。不過, 話又說回來, 人情欠著不還比欠人錢還難受。得, 就**依著**你吧。

————■————

词语注释

- 生日**有什么好过的?**
  有什么好...的? Also as 有什么可...的? A rhetorical question to express disapproval, it has the same meaning as the frequently used expression, 没什么好...的, "It is not worth it to do ...." For example, 这点事儿有什么好说的? "Why talk about something so minor."

- 现在人人都兴过生日, 咱**不过不过也得过一回**。
  不...不...也得... **(B)** This pattern is used to provide contrast: "even if we don't want to ..., we still have to ...." Here ... is a verb, and ... is its object or complement. For example, 你们都说过了, 该我说了. 我不说不说也得说几句。 "You have all spoken, now it's my turn. Even if I don't want to, I still have to say something."

- **就算你过不过都无所谓, 也该趁这个机会请请客、还还人情了吧?**
  就算..., 也... "Even if ..., (B)." This pattern is used to express an assumed situation and the results or inference drawn from it. For example, 就算她没去过那个店, 也不会找不到. "Even if she has never been to that store, she still should be able to find it."

- 就算你过不过都**无所谓**
  无所谓 "Be indifferent"; "doesn't matter." For example, 吃什么

我都无所谓, 只要你们高兴就行。 "Whatever we eat is okay with me, as long as you are all happy."

- 也该**趁这个机会**请请客、还还人情了吧?
  趁这个机会 (趁 [chèn] take advantage of; avail oneself of; "Take this chance," "use this opportunity." For example, 咱们明天都没课, 还不趁这个机会出去玩儿玩儿? "There is no class tomorrow. Why don't we take this chance to go out have some fun?"

- 也该趁这个机会请请客、**还还人情**了吧?
  还人情 (人情 [rénqíng] a favor, feelings) "Return a favor," "send gifts in return." For example, 几个月以前她给过我一件礼物, 现在就要过年了, 我也准备给她买一件礼物还人情。 "She gave me a gift a few months ago. Now that it's New Year's I'm going to return the favor."

- 咱现在是要钱没钱, 要时间没时间, 每天**穷忙**, 哪儿请得起客呀!
  穷忙 This expression means "fully occupied," and contains a passive connotation. For example, 昨天我穷忙了一整天。 "I was very busy for all day yesterday."

- **存着也是存着, 不如拿它过生日,**
  ...着也是...着, 不如... A colloquial way to express "rather ... than ...." For example, 咱们等着也是等着, 不如自己试试看。 "Since we're going to wait anyway, why don't we try it ourselves."

- **我把你这个人哪,** 一点儿办法也没有
  我把你这... 啊, ... "To you, ..., I ..." This pattern is used to show the speaker's frustration and inability to deal with his listener. The first "..." should be a noun phrase, and the second "..." should be the speaker's comments. 你 could be replaced by 你们. For

example, 我把你们这些小东西啊, 真没办法。 "To you little guys, I can't do anything at all."

- 手里刚有几个奖金, 就**烧得坐不住了**。
  烧得... "Burning a hole in one's pockets." A colloquial way to say that someone is getting carried away with their wealth. For example, 有点儿钱就烧得不知道干什么好了。 "He got a little bit of money and now it's burning a hole in his pocket."

- **钱花少了吧, 怕人笑话; 钱花多了吧, 根本就没个边儿,**
  ...吧, ...; ...吧, ... "If …, then …; if …, then ..." This pattern implies a difficult choice. The conditions are expressed by "if...," and the corresponding consequences are expressed by "then...". For example, 你说这个长周末咱怎么过? 在家呆着吧, 太没劲; 出去旅行吧, 路上车太多, 太烦人。 "What do you think we should do this long weekend? We can stay home, but it'll be too boring; or we can go out, but there'll be too many cars on the road."

- 你怎么那么**抠门儿**?
  抠门儿 (抠 [kōu] to dig or dig out with a finger.) This is a colloquial expression, that means "stingy" or "miserly." For example, 他有时候是挺抠门儿, 可有时候还挺大方的。 "Although sometimes he is stingy, sometimes he is quite generous."

- 要是**不声不响**地过去, 怎么好意思见人?
  不声不响 A fixed expression for "not say a word" or "not utter a sound." For example, 别看他不声不响的, 他心里比谁都清楚。 "Don't be fooled by him not saying anything all the time, he's clearer than anyone else inside."

- 要是不声不响地过去, 怎么**好意思**见人?
  怎么**好意思** 好意思 stands for "having the nerve." For example,
  她怎么好意思说这种话! "How could she have the nerve to
  say something like this!"

- **我看呀**, 这个客请也得请, 不请也得请。
  我看 "I think"; "in my opinion." For example, 我看你还是晚一
  点走好, 现在路上一定正堵车呢。 "I think you'd better leave
  a little later. I bet there's a traffic jam right now. "

- 我看呀, 这个客**请也得请, 不请也得请**。
  …也得…, 不…也得… This is a colloquial pattern in duplicated
  form to emphasize "have to," "there is no choice," or "no matter …
  or not." It literally means that "(If somebody) wants to …, then …,
  (if somebody) does not want to …, he (or she) still has to do it."
  Here "…" is usually a verb or verbal phrase. For example, 今天的
  会很重要, 咱们去也得去, 不去也得去。 "Today's meeting
  is very important. If we want to go, we go. If we don't want to go,
  we still have to go."

- **出得起多少出多少**, 没什么可丢人的。
  …得…多少…多少 "To … as much as one can." In this expression, the first and the third "…" are the same verb, and the second
  "…" is its complement. The structure …得… indicates possibility.
  For example, 咱们今天干得了多少干多少, 明天接着干。
  "We do as much as we can today, and we'll continue tomorrow."
  这些书, 你看得完多少看多少。 "These books, you just read
  as much as you can."

- 话是这么说, 可真的请起来, 没个几千块根本**下不来**。
  下不来 "Cannot be done." For example, 造这么大个房子, 没有几个月下不来。 "Building such a big house can't be done in less than several months."

- 得, 就**依着**你吧。
  依着 "Comply with"; "go with." For example, 他还是个孩子, 你可不能什么事儿都依着他。 "He is still a child, you can't give in to him on everything."

▌VOCABULARY

商量	shāngliang	discuss
旅行	lǚxíng	travel; journey
光	guāng	solely; only
归来	guīlái	go back to; return
满眼	mǎnyǎn	to see the same thing everywhere
泰山	tàishān	Mount Taishan
白洋淀	báiyángdiàn	Baiyang Lake
折腾	zhēteng	cause physical or mental suffering
猛	měng	fierce; violent
涨价	zhǎngjià	rise in price
狠	hěn	ruthless; relentless
宰人	zǎirén	overcharge customers; rip off
值得	zhíde	be worth
过瘾	guòyǐn	enjoy oneself to the fullest
讨论	tǎolùn	discuss; talk over

锅	guō	(measure word, similar to "number of pans")
同事	tóngshì	colleague; fellow worker
哭穷	kūqióng	complain of being hard up
年终	niánzhōng	the end of the year
奖金	jiǎngjīn	money award; bonus
欠	qiàn	owe
轮	lún	take turns
放血	fàngxuě	bloodletting; spend money
实力	shílì	actual strength; strength
笑话	xiàohua	laugh at
寿	shòu	birthday
主意	zhǔyì	decision
拿	ná	make (decision)
量力而行	liànglìérxíng	act according to one's capability
丢人	diūrén	lose face; be disgraced
根本	gēnběn	simply

练习/EXERCISES

A. Fill in the spaces with the appropriate words or phrases:

> 说来说去　　有山有水　　满眼　　多好
> 还不够忙呢　除了学习　再说　　扎堆儿

1　这地方_____, 风景真美, 以后我还要再来玩。

2　明天别跟他们去_____了, 好好在家休息吧。

3 这事儿别等到最后一天才做呀, 早一点做完_____。

4 咱们明天再去看她吧, 今天没时间,_____她也需要多休息。

5 这些鞋不是式样旧就是价钱贵,_____, 没一双合适的。

6 中午只有半小时时间, 你又要作这又要作那,_____。

7 到了服装市场,_____都是衣服, 准能买到适合你穿的。

8 你每天_____还是学习, 什么也不玩, 不觉得没意思吗?

B. Choose the expression from the following list that best corresponds to the underlined words or phrases:

惹一肚子气   琢磨   呆着   没劲   猫
有什么看头   想想   转转   紧了点儿

1 什么? 你觉得上网玩游戏还没意思? 那什么有意思呀?

2 我这么作都是为你好, 你琢磨琢磨, 我说得对不对。

3 你想了这么半天, 有没有想出什么好办法?

4 我打电话告诉她我马上就要去接她, 让她在家别出去。

5 你老一个人呆在这儿有什么意思? 走, 跟我们一块儿玩儿去。

6 快过年了, 商店都在大减价, 咱们也去逛逛吧。

7 为这么点儿小事生这么大气, 太不值得了。

8 这种电影没什么好看的, 还是看个别的吧。

9 时间是有点儿紧, 不过只要安排得好, 还是没问题。

C. Fill in the spaces with the appropriate words or phrases:

不学不学   还人情   我把你   下不来   穷忙
不干也得干 不声不响   好意思   在家吧   烧得

1 他请我吃了好几次饭了,这次该_____了,我来请请他。

2 这几天给你打电话老是没人接,你又在____什么呢?

3 有人叫得挺响,可是没作什么事；有人_____,可是事情作了很多。

4 到朋友家去聚会、吃饭,她从来都不_____空着手去。

5 现在物价这么贵,办个婚礼只花几千块钱可_____。

6 他手里一有钱,就_____非花光不可,所以从来存不下钱。

7 现在人人会用电脑,咱_____也得学一点儿吧?

8 这是命令,他干也得干,_____。

9 我还没想好今天怎么过。出去吧,怕 雨；_____,又没事做。

10 _____这个老王啊,一点办法也没有。

D. Choose the expression from the following list that best corresponds to the underlined words or phrases:

有什么   闲着   我看   抠门儿   趁
无所谓   就算   依着   吃得了多少

1 他可小气了,平常连一分钱都舍不得花。

2 去公园还是看去电影,我都没意见,你决定吧。

3 你不舒服好几天了,<u>我想</u>你最好去看看医生。

4 以前商量去哪玩儿的时候都听你的,这次<u>听我的</u>吧。

5 我陪你好多次了,<u>即使</u>你不想看电影,也该陪我去一
   回吧?

6 这游戏<u>没什么</u>好玩儿的,一点意思都没有。

7 这次去中国旅游,咱们可以<u>利用</u>这个机会练练中文。

8 今天的点心我请客,你<u>能吃多少</u>吃多少。

9 住在这旅馆里,闲着<u>没事儿</u>,不如出去走走。

———————■———————

ANSWER KEY

Exercise A (Dialogue 1)

1 有山有水
2 扎堆儿
3 多好
4 再说
5 说来说去(说来说去, ...)
6 还不够忙呢(还不
   够...呢)
7 满眼(满眼都是...)
8 除了学习(除了... 还
   是...)

Exercise B (Dialogue 1)

1 没劲
2 想想(你想想)
3 琢磨
4 呆着
5 猫
6 转转
7 惹一肚子气
8 有什么看头(有什
   么...头)
9 紧了点儿(...了点儿)

Exercise C (Dialogue 2)

1 还人情

2 穷忙

3 不声不响

4 好意思

5 下不来

6 烧得（烧得…）

7 不学不学(不…不…也得…)

8 不干也得干（…也得…，
不…也得…）

9 在家吧（…吧，…；…吧，
…）

10 我把你（我把你这
个…啊),…

Exercise D (Dialogue 2)

1 抠门儿

2 无所谓

3 我看

4 依着

5 就算（就算…, 也…）

6 有什么（有什么好…的）

7 趁（趁这个机会）

8 吃得了多少（…得…多
少…多少）

9 也是闲着（…着也是…着，
不如…）

CULTURE NOTES

According to the Chinese-English Dictionary 人情 has several meanings: human feelings; human sympathy; sensibilities; human nature; human relationships; favor; gift; present; etiquette; custom. In fact, it's easy to understand Chinese 人情 if you connect these definitions with sentences: All human beings have feelings, such as sympathy or sensibilities; this is human nature. When you have relationships with others, such as a friend or colleague, you should pay close attention to their feelings. If you receive a gift from someone, you'd better send a present in return. When you get a favor from a friend, you owe him or her one and need to return the sentiment. This is the established etiquette and custom in China.

人情 is a very common topic in Chinese daily life. There are quite a few related words. For example, to do somebody a favor is 做个人情; to owe somebody a favor is 欠人情; lip service is 空头人情; to seek somebody's favor through a third person is 托人情; to present a gift could be 送人情; not amenable to reason is 不近人情; to lose sight of the human side of things is 不讲人情; to observe social etiquette is 尽人情.

你以为说戒就戒得了啊 要真考砸了也没什么了不起 的

WORRYING
•
PERSUADING, ADVISING
•
ENCOURAGING
•
CONVINCING, REASONING

CONVERSATION A:

Simplified

张先生和张太太在说话。

张太太: 哎,你怎么**又抽上**了? 昨天不是说戒了吗? **真拿你没办法**!

张先生: 都抽了十来年了,你以为**说戒就戒**得了啊?

张太太: 你**又不是不**知道抽烟的坏处,抽一支起码少活五分钟。

烟鬼 (lit: "cigarette demon") cigarette demon (see page 252.)

Mr. Zhang is talking with Mrs. Zhang.

Mrs. Zhang: Hey, what are you doing? Smoking again? Didn't you say you'd quit tomorrow? I really don't know what to do with you!

Mr. Zhang: I've been smoking for ten years. You think I can quit just like that?

Mrs. Zhang: It's not like you to not know why it's bad for you; you live at least five minutes less for every one you smoke.

张先生： 诶, 少活几年就少活几年吧! 没什么**大不了**的, 省得**活受罪**。

张太太： 这可不是你一个人的事儿。你得对老婆孩子负责, 还得对你老爸老妈负责! 当然啦, 我们也都有责任帮你戒。你看这么着行不行...

张先生： **谢了**, **谢了**, 我还是自己来吧。我又不是**成心**不戒! 这得慢慢儿来。

张太太： 可你不能老这样儿天天戒天天开戒吧? 这么**戒来戒去**, **还是戒不了**。

张先生： **什么事儿就怕上瘾**。你看这 "瘾" 字是个病字头, 抽烟是一种病。

张太太： 得了病**咱**得赶紧治, 你自己也要有决心。

张先生： 话是这么说, 可总得有个过程吧? 不过, 你放心, 为了你和孩子, 为了我的健康, 这烟我是戒也得戒, 不戒也得戒! 怎么样? 高兴了吧?

张太太： 嗨, 你呀, 就会耍贫嘴! 我把你这**烟鬼**啊, 真没办法!

———————■———————

Traditional

張先生和張太太在說話.

張太太： 哎, 你怎麼又**抽上了**? 昨天不是說戒了嗎? **真拿你沒辦法**!

張先生： 都抽了十來年了, 你以為說戒就戒得了啊?

Mr. Zhang: If I die a few years sooner, I'll die sooner. No big deal; better than living and suffering.

Mrs. Zhang: This isn't just about you. You have to take responsibility for your wife and your son, and for your mom and dad! Of course, we have a responsibility to help you quit. How about ... ?

Mr. Zhang: Thank you, but I'd rather do it myself. It's not like I'm keeping it up on purpose! You have to do this slowly.

Mrs. Zhang: But you can't go on like this, quitting one day and starting the next! If you keep on trying to quit like this you'll never quit.

Mr. Zhang: Anything's hard when you get addicted. Addiction is a disease, and so is smoking.

Mrs. Zhang: Well, if you get sick we have to find a cure. You have to have self discipline, too.

Mr. Zhang: That all sounds good, but everything is a process, right? But, rest assured, for you and our son, for my own health, I'll quit smoking no matter what! There, you happy?

Mrs. Zhang: Oh, brother! All you ever do is clown around! What am I going to do with you, you big chain smoker?

張太太: 你**又不是不知道**抽煙的壞處, 抽一支起碼少活五分鐘。

張先生: 誒, 少活幾年就少活幾年吧!沒什麼**大不了**的, 省得**活受罪**。

張太太: 這可不是你一個人的事兒。你得對老婆孩子負責, 還得對你老爸老媽負責!當然啦, 我們也都有責任幫你戒。 你看這麼著行不行?

張先生: **謝了**, 謝了, 我還是自己來吧. 我又不是**成心**不戒!這得慢慢兒來。

張太太: 可你不能老這樣兒天天戒天天開戒吧? 這麼**戒來戒去, 還是戒不了**。

張先生: **什麼事兒就怕上癮**。你看這 "癮" 字是個病字頭, 抽煙是一種病。

張太太: 得了病**咱**得趕緊治, 你自己也要有決心。

張先生: 話是這麼說, 可總得有個過程吧? 不過, 你放心, 為了你和孩子, 為了我的健康, 這煙我是戒也得戒, 不戒也得戒! 怎麼樣? 高興了吧?

張太太: 嗨, 你呀, 就會耍貧嘴!我把你這**煙鬼**啊, 真沒辦法!

———————■———————

词语注释

- 哎, 你怎么又**抽上了**
  …上了 "Started to… already." This pattern indicates that an action has started. For example, 他已经吃上了。 "He started eating already." 她爱上我了。 "She's fallen in love with me."

- **真拿你没办法**
  拿…没办法 A colloquial expression with a note of impatience: "Can't do any thing about …." In this pattern, … is often a noun or noun phrase. For example, 我简直拿他们没办法。 "I simply can't do anything about them."

- 你**又**不是不知道抽烟的坏处

  又… It is often used in a negative sentence or a rhetorical question to add emphasis. For example, 我又没去过那儿, 怎么会知道那儿好不好? "I've never been there, so how would I know if that place is any good?"

- 你又**不是不**知道抽烟的坏处

  不是不… This pattern is a double negative in form but affirmative in meaning, and is used for showing emphasis. 不是不… simply means 是…. The sentence from the text 你又不是不知道抽烟的坏处 means 你知道抽烟的坏处。 It's not as if you don't know the dangers of smoking." Another example: 你不是不会, 只是不愿意教我。 "It's not like you don't know, you just don't want to teach me."

- 没什么**大不了**的, 省得活受罪。

  大不了 A colloquial expression. When used in a negative form, 大不了 usually means "alarming" or "serious." It is often used in the negative statement 没什么大不了的 or in a rhetorical question 有什么大不了的? Both of these mean: "It's nothing serious." "It's not a big deal." For example, 不就是几百块钱吗, 没什么大不了的。 "It's just a few hundred dollars; it's nothing." When 大不了 is used in a positive statement, it means "at the worst" or "if worst comes to worst." For example, 大不了花几百块钱。 "It'll cost us a few hundred dollars at worst."

- 没什么大不了的, 省得**活受罪**。

  活受罪 (受罪 [shòuzuì] endure hardships; tortures) A colloquial expression: "to suffer." For example, 与其待在家里活受罪, 不如早点儿去医院开刀把它割了。 "Rather than suffer at home, it's better to hurry to the hospital and have an operation."

- **谢了**, **谢了**, 我还是自己来吧。

  谢了 A colloquial expression that is the same as 谢谢. For example, "这是我替你买的书。" "谢了。" "Here is the book I bought for you." "Thanks."

- 我又不是**成心**不戒!

  成心 "Intentionally"; "on purpose." For example, 你说, 他是不是成心跟我找麻烦? What do you think? Is he causing trouble for me on purpose?" 对不起, 我不是成心的。 "I'm sorry. I didn't mean to."

- **戒来戒去**, 还是戒不了

  …来…去, … "No matter how much you …, the fact remains that…." In this pattern, the first and the second "…" are the same verb or verb phrase, so. …来…去 means that after repeatedly doing …, the fact is still…. For example, 我找来找去, 就是找不到车钥匙。 "No matter how much I looked, I just couldn't find my car key."

- **什么事儿就怕上瘾**。

  什么事儿就怕… This statement expresses the idea that things will be positively or negatively affected if "…" happens. 什么 denotes indefinite indication, and 什么事儿 stands for "all things." 怕 means "cannot stand" or "will be affected by." For example, 什么事儿就怕上瘾, 上了瘾就跟得了病一样难治。 "Everything goes wrong if you get addicted. Addiction is just as hard to cure as a disease." 什么事儿都怕认真, 只要认真了, 一定会想出办法来。 "Anything goes easier if you get serious; once you get serious, you will find the answer no matter what."

- 得了病**咱**得赶紧治

  咱 or 咱们 usually refers to both speaker and listener, and means "we" or "us," but sometimes this colloquial word could also mean "you." For example, 服务员, 咱这儿有螃蟹吗? "Waiter, do you serve crab here?"

- 我把你这**烟鬼**啊, 真没办法!

  烟鬼 (烟 [yān] tobacco; cigarette; 鬼 [guǐ] ghost) With a negative connotation, this is a colloquial form for "opium addict" or "heavy smoker." For example, 她跟你一样, 也是个烟鬼, 一天要抽两包烟。 "He is also a heavy smoker, just like you; he smokes two packs of cigarettes a day."

———————◼———————

CONVERSATION B:

Simplified

快到期末了, 李林和云云在说考试的事儿。

李林: **瞧你那样**儿, 没精打采的, 饭也不吃, 是不是病了?

云云: 哪儿啊, 还不是**让考试闹的**。**眼看**就要大考了, 我这儿八字还**没一撇**呢, 你说**急人**不急人? 弄得我这几天是 吃也吃不下, 睡也睡不着, 昨天还开了个夜车。

李林: 我说你 也**忒**认真了吧? **至于吗**? **不就是**期末考试吗? 你看我, **牌照打**, **舞照跳**, 该干什么干什么。

云云：　嗨,**要不怎么说 "人比人该死,货比货该扔"呢**？你是天生的乐天派,我和你比不了。可是话又说回来,大考临头,你不复习不复习也得多少复习复习吧,**要是真考砸了,看你怎么跟你爸妈和老师交代？**

李林：　话是这么说,可要真考砸了也没什么大不了的。**砸了就砸了呗**,我才不在乎呢,我又不是给他们活着的。**叫我说**,你不用劝我,倒是我该劝劝你。你平常学习那么好,有什么好愁的？

云云：　唉,**不复习不要紧,一复习吓一跳**。好多地方我都背不下来,要真考到那些地方,我就一**点儿辙都没了**。

李林：　我的小姐,我还当你是愁什么呢,闹了半天,你想把书都背下来呀! 哪点儿没背下来就愁成这样,这日子还有什么过头! 我把你这个书虫啊,一点儿办法也没有! **叫我怎么说你才好？**

云云：　我也知道自己有点儿太死心眼儿,可知道是知道,就是改不了。再说,我跟老师保证说我能考好,考不好哪儿行？我向来说话算数,**说什么就是什么**。

李林：　**考好也好,考砸也好**,你都别不吃不睡呀! 身体垮了,你还能干什么？连这么简单的道理都不明白,**还好学生呢!**

The semester is ending, and Li Lin and Yun Yun are talking about the final.

Lin Li: Look at you, all sad and depressed, and you're not eating, either. Are you sick?

Yun Yun: What are you talking about; it's the final doing it to me. It's almost the final exam, and I've barely started to study. Tell me, shouldn't I be going crazy? Because of it these past few days I haven't been able to eat or sleep, and I pulled an all nighter last night.

Lin Li: I think you're being too serious. Aren't you going too far? It's only a final exam, right? Look at me, I play cards just like I always do, dance just like I always do, and do whatever I want.

Yun Yun: Man, that's why they say you can't compare people. You're laid-back by nature. I can't compare to you at all. But now that you mention it, it's almost the final. No matter how much you say you don't study, you have to study a little. If you fail, what do you think you're going to say to your parents and teacher?

Lin Li: That's what they say, but even if I really fail it's no big deal. If I fail I fail; I don't care, and I'm not living for their sake. As I see it, you shouldn't be preaching to me, but I should be preaching to you. Your grades are so good normally, what do you have to worry about?

Yun Yun: Man, it's okay if you don't review, but once you start it's scary. A lot of information I haven't memorized. If they really test that, there won't be anything I can do.

Lin Li: My dear miss, I was wondering what you were worrying about. So all this time you were trying to memorize the whole book! If you start killing yourself every time you don't memorize one little thing, what is there to live for! What am I going to say to you, my little bookworm? There's nothing I can do!

Yun Yun:　I know I'm sometimes a little pigheaded, but knowing is knowing, and there's nothing I can do about it. Besides, I told my teacher I'd do well, so now how can I not? I've always kept my promises. If I made a promise, then I have to honor it.

Lin Li:　You can do well or you can fail, but don't skip food and sleep! If you ruin your health, what can you do? You don't even get something this simple, and you're a good student!

———■———

Traditional

快到期末了, 李林和云云在說考試的事兒。

李林:　**瞧你那樣兒,** 沒精打采的, 飯也不吃, 是不是病了?

雲雲:　哪兒啊, 還不是**讓考試鬧的**。**眼看**就要大考了, 我這兒**八字還沒一撇**呢, 你說**急人**不急人? 弄得我這幾天是 吃也吃不下, 睡也睡不著, 昨天還開了個夜車。

李林:　我說你也**忒**認真了吧? **至於嗎? 不就是期末考試嗎?** 你看我, **牌照打, 舞照跳, 該幹什麼幹什麼**。

雲雲:　嗨, 要不怎麼說 "人比人該死, 貨比貨該扔" 呢? 你是天生的樂天派, 我和你比不了。可是話又說回來, 大考臨頭, 你不復習不復習也得多少復習復習吧, **要是真考砸了, 看你怎麼跟你爸媽和老師交代?**

李林： 話是這麼說，可要真考砸了也沒什麼大不了的。**砸了就砸了唄，**我才不在乎呢，我又不是給他們活著的。**叫我說**，你不用勸我，倒是我該勸勸你。你平常學習那麼好，有什麼好愁的?

雲雲： 唉**不復習不要緊，一復習嚇一跳**。好多地方我都背不下來，要真考到那些地方，我就**一點兒轍都沒了**。

李林： 我的小姐，我還當你是愁什麼呢，鬧了半天，你想把書都背下來呀!哪點兒沒背下來就愁成這樣，這日子還有什麼過頭!我把你這個書蟲啊，一點兒辦法也沒有!**叫我怎麼說你才好?**

雲雲： 我也知道自己有點兒太死心眼兒，可知道是知道，就是改不了。再說，我跟老師保證說我能考好，考不好哪兒行? 我向來說話算數，**說什麼就是什麼**。

李林： **考好也好，考砸也好**，你都別不吃不睡呀!身體垮了，你還能幹什麼? 連這麼簡單的道理都不明白，**還好學生呢!**

———■———

词语注释

• **瞧你那样儿**, 没精打采的
  瞧你那样儿 Also as 看你那样儿 "Look at yourself." This pattern is usually used to blame or to tease. For example, 瞧你那样儿, 像个饿狼似的. "Look at you, you're just like a hungry wolf." In fact, this pattern is a short form of 瞧你那...样儿, and ... should be a description of the look. For example, 看你那傻

样儿, 还不快过来和大家打招呼。 "Look at you, you look foolish. Come over and say hello to everybody."

- 哪儿啊, 还不是**让考试闹的**。
  让…闹的 "Troubled by …" or "suffer from …." In this pattern, 让 is a preposition to introduce the doer … of the action. 闹 means "trouble" here. For example, 我这几天吃不下睡不着, 都是让我小儿子得病闹的。 "I didn't eat or sleep well these past few days, because I was troubled by my young son's illness."

- **眼看**就要大考了
  眼看 "Soon," "in a moment." The context is: "Nowhere near done." For example, 眼看天就要黑了。 "It will be dark soon." 电影眼看就要开始了, 你还要去哪儿? "The movie will start any moment, where are you going?"

- 眼看就要大考了, 我这儿**八字还没一撇**呢,
  八字还没一撇 Literally: "There's not even the first stroke of the character 八." The contextual meaning is: "nowhere near done." For example, "你的论文写得差不多了吧? ""哪儿啊, 八字还没一撇呢。 ""Your dissertation is almost complete, isn't it?""No, I have a long way to go."

- 你说急人不急人
  急人 "worrying," "troubling." For example, 她怎么这么晚还不来啊? 真急人! "It's so late, why hasn't she come already? It's so troubling!"

- 也**忒**认真了吧
  忒 ([tuī]) A colloquial word meaning "too" or "very." For example, 今天老师留的作业忒难了, 没一个人能做得出来。 "Today's homework is too hard. Not a single person could do it."

- 至于吗? 不就是期末考试吗?

  至于吗 An expression for "to make a mountain out of a molehill." It is in the form of a rhetorical question with the connotation "it does not need to go so far as that." 至于 means "go so far as to." For example, "今天吃了一杯冰淇凌, 我得去减肥了。""至于吗? 不就是一杯冰淇凌吗!""I had a cup of ice cream today, so I have to lose weight." "Aren't you going too far? It's just a cup of ice cream!"

- 至于吗? **不就是期末考试吗?**

  不就是…吗 This is a rhetorical question that emphasizes …. It has the same meaning as 就是 …, "It's merely …." 就 means "merely," "just," or "only." For example, 不就是过个生日吗? 有什么可大惊小怪的? "Isn't it just a birthday celebration? What's the fuss about?"

- **牌照打**, **舞照跳**, 该干什么干什么.

  …照…, …照… "To … and … as usual." This is a parallel structure, in each …照…, the second "…" is a verb and the first "…" is its object; and 照 means "in the same old way" or "as usual." For example, 虽然有心脏病, 可是他烟照抽, 酒照喝, 一点儿也不在乎。 "Although he has heart problems, he smokes as usual, and drinks as usual."

- 牌照打, 舞照跳, **该干什么干什么**。

  该…什么…什么 "Just … whatever should be …." In this pattern, … is a verb, and 该 means "should." For example, 今天客人不来, 你们该做什么做什么。 "The guests aren't coming today; you guys do whatever needs to be done." 不管他会怎么想, 咱们该说什么说什么。 "No matter what he might think, we just say whatever should be said."

- **要不怎么说 "人比人该死, 货比货该扔" 呢?**
  要不怎么说…呢? This pattern introduces a rhetorical question.
  Literally it means: "Otherwise how come it is said …." The
  contextual meaning is: "That's why they say …." For example, upon
  hearing about a large company going bankrupt, people may say: 要
  不怎么说天下没有不散的戏呢。"That's why they say every
  play must end sometime."

- 要不怎么说**"人比人该死, 货比货该扔**"呢?
  人比人该死, 货比货该扔 (货 [huò] goods; 扔 [rēng] throw
  away) Literally it means: "When comparing two persons, the inferior
  one should die; when comparing two products, the inferior one
  should be thrown away." The figurative meaning of the expression
  is that you should not simply compare two persons. The expression
  is often used as advice to encourage people to build up self-
  confidence. For example, 人比人该死, 货比货该扔. 要是你
  总拿自己的缺点和别人的优点比, 你还活不活了? "You
  shouldn't compare yourself with others. If you keep comparing your
  shortcomings with other's strengths, how can you go on living?"

- **要是真考砸了**, 看你怎么跟你爸妈和老师交代?
  要是…, 看你怎么… "In case …, how could you …?" This is a
  colloquial pattern in the form of a rhetorical question, and is used
  to impose an opinion. For example, 你就是不肯买汽车保险,
  要是真出了车祸, 看你怎么赔得起。"You persist in not
  buying auto insurance; if you have an accident how could you afford
  the damages?"

- **砸了就砸了呗**, 我才不在乎呢
  …了就…了呗 This is a colloquial pattern for "It's not a big deal
  to do …." In this pattern, … is usually a verb or verbal phrase. For
  example, 成功就成功了呗, 有什么好吹的。"It's not a big

deal to succeed and there is nothing to brag about." 输了就输了呗, 没有什么好灰心的。 "So you fail; there's no reason to get discouraged."

- **叫我说**, 你不用劝我, 倒是我该劝劝你。
  叫我说 "I would say." This is a colloquial expression that is often used to initiate a comment or opinion. For example, 叫我说, 你的话没错。 "I would say that your words are right." 叫我说, 咱们一起作最好。 "In my opinion, we should do this job together."

- **不复习不要紧, 一复习吓一跳**
  不...不要紧, 一...吓一跳 This is a colloquial pattern for "It seems alright when he (or she) did not ..., but he (or she) was frightened as soon as he (or she) started to .... " ... is the verb or verbal phrase in the pattern. For example, 不看不要紧, 一看吓出了我一身冷汗。 "It was alright when I was not looking, but I broke out in a cold sweat as soon as I looked at it."

- 要真考到那些地方, 我就**没辙了**
  没辙 (辙 [zhé] the track of a wheel) "One can find no way out." "Be at the end of one's rope." This is a colloquial expression, and 辙 stands for "way" or "idea." When emphasized, 没辙 is often expressed as 一点儿辙都没有 or 没一点儿辙, "just cannot find any way out." For example, 车坏成这样, 我是没辙了。 "With the car being broken to this extent, I've got no ideas."

- **叫我怎么说你才好?**
  叫我怎么说你才好? "What can I say about you?" This is a rhetorical question that contains a connotation of mild blame. For example, 每次约会你都迟到, 叫我怎么说你才好? "You're late on every date. What can I say about you?"

- 我向来说话算数, **说什么就是什么**。
  说什么就是什么 This is a synonym of 说话算数. Literally, "Whatever is said, is counted." The context meaning of this expression is: "To live up to one's words." "To mean what one says." For example, 他一向说什么就是什么, 从不反悔。 "He is always as good as his word, and never goes back on it."

- **考好也好**, **考砸也好**, 你都别不吃不睡呀!
  ...也好, ...也好 The reduplicated 也好 structure means "whether ... or ...." For example, 你喜欢也好, 不喜欢也好, 都应该表示感谢。 "Whether you like it or not, you should express your gratitude for it." 你坐火车也好, 坐飞机也好, 都得在这个星期五以前到那儿。 "Whether you take the train or airplane, you must be there before this Friday."

- 连这么简单的道理都不明白, **还好学生呢**!
  还...呢 This is a colloquial pattern used to express a tone of complaint. It often contains a sarcastic tone or the connotation of blame. The basic meaning of this pattern is that some thing should have been done but was not, or that expectations are not borne out by reality. This pattern is often used together with a negative comment or a rhetorical question to emphasize the meaning. For example, 连我的名字都叫错了, 还老朋友呢! "You got my name wrong, and you're my old friend!" 还说给我打电话呢! 他问过我的电话号码吗? "And he said he would call me! Did he even ask for my phone number?"

———————■———————

VOCABULARY

抽烟	chōuyān	smoke (a cigarette or a pipe)
戒	jiè	give up; stop
负责	fùzé	be responsible for
责任	zérèn	duty; responsibility
开戒	kāijiè	break an abstinence (from smoking, drinking, etc.)
赶紧	gǎnjǐn	lose no time; hasten
决心	juéxīn	determination
过程	guòchéng	course; process
健康	jiànkāng	health
耍贫嘴	shuǎpínzuǐ	be garrulous
期末	qīmò	end of term or semester
没精打采	méijīngdǎcǎi	listless; in low spirits
大考	dàkǎo	final exam
天生	tiānshēng	inborn; innate
乐天派	lètiānpài	a happy-go-lucky person
临头	líntóu	befall; happen
交代	jiāodài	justify oneself; explain
不在乎	bùzàihu	not mind; not care
劝	quàn	advise; persuade
书虫	shūchóng	pedant; bookworm
死心眼儿	sǐxīnyǎnr	a person with a one-track mind
保证	bǎozhèng	pledge; guarantee; ensure
向来	xiànglái	always; all along
垮	kuǎ	collapse; break down

简单	jiǎndān	simple
道理	dàoli	principle, truth

---■---

EXERCISES

A. Fill in the spaces with the appropriate words or phrases:

什么事儿   烟鬼   又

不是不喜欢   没办法   咱

1 服务员,＿＿＿＿这旅馆里有传真机吗?

2 我那个朋友啊, 既是＿＿＿＿, 又是酒鬼。

3 他＿＿＿＿不是没去过那儿, 不可能找不到。

4 我那两个孩子特别不听话, 我真拿他们＿＿＿＿。

5 他＿＿＿＿那个女孩儿, 只是不好意思说。

6 ＿＿＿＿就怕不用心, 不用心就什么也干不好。

B. Choose the expression from the following list that best corresponds
   to the underlined words or phrases:

活受罪   吃上了   谢了

看来看去 大不了   成心

1 昨天开会我看他是<u>故意</u>迟到的。

2 今天吃饭又是你请的客。<u>谢谢</u>。

3 不就是做个心脏手术吗, 没什么<u>了不起</u>的。

4 那个地方这几天热极了, 去那儿旅游肯定<u>难受死了</u>。

5 她说那件衣服好, 可我不管怎么看, 就是看不出怎么好。

6 你们怎么也不等等我就开始吃了?

C. Fill in the spaces with the appropriate words or phrases:

还爸爸呢	没辙	让胃病闹的	去也好
事儿照作	要不	人比人该死	至于吗
叫我怎么说你才好		八字还没一撇	不就是

1 你要是真的不听他的话, 他就_____了。

2 他才感冒就要求住院, 你说他_____?

3 连儿子的生日都不知道, _____!

4 你_____, 不去也好, 都得通知他们一下。

5 他一个月体重减了好几斤, 都是_____。

6 你问他什么时候结婚? 他连女朋友都没有, _____呢!

7 _____一次考试没及格吗? 值得这么难受吗?

8 他得了病也不休息, 班照上, _____。

9 你连这个都不会, _____怎么说你不行呢?

10 我从来没忘过你的生日, 可你呢? _____?

11 _____, 货比货该扔。我哪能跟你比呀?

D. Choose the expression from the following list that best corresponds to the underlined words or phrases:

不要紧	要是	急人	忒	瞧你那样儿
叫我说	眼看	就丢了呗	该	说什么就是什么

1 火车<u>马上</u>就要开了,你赶不上了。

2 飞机都要起飞了,他还没到,真<u>叫人</u>着急。

3 踩了我的脚还说我的脚没放对地方,你这人也<u>太缺</u>德了。

4 <u>我看</u>咱们根本就不应该参加那个活动。

5 不管会不会长胖,我还是<u>想吃什么吃什么</u>。

6 这么晚了你还不走,<u>如果</u>赶不上飞机,看你怎么办?

7 钱包丢了<u>有什么办法</u>,着急也没什么用?

8 外面下雨了吧? <u>你看看你自己</u>,从头到脚都湿了。

9 <u>我们老板说要怎么办就一定会怎么办</u>,值得信任。

10 那些话不听<u>没关系</u>,一听吓一跳。

ANSWER KEY

Exercise A (Dialogue 1)

1 咱

2 烟鬼

3 又 (又...)

4 没办法 (拿...没办法)

5 不是不喜欢(不是不...)

6 什么事儿 (什么事儿就怕...)

Exercise B (Dialogue 1)

1 成心

2 谢了

3 大不了

4 活受罪

5 看来看去 (...来...去), (B)

6 吃上了 (...上了)

Exercise C (Dialogue 2)

1 没辙
2 至于吗
3 还爸爸呢 (还...呢)
4 去也好 (...也好,...也好)
5 让胃病闹的 (让...闹的)
6 八字还没一撇
7 不就是 (不就是...吗)
8 事儿照作 (...照...,...照...)
9 要不 (要不怎么说...呢?)
10 叫我怎么说你才好?
11 人比人该死 (人比人该死,货比货该扔)

Exercise D (Dialogue 2)

1 眼看
2 急人
3 忒
4 叫我说
5 该 (该...什么...什么)
6 要是 (要是..., 看你怎么...)
7 就丢了呗 (...了就...了呗)
8 瞧你那样儿
9 说什么就是什么
10 不要紧 (不...不要紧, 一...吓一跳)

CULTURE NOTES

There are many Chinese expressions that contain the word 鬼. When 鬼 is used as a noun, it means "ghost"; "spirit" or "apparition." Read the following examples:

鬼火　　well-o'-the-wisp; jack-o'-lantern

鬼哭狼嚎　wail like ghosts and howl like wolves; set up wild shrieks and howls

鬼脸　　funny face; wry face; grimace; mask used as a toy

鬼门关	the gate of hell; danger spot; a trying moment
鬼迷心窍	be possessed; be obsessed
不人不鬼	in miserable physical condition
活见鬼	it's sheer fantasy; you're imagining it
见鬼	fantastic; preposterous; absurd; go to hell
闹鬼	be haunted; play tricks behind sb.'s back; use underhanded means
死鬼	devil
替死鬼	scapegoat; fall guy
吸血鬼	bloodsucker; vampire
小鬼	imp; goblin; little devil; (a term of endearment in addressing a child)

With the same meaning, 鬼 is often used in certain terms that refer to human beings. For example:

胆小鬼	craven; piker; scaramouch
饿鬼	ghoul
酒鬼	drunkard; sot; toper; wine bibber
烟鬼	opium addict; heavy smoker
色鬼	satyr
鬼子	devil (an epithet for foreign invaders)
洋鬼子	foreign devil (a term used in preliberation China for foreign invaders)

鬼 is also used as an adjective, and it means "sinister (plot)," "dirty (trick)," "terrible," or "damnable." Read the following examples:

鬼把戏	sinister plot; dirty trick
鬼点子	wicked idea; trick
鬼怪	ghosts and monsters; monsters of all kinds; forces of evil

鬼魂	ghost; spirit; apparition
鬼话	lie
鬼话连篇	full of lies and deceptions
鬼混	lead an aimless or irregular existence; fool around
鬼胎	sinister design; ulterior motive
鬼头鬼脑	thievish; stealthy; furtive
鬼主意	evil plan; wicked idea
搞鬼	play tricks; be up to some mischief
有鬼	there's something fishy
做鬼	play tricks; play an underhanded game; up to mischief

Although in most expressions, 鬼 refers to something negative, it also has a positive meaning, "clever" or "smart," when used informally.

你看看都什么时候了?
人再多也得有个先来后到吧?

BLAMING
•
CRITICIZING
•
EXPLAINING

CONVERSATION A:

Simplified

李琳跟男朋友方明下班后有一个约会，方明迟到了。

方明： 真对不起,又来晚了。

李琳： 你看看,**都什么时候了?** 让人家在冷风里**干等着,真不是事儿!**

方明： 对不起,对不起,临时有点儿急事儿**走不开**。你看,我紧着往这儿赶,出了一身汗。

李琳： 什么急事儿? **动不动就找借口!** 这可不是头一回了,你心里根本就没我。

274

酒香不怕巷子深 (lit: "When your wine is fragrant you need not be afraid that your store is hidden.") Quality will sell itself. (see page 286.)

Lin Li and her boyfriend, Ming Fang, have a date after work, but Ming Fang is more than half an hour late.

Fang:	I'm really sorry I came late again.
Li:	Look, do you know what time it is? Making me wait in the cold like that, what the hell!
Fang:	I'm sorry, I'm sorry, something urgent came up and I couldn't get away. See, I got here as fast as I could, and now I'm all sweaty.
Li:	Oh really, something urgent? You have an excuse for everything! This isn't the first time; you don't care about me at all.

方明:　哎,你可别这么说! 我心里就想着你。前天刚一分手,我就盼着再看见你。你瞧我跑得**上气不接下气**的,不就是想让你少等会儿吗?

李琳:　**说的比唱的还好听!** 你要是真心爱我,有什么事儿比咱俩的事儿还重要?

方明:　没错儿,当然是咱俩的事儿最重要! **你不知道**,我的心早就飞到这儿来了。为了能按时下班,我今儿干活儿特别**麻利**,**早早儿的**就把什么事儿都干完了。没想到我们老板**早也不去**,**晚也不去**,偏偏在下班前五分钟去了公司,把我们叫到一块儿开会。我走也不是,不走也不是,你说急人不急人?

李琳:　反正你老是**有的说**,就是不能按时来。

方明:　**你千万别误会**,我可不是**故意**来晚的。不过,话又说回来,这事儿也是该**怨我**,谁让我把手机给丢了呢? 要不一个电话就行了,哪儿能让你等这么久? 我已经打电话去买新手机了,明天就能拿到。我保证以后一定不迟到,这是最后一次。这回行了吧?

———■———

Fang: Oh, don't say that! I think about nothing but you. Ever since I left you the day before yesterday, I've been thinking about seeing you again. Look how I'm huffing and puffing from running. It's because I didn't want to keep you waiting!

Li: Well that sounds just beautiful! If you really loved me, what was it that was more important than us being together?

Fang: You're right, of course there's nothing more important than us! You didn't know, but my heart was over here the whole day. Just so I can get off work on time, I was really quick about my work today, and finished everything early. But who knew the boss would show up at the company—not earlier, not later, but 5 minutes before work let out, to call a meeting! I couldn't go, and I couldn't stay; what was I supposed to do?

Li: Well you always have something to say, but you can never make it on time.

Fang: Now please don't jump to conclusions; I didn't come late on purpose. But, speaking of that, it is my fault; I was the one who lost my cell phone, right? Otherwise it would've been just a phone call. How could you have waited for so long? I've put in a call for a new cell phone, I'll get it tomorrow. I guarantee that I'll never be late again, this is the last time. There, you forgive me?

Traditional

李琳跟男朋友方明下班後有一個約會，方明遲到了。

方明：　真對不起, 又來晚了。

李琳：　你看看, **都什麼時候了**? 讓人家在冷風裏**幹等著, 真不是事兒**!

方明：　對不起, 對不起, 臨時有點兒急事兒**走不開**。你看, 我緊著往這兒趕, 出了一身汗。

李琳：　什麼急事兒? **動不動就找藉口**! 這可不是頭一回了, 你心裏根本就沒我。

方明：　哎, 你可別這麼說! 我心裏就想著你。前天剛一分手, 我就盼著再看見你。你瞧我跑得**上氣不接下氣**的, 不就是想讓你少等會兒嗎?

李琳：　**說的比唱的還好聽**! 你要是真心愛我, 有什麼事兒比咱倆的事兒還重要?

方明：　沒錯兒, 當然是咱倆的事兒最重要! **你不知道**, 我的心早就飛到這兒來了。為了能按時下班, 我今兒幹活兒特別**麻利**, **早早兒的**就把什麼事兒都幹完了。沒想到我們老闆**早也不去, 晚也不去, 偏偏在下班前五分鐘去了公司**, 把我們叫到一塊兒開會。我走也不是, 不走也不是, 你說急人不急人?

李琳：　反正你老是**有的說**, 就是不能按時來。

方明：　**你千萬別誤會**, 我可不是**故意**來晚的。不過, 話又說回來, 這事兒也是該**怨我**, 誰讓我把手機給丟了呢? 要不一個電話就行了,哪兒能讓你等這麼久? 我已經打電話去買新手機了,明天就能拿到。我保證以後一定不遲到,這是最後一次。這回行了吧?

词语注释

- 你看看, **都什么时候了**?
  都什么时候了 "What time do you think it is?" This is a rhetorical question with a tone of blame, with the connotation of the subject being late. For example, 都什么时候了,还在玩儿游戏! "What time do you think it is? You are still playing games!"

- 让人家在冷风里**干等着**,真不是事儿!
  干...着 "To … for nothing." "To … in vain." For example, 今天早上中平没来,他们谁也干不了这活儿,干着急,没办法。"This morning Zhongping did not come. None of the other people know how to do the job, so they worried without being able to do anything."

- 让人家在冷风里干等着, **真不是事儿**!
  真不是事儿 "It's unreasonable." "It's annoying." For example, 我今天一大早就吃了一张超速的罚单,真不是事儿! "Today I got a ticket for speeding early in the morning. It's so annoying!"

- 临时有点儿急事儿**走不开**
  走不开 When used after a verb, one meaning of 开 is to indicate separation. 走不开 means "Couldn't leave at the moment." For example, 明天你下飞机的时候,我正上班,走不开。我叫

我弟弟去接你吧。"When you arrive at the airport tomorrow, I'll be working, and will not be able to get away. I'll ask my brother to pick you up."

- **什么急事儿? 动不动就找借口!**
  动不动就… (Of an act or situation, usually unwished) "occurring easily or frequently." For example, 他身体不好, 动不动就着凉。"His health isn't good, and he frequently catches colds."

- **你瞧我跑得上气不接下气的**
  上气不接下气 "To be out of breath." For example, 你看你, 走这么一点儿路就上气不接下气的。你真该好好运动运动了。"Look at you, you are out of breath after walking such a short distance. You really need to exercise more."

- **说的比唱的还好听!**
  说的比唱的还好听 This is a fixed idiom with the literal meaning: "What (you) said sounds better than singing." The contextual meaning is: "It sounds too good to be true." For example, 别看他说的比唱的还好听, 其实连他自己也不信自己说的话。"In spite of his beautiful words, even he didn't believe them."

- **你不知道, 我的心早就飞到这儿来了。**
  你不知道 "To tell you the truth," or "You know." For example, 你不知道, 听说你出了车祸, 我都快吓死了。"To tell you the truth, I was scared to death when I heard that you had an accident."

- **我今儿干活儿特别麻利,**
  麻利 "Quick and neat"; "dexterous." For example, 她手脚麻利极了, 每天下班后连做饭带收拾屋子, 一会儿就都干完了。"Her hands are very fast. Every day after work she both cooks and cleans, and finishes in an instant."

- **早早儿的**就把什么事儿都干完了。
  早早的 "Well in advance"; "as early as possible." For example, 新年还没到, 可他早早儿的就做好了过年的准备。"Although it's not yet New Year, he got everything ready in advance to celebrate."

- 没想到我们老板**早也不去, 晚也不去, 偏偏**在下班前五分钟去了公司,
  早也不..., 晚也不..., 偏偏... In this pattern, ... is usually a verb or verbal phrase. Literally, "(One) does not do ... early nor late, but does it just at the time of ... ." This pattern is usually used to show that something happened that was not expected. For example, 这雨是早也不下, 晚也不下, 偏偏在我们开运动会的时候下了起来。"It didn't rain earlier and didn't rain later, but at the exact time of our sports tournament it started raining."

- 反正你老是**有的说**
  有的说 Literally, "have something to say." The contextual meaning is often "have an excuse" or "have pretext." For example, 不管怎么样, 反正他有的说。"No matter what happens, he can always find some excuse for his behavior."

- 你**千万别**误会,
  千万别... "Make sure not to ...." Usually used in the imperative to sincerely urge somebody not to do something. For example, 她妈妈叮嘱她千万别去不安全的地方。"Her mother urged her never to go anywhere unsafe."

- 我可不是**故意**来晚的。
  故意 "On purpose" or "intentionally." For example, 他见到我假装没看见, 故意不理我。"He pretended not see me, and ignored me intentionally."

• 这事儿也是该**怨我**

怨… (怨 [yuàn] resentment; blame) "Blame …" For example, 这事儿谁也怨不得, 只能怨咱们自己。 "There is nobody but ourselves to blame for this matter." 他不是故意的, 你别怨他。 "He did not do it on purpose; don't blame him."

CONVERSATION B:

Simplified

两个顾客在一家饭馆里等待点菜。

顾客甲: 咱们都**傻等**了二十几分钟了, 怎么连服务员的人影儿都不见啊?

顾客乙: 这家馆子上菜慢是出了名的, 这就叫 "酒香不怕巷子深", 这儿的菜比哪儿的**味儿**都**正**, 别看上菜慢, 买卖照样儿火, 你看门口都排上队了。

顾客甲: 这叫什么事儿啊, 有这工夫咱们自己做也吃上了。**我催催**他们。哎, 服务员, 过来一下。

服务员: 是叫我吧? 什么事?

顾客甲: 还什么事呢! 我们来这儿**还能有什么事?** 我们在这儿坐半天了, 怎么连个人影儿都没有啊?

服务员: 实在对不起, 今天特别忙。**来, 来, 来,** 我给您倒杯茶, 您**消消火儿**。刚才我以为**二位**还没商量好吃什么呢。我这就给您点。今天吃点儿什么?

顾客乙: 就要你们最**拿手**的香酥鸡和烤鸭吧, 得等多
长时间?

服务员: 这**俩**菜, 快! 顶多二十分钟。
（又过了三十五分钟）

顾客甲: 怎么搞的, 咱点完菜又等了半个多钟头了。刚
才他说二十分钟我就有点不信, 这么多人吃
饭, 二十分钟哪儿成啊? 我再催催。服务员!

服务员: **等急了吧?** 我去给您催催去, 您再喝口茶, 聊
聊天儿。

顾客甲: **还喝什么喝**! 再喝就喝饱了。我们干等一个
钟头了, 你们也太**不像话**了。

服务员: 真对不起。今天人实在太多了, 哪天也没今天
多。

顾客乙: **人再多也得有个先来后到**吧? 为什么比我们
晚来的都早就吃上了?

服务员: 是吗? **都怪我**, 我**忙活**得**晕头转向**的, 没**钉着
催**您的菜。

顾客甲: 去把你们经理叫来, 我跟他**讲讲理**。你们菜做
得再好, 也不能这么**涮人**吧? 告诉我们顶多二
十分钟, 现在一个钟头过去了。闹了半天, 才
开始催!

服务员: 我**给您赔不是**了。我这就叫经理去。

经理: 你们好! 真对不起, 你们来这儿吃饭是**看得起**我们。可我们工作没做好, 让你们浪费时间不说, 还闹一肚子气。这么着吧, 今天你们要的两个菜收一个菜的钱。贵的那个算是本店送二位品尝的。要是十分钟之内还不上菜, 今天的菜就都不收钱了。你们看怎么样?

顾客甲、乙: 这还差不多。

———————————■———————————

Two customers are seated in a restaurant, waiting for service.

Customer A: We've been sitting for over twenty minutes; why haven't we seen so much as a waiter's shadow?

Customer B: This restaurant is famous for how slow it is. That's why the saying goes "When your wine is fragrant you need not be afraid that your store is hidden." The food here is more authentic than anywhere else, so even if they're slow, they still do a roaring business. See, there's a line forming at the door.

Customer A: This is unacceptable. With this amount of time we could have cooked the food ourselves, and we'd be eating already. I'll tell them to hurry up. Hey, waiter, come over for a second.

Waiter: You're calling me? What is it?

Customer A: What is it! What else would we come here for? We've been sitting here forever; how come we haven't seen even a shadow?

Waiter: I'm very sorry. We're extremely busy today. Here, let me pour you some tea. Please calm down. Just now I thought you two were still discussing what to eat. I'll take your order right away. What would you like today?

Customer B: We'll take your specialties—the crispy chicken and the roast duck. How long do we have to wait?

Waiter: These two dishes, they're fast! Twenty minutes at most!

(Thirty-five minutes later)

Customer A: What's going on, it's been over half an hour since we ordered. I was a little suspicious even when he said twenty minutes, with this many people eating, how can they take only twenty minutes? I'll talk to them again. Waiter!

Waiter: Tired of waiting? I'll go tell them to hurry up, please have some more tea and chat a bit.

Customer A: Drink more tea! Any more and we'll be full. We've been waiting for an hour; you people have gone way too far!

Waiter: I'm truly sorry. There's an extraordinary number of people here today, more than any other day.

Customer B: It should be first come, first serve, no matter how many people there are, am I right? Why were people later than us served a long time ago?

Waiter: Oh, really? It's my fault. I'm so busy that my head's turned around, and didn't pay attention to hurrying your dishes along.

Customer A: Go get your manager, I want him to hear our case. I don't care how good your food is, you can't treat people like this! You told us twenty minutes tops, and now it's been an hour. After all that, now you're going to tell them to hurry up!?

Waiter: I apologize. I'll go get the manager right now.

Manager: Hello! I'm very sorry; by coming to eat you gave us your trust. But we did not do our jobs well, and not only wasted your time, but also caused you displeasure. How about this: we'll charge you for only one of the dishes you ordered. The more expensive one is on the house, for you to sample. If within ten minutes the food is not here, everything will be free today. What do you guys think?

Customer A, B: That's more like it.

———————■———————

Traditional

兩個顧客在一家飯館裏等待點菜。

顧客甲: 咱們都**傻等**了二十幾分鐘了, 怎麼連服務員的人影兒都不見啊?

顧客乙: 這家館子上菜慢是出了名的, 這就叫 "酒香不怕巷子深", 這兒的菜比哪兒的**味兒**都正, 別看上菜慢, 買賣照樣兒火, 你看門口都排上隊了。

顧客甲: 這叫什麼事兒啊, 有這工夫咱們自己做也吃上了。**我催催**他們。哎, 服務員, 過來一下。

服務員: 是叫我吧, 什麼事?

顧客甲: 還什麼事呢! 我們來這兒**還能有什麼事?** 我們在這兒坐半天了, 怎麼連個人影兒都沒有啊?

服務員: 實在對不起, 今天特別忙。**來來來,** 我給您倒盃茶, 您**消消火兒**。剛才我以為**二位**還沒商量好吃什麼呢。我這就給您點。今天吃點兒什麼?

顧客乙: 就要你們最**拿手**的香酥雞和烤鴨吧, 得等多
　　　　長時間?

服務員: 這**倆**菜, 快! 頂多二十分鐘。

　　　　(又過了三十五分鐘)

顧客甲: 怎麼搞的, 咱點完菜又等了半個多鐘頭了。剛
　　　　才他說二十分鐘我就有點不信, 這麼多人吃
　　　　飯, 二十分鐘哪兒成啊? 我再催催。服務員!

服務員: **等急了**吧? 我去給您催催去, 您再喝口茶, 聊
　　　　聊天兒。

顧客甲: **還喝什麼喝**! 再喝就喝飽了。我們幹等一個
　　　　鐘頭了, 你們也太**不像話**了。

服務員: 真對不起。今天人實在太多了, 哪天也沒今天多。

顧客乙: 人**再多也得有個先來後到**吧? 為什麼比我們
　　　　晚來的都早就吃上了?

服務員: 是嗎? **都怪我**, 我**忙活**得**暈頭轉向**的, 沒**釘著
　　　　催**您的菜。

顧客甲: 去把你們經理叫來, 我跟他**講講理**。你們菜做
　　　　得再好, 也不能這麼**涮人**吧? 告訴我們頂多二
　　　　十分鐘, 現在一個鐘頭過去了。鬧了半天, 才
　　　　開始催!

服務員: 我**給您賠不是**了。我這就叫經理去。

經理:　　先生們, 你們好! 真對不起, 你們來這兒吃飯
　　　　是**看得起**我們。可我們工作沒做好, 讓你們浪
　　　　費時間不說, 還鬧一肚子氣。這麼著吧, 今天
　　　　你們要的兩個菜收一個菜的錢。貴的那個算

是本店送二位品嘗的。要是十分鐘之內還不
上菜, 今天的菜就都不收錢了. 你們看怎麼樣?

顧客甲、乙: 這還差不多。

——————■——————

词语注释

- 咱们都**傻等**了二十几分钟了
  傻… (傻 [shǎ] stupid; muddleheaded) 傻… means "foolishly …" or
  "simple-mindedly …." In this pattern, … is usually a verb or verbal phrase.
  For example, 你傻笑什么? "Why are you laughing stupidly?"

- 这儿的菜比哪儿的**味儿都正**
  味儿正 "The flavor is right." 正 means "pure" or "right" when it is
  used to describe flavor or color. For example, 这酒味道不正, 别喝
  了。 "The taste of this wine is not pure. Don't drink it any more."

- 我**催催**他们.
  催 ([cuī]) A colloquial word meaning, "urge," "hurry," or "press."
  For example, 别催他, 让他想想。 "Don't hurry him. Let him
  think it over."

- 还什么事呢! 我们来这儿**还能有什么事?**
  还能…什么… "What else could I …?" The first "…" is a verb.
  The second "…" is its object, and is optional for the pattern. This is
  a rhetorical question and usually contains the connotation:"You are
  asking while knowing the answer." For example, "你找我干什
  么? ""还能干什么? 你欠我的钱该还了! " "What did you
  come here for?" "What else could I come here for? You should pay
  back the money you owe!"

- **来来来,** 我给您倒杯茶, 您消消火儿。
  … … … "…" is often a verb or the adjective 好. Repeating the "…" three times reveals a mood, such as excitement, dislike, impatience, solicitousness, or contentment. For example, 去去去, 谁爱理你! "Go, go, go, nobody wants to talk to you!" 好好好, 你怎么办都行! 我不管。 "OK OK OK, do whatever you want! I don't care."

- 来来来, 我给您倒杯茶, 您**消消火儿**。
  消火 (消 [xiāo] disappear; vanish; eliminate) 消火, also appear as 消气, meaning "to calm one's anger." For example, 你去赔个不是, 让她消消火儿。 "You'd better go and apologize to calm her anger."

- 刚才我以为**二位**还没商量好吃什么呢。
  二位 A polite way of saying "You two," usually used for customers or guests. For example, 二位今天吃点儿什么? "What would you two like to eat today?"

- 就要你们最**拿手**的香酥鸡和烤鸭吧
  拿手 "Be good at" or "be at one's best in doing something." For example, 唱歌她很拿手。 "Singing is her forte."

- 这**俩**菜, 快! 顶多二十分钟。
  俩 ([liǎ]) "Two"; "a few." No classifier should be added after 俩. For example, 那儿一共有五个, 俩红的, 仨黄的。 "There are five in total; two red ones and three yellow ones." 怎么一共就这么俩人啊? "How come there are only a few people?"

- **等急了**吧? 我去给您催催去
  …急了 "Impatient because of …" "irritated because of …." … is usually a monosyllabic verb in this pattern. For example, 你老说他, 会把他说急了的。 "If you keep nagging him, you'll make him very annoyed."

- **还喝什么喝!** 再喝就喝饱了。

  还...什么... A colloquial pattern to express discontent, censure, or disagreement. ... is usually a monosyllabic verb in this pattern. For example, 还等什么等! 等到半夜他也来不了! "We can't wait any longer! We won't see him even if we wait till midnight!"

- 你们也太**不像话**了。

  不像话 "Unreasonable," "unacceptable." For example, 每次开会你都迟到, 真不像话! "You're late to every meeting; it's unacceptable!"

- 人**再**多**也**得有个先来后到吧?

  再...也... "No matter how ..., still ...." In this pattern, the second "..." is often a negative expression. For example, 他不注意休息, 所以再锻炼身体也好不了。 "He doesn't give himself a rest; so no matter how much he works out he won't improve."

- 人再多也得有个**先来后到**吧?

  先来后到 "In the order of arrival"; "first come, first served." For example, 请大家排好队, 我们按先来后到的次序给大家服务。 "Everyone please line up. You'll be served in the order of arrival."

- **都怪我**, 我忙活得晕头转向的, 没钉着催您的菜。

  都怪... (怪 [guài] blame) "It's all ...'s fault." For example, 这件事都怪他没讲清楚。 "It's his fault for not explaining things clearly."

- 都怪我, 我**忙活**得晕头转向的, 没钉着催您的菜。

  忙活 ([máng huo]) A colloquial form, "bustle about," "be busy." For example, 我们忙活了一天, 也没干完。 "We were busy for a whole day, but still couldn't finish."

- 都怪我, 我忙活得**晕头转向**的, 没钉着催您的菜。

  晕头转向 (晕 [yūn] dizzy) "Dizzy," "giddy," "confused and disoriented." For example, 你一会儿说西, 一回说东, 把我弄得晕头转向的。 "You tell me to go west one moment, and east the next, and turned me completely around."

- 都怪我, 我忙活得晕头转向的, 没**钉着催**您的菜。
  钉着... (钉 [dīng] urge; press) "Keep doing ...." ... should be a verb in this pattern. For example, 要是你钉着问他, 他就会告诉你。 "If you keep asking him, he will tell you." 你要盯着催她吃药, 别让她忘了。 "You must keep urging her to take her medicine, in case she forgets."

- 去把你们经理叫来, 我跟他**讲讲理**
  讲理 "Argue with somebody." "Reason with somebody." For example, 他们欺骗顾客不对, 咱们跟他们讲理去。 "They are wrong for cheating their customers. Let's go reason with them."

- 你们菜做得再好, 也不能这么**涮人**吧?
  涮人 (涮 [shuàn] rinse; instant-boil) This is a colloquial expression for "cheat" or "make a fool of someone." For example, 你刚登了广告我就来买, 可你说卖完了, 你这不是成心涮人吗? "I came as soon as you published the ad, but you say it's sold out already. Are you making a fool out of me intentionally?"

- 我给您**赔不是**了
  赔不是 (赔 [péi] compensate; pay for) "Apologize for a fault." For example, 你错了, 去给她赔个不是。 "You're wrong. Go tell her you're sorry."

- 你们来这儿吃饭是**看得起**我们
  看得起 "Have a good opinion of," "not look down upon." For example, 你要是看得起我, 就给我这个机会。 "If you really respect me, then give me this chance."

VOCABULARY

临时	línshí	at the time when something happens; temporary
头一回	tóuyīhuí	the first time
分手	fēnshǒu	part company; say good-bye
盼	pàn	hope for; long for
没错儿	méicuòr	I'm quite sure, you can rest assured; can't go wrong
按时	ànshí	on time; on schedule
误会	wùhuì	misunderstand
迟到	chídào	be late; arrive late
巷子	xiàngzi	lane; alley
照样	zhàoyàng	after a pattern or model; in the same old way; all the same; as before
排队	páiduì	form a line; line up
火	huǒ	(for business) prosperous; flourishing
催	cuī	urge; hurry; press; hasten
实在	shízài	really; honestly
经理	jīnglǐ	handle; manage; manager; director
浪费	làngfèi	waste; squander; be extravagant
品尝	pǐncháng	taste; sample

EXERCISES

A. Fill in the spaces with the appropriate words or phrases:

早早儿的　　　走不开　　　还好听　　　故意
真不是事儿　　千万别去　　怨他们　　　麻利

1　咱们今天干活都_____点儿, 早点儿下班回家过节。

2　为了躲过那天的考试, 他_____迟到了半个钟头。

3　这次过圣诞节前, 他们都_____就准备好了圣诞树。

4　他现在正在开会, _____, 你去找别人吧。

5　他们两个大人跟一个孩子打架, _____。

6　这次把事情作错应该_____, 咱们没责任。

7　现在那个地区的传染病很厉害, 你_____。

8　别看他说的比唱的_____, 我可不相信他的话。

B. Choose the expression from the following list that best corresponds
to the underlined words or phrases:

上气不接下气　　你不知道　　　有的说　　　偏偏
都什么时候了　　动不动就　　　干站着

1　<u>说真的</u>, 我第一次见到你就喜欢上你了。

2　你每次迟到都<u>有借口</u>, 好像根本就没你的错。

3　<u>已经这么晚了</u>, 你再不起床肯定要迟到了。

4　你先休息一下, 像这样<u>气都喘不过来</u>怎么讲话?

5　咱们不能让客人<u>站在那里</u>, 既没吃的, 又没玩儿的。

6 他最近<u>总是</u>迟到, 不知道是什么原因。

7 他早也不来,晚也不来,<u>正好</u>在我最忙的时候来了。

C. Fill in the spaces with the appropriate words or phrases:

消消火　　傻等　　　催　　　俩
还能有　　二位　　　逗急了

1 他借了别人的钱以后, 常常要_____好几次才会还。

2 你们明天就走吗? 祝你们_____一路平安。

3 这苹果不错, 我给你买了___, 你尝尝喜欢不喜欢吃。

4 你没有钥匙呀? 我还以为你有呢, 在这儿_____
   了你半天。

5 他现在正在火头上, 听不进话去, 你得让他_____
   再跟他说。

6 我来医院_____什么事? 看病呗。

7 别逗那条狗, _____它会咬人的。

D. Choose the expression from the following list that best corresponds
    to the underlined words or phrases:

钉着要　　行行行　　忙活　　　再喜欢
都怪我　　味儿正　　拿手　　　还去什么去

1 你尝尝这个菜, 怎么样? <u>味儿好</u>吗?

2 你给我们说说这个大师傅<u>做得最好</u>的菜是什么。

3 这么晚了还没做饭, 你在厨房<u>王</u>什么呢?

4 这件事情是弄错的,<u>就是因为我</u>记性不好。

5　你把书借给他以后, 如果<u>不催着要</u>, 他就不会还。

6　<u>好好好</u>, 我都听你的, 这下满意了吧?

7　你<u>不管多喜欢</u>玩儿游戏机, 也得先作完作业才能玩
　　儿。

8　现在飞机已经起飞了, <u>还去干什么</u>!

E. Fill in the spaces with the appropriate words or phrases:

先来后到　　　不像话　　　讲理　　　　　　涮人
晕头转向　　　看得起　　　赔不是

1　骂完了人还说别人态度不好, 哪有这么不_____的!

2　这孩子今天太_____了, 打了同学还说谎。

3　他就____象王东这样的人, 喜欢跟这样的人交朋友。

4　我们老板一会儿要这么着, 一会儿要那么着, 是不
　　是_____哪?

5　他可能是作错什么事了, 紧着向别人_____。

6　这么多人等着买东西, 你们得按_____的顺序卖吧?

7　我连着几天没睡好觉, 觉得_____的。

ANSWER KEY

Exercise A (Dialogue 1)

1 麻利
2 故意
3 早早儿的
4 走不开
5 真不是事儿
6 怨他们（怨…）
7 千万别去（千万别…）
8 还好听（说的比唱的还好听）

Exercise B (Dialogue 1)

1 你不知道
2 有的说
3 都什么时候了
4 上气不接下气
5 干站着（干…着）
6 动不动就（动不动就…）
7 偏偏（早也不…，晚也不…，偏偏…）

Exercise C (Dialogue 2)

1 催
2 二位
3 俩
4 傻等（傻…）

5 消消火（消火）
6 还能有（还能…）
7 逗急了（…急了）

Exercise D (Dialogue 2)

1 味儿正
2 拿手
3 忙活
4 都怪我（都怪…）
5 钉着要（钉着…）
6 行行行（……）
7 再喜欢（再…也…）
8 还去什么去（还…什么…）

Exercise E (Dialogue 2)

1 讲理
2 不像话
3 看得起
4 涮人
5 赔不是
6 先来后到
7 晕头转向

CULTURE NOTES

China has a long history of wine culture. Therefore, there are many words or expressions that contain 酒, "alcoholic," "drink," "wine," "liquor," or "spirits." Please see the following four groups of examples:

Group (1)

酒吧	Bar; taproom
酒杯	wine-glass
酒菜	food and drink; food to go with wine or liquor
酒厂	brewery; winery; distillery
酒店	wineshop; public house; hotel (used in names of hotels)
酒馆	public house
酒鬼	drunkard; sot; toper; wine bibber
酒会	cocktail party
酒家	wineshop; restaurant (used in names of restaurants)
酒量	capacity for liquor
酒钱	beer money; cumshaw; pourboire
酒徒	wine and bibber
酒糟	distiller's grains
酒糟鼻	brandy nose
酒席	feast

Group (2)

白酒	spirit usu. distilled from sorghum or maize; white spirit
陈酒	old wine; mellow wine
干红葡萄酒	dry red wine
果酒	cider; ratafia 酒
喝酒	drinking; tipsiness 酒
黑啤酒	dark beer; stout
虎骨酒	tiger-bone liquor
鸡尾酒	cocktail
老酒	wine; Shaoxing rice wine
料酒	cooking wine
露酒	alcoholic drink mixed with fruit juice
茅台酒	Maotai (a famous Chinese spirit)
米酒	rice wine
啤酒	beer; stout
葡萄酒	grape wine
汽酒	light sparkling wine
甜酒	rum
喜酒	wine drunk at wedding feast; wedding feast
药酒	medicinal liquor
香槟酒	champagne

Group (3)

罚酒	be made to drink as forfeit
酿酒	make wine; brew beer

敬酒	propose a toast; toast
劝酒	urge sb. to drink (at a banquet)
下酒	go with wine; go well with wine
醒酒	dispel the effects of alcohol; sober up
酗酒	excessive drinking
饮酒	potation
祝酒	drink a toast; toast

Group (4)

酒肉朋友	wine-and-meat friends; fair weather friends
茶余酒后	over a cup of tea or after a few glasses of wine – at one's leisure
灯红酒绿	red lantern and green wine; scene of debauchery
滴酒不沾	not even a sip
新瓶装旧酒	old wine in a new bottle—the same old stuff with a new label
醉翁之意不在酒	have ulterior motive
敬酒不吃吃罚酒	refuse a toast only to drink a forfeit; submit to somebody's pressure after first turning down his request; be constrained to do what one at first had declined

她这是杀鸡给猴儿看
家家都有一本难念的经

GETTING ANGRY
·
ADVISING
·
COMFORTING

CONVERSATION A:

Simplified

吴安在跟李友说他们单位的事。

吴安: 我们头儿真不是人,我又跟她干了一架。

李友: 她又**找你茬儿**啦?

吴安: **可不!** 她**愣**说我一条臭鱼弄腥了一锅汤。

李友: 我这可有点儿不明白了。她**凭什么**呀? **她一个领导**,总不该**没事儿找事儿**吧。

吴安: 我不过是请了几次假,迟到了几次,她就借口我**泡病号**,**磨洋工**,把我骂得**狗血淋头**。

杀鸡给猴儿看 (lit: "to kill a chicken to scare the monkeys") to make an example of. (see page 302.)

An Wu and You Li are talking about work.

Wu: Our boss is a horrible jerk. I had another fight with her.

Li: She was finding fault with you again?

Wu: Of course! She kept saying I was the bad apple in the barrel.

Li: Now there's something I don't get. Why's she doing it? She's a leader; she shouldn't be making things up out of the blue.

Wu: All I did was take a few days off, get here late a couple of times, and she accused me of faking illness and sitting around, and gave me bloody hell about it.

李友：　一个巴掌拍不响,还是让人家抓住你的辫子了.

吴安：　我从来是少说话,多做事,可我是个老病号,
　　　　她再霸道也不能不让人得病吧!

李友：　她这是杀鸡给猴儿看。

吴安：　她仗势欺人! 急了我就豁出去给她来个躺倒
　　　　不干,让她抓瞎去。

李友：　别价,万一她狗急跳墙,把你炒了鱿鱼,你喝
　　　　西北风去不成?

吴安：　她敢! 我又没做错事儿,我才不怕她呢。

李友：　你得有点儿长远打算,大丈夫能伸能屈,我劝你
　　　　这次就跟她说两句软话,息事宁人得了。

吴安：　你不知道,她那个人不知好歹,跟她说软话完
　　　　全是白费口舌。再说我也不是那种能忍气吞
　　　　声的人。

李友：　你俩不对付也不是一天两天了,难办!

吴安：　我干脆打开天窗说亮话,告诉她,要是再出口
　　　　伤人,我就跟她对着干。

李友：　那她肯定发火。她是你顶头上司,权在她手
　　　　里,真要撕破脸整你,你能得了好儿吗?

吴安：　我也知道吃小亏占大便宜的理儿,可她小题
　　　　大作,实在太气人了。

李友：　好男不和女斗,忍一忍,咽下这口气吧。

吴安：　君子报仇十年不晚,这次我就先饶了她。

Li: Where there's smoke there's fire, so she caught you red-handed.

Wu: I've always been the quiet but diligent type, but my health is bad. No matter how much of a dictator she is, she can't ban us from getting sick!

Li: She's making an example out of you.

Wu: She's abusing her power! If she pushes me too far, I'll just refuse to do anything more for her, and she can go kiss my butt.

Li: Don't, the odds are against you on this one. If she gets desperate and gives you the pink slip, what are you going to live on? Air?

Wu: She wouldn't dare! I've never done anything wrong, I've got nothing to be afraid of.

Li: You have to look at the big picture. A real man can be flexible when the situation calls for it. I think you should go and apologize to her, and put all of this behind you.

Wu: You don't know, she's not a reasonable person. Apologizing to her is a complete waste of time. Besides, I'm not the kind of person who can stand there and take that.

Li: You guys have been fighting for quite some time; it won't be easy to take care of!

Wu: Why don't I give her tit for tat, and put my cards on the table. I'll tell her. If she keeps on slandering me, I'll oppose her with everything I have.

Li: She'll be outraged! She's your immediate superior; the power is in her hands. If she really tried to make life hard for you, what good is there in it for you?

Wu: I know I shouldn't get hung up on the little stuff, but she makes a giant fuss over every little thing, and it makes me so mad!

Li: Forget it, a real man also doesn't fight with women. Swallow your anger, and forget about it.

Wu: They say revenge is a dish best served cold. I'll forgive her this time.

———————■———————

Traditional

吳安在跟李友說他們單位的事。

吳安: 我們頭兒真不是人, 我又跟她幹了一架。

李友: 她又**找你茬兒**啦?

吳安: **可不!** 她**愣**說我一條臭魚弄腥了一鍋湯。

李友: 我這可有點兒不明白了。她**憑什麼**呀? **她一個領導**, 總不該**沒事兒找事兒**吧。

吳安: 我不過是請了幾次假, 遲到了幾次, 她就藉口我**泡病號**, **磨洋工**, 把我罵得**狗血淋頭**。

李友: **一個巴掌拍不響**, 還是讓人家**抓住你的辮子**了。

吳安: 我從來是少說話, 多做事, 可我是個**老病號**, 她再**霸道**也不能不讓人得病吧!

李友: 她這是**殺雞給猴兒看**。

吳安: 她仗勢欺人! 急了我就**豁出去**給她來個**躺倒不幹**, 讓她**抓瞎**去。

李友: **別價**, 萬一她**狗急跳牆**, 把你**炒了魷魚**, 你**喝西北風**去不成?

吳安: 她敢! 我又沒做錯事兒, 我才不怕她呢。

李友: 你得有點兒長遠打算, **大丈夫能伸能屈,** 我勸你這次就跟她**說兩句軟話,**息事寧人得了。

吳安: 你不知道, 她那個人**不知好歹,** 跟她說軟話完全是白費口舌。再說我也不是那種能忍氣吞聲的人。

李友: 你倆**不對付**也不是一天兩天了, 難辦!

吳安: 我乾脆**打開天窗說亮話**, 告訴她, 要是再出口傷人, 我就跟她**對著幹**。

李友: 那她肯定發火。她是你頂頭上司, 權在她手裏, 真要**撕破臉整你**, 你能**得了好兒**嗎?

吳安: 我也知道**吃小虧占大便宜**的理兒, 可她**小題大作,** 實在太氣人了。

李友: **好男不和女鬥**, 忍一忍, **咽下這口氣吧**。

吳安: **君子報仇十年不晚,** 這次我就先饒了她。

———— ■ ————

词语注释

* 她又**找你茬儿**啦?
  找茬儿 (茬 [chá] stubble) To "find fault," or "pick a fight." For example, 今天我太太总想找茬儿跟我吵架。"Today my wife keeps trying to pick a fight with me."

- **可不!** 她愣说我一条臭鱼弄腥了一锅汤。

  可不 Also 可不是 or 可不是吗。 These are all colloquial ways to express agreement: "Right!" "Exactly!" For example, "今天都星期五了吧？" "可不，我还觉得才星期三呢。日子过得真快。" "Today is already Friday. Isn't it?" "Right. I still feel like it's Wednesday. Time flies."

- 她**愣说**我一条臭鱼弄腥了一锅汤。

  愣说 (愣 [lèng] rash, reckless, foolhardy) To "insist stubbornly." For example, 他病得直发烧，可他愣说他没病。 "He was so sick that he had a fever, but he stubbornly insists that he was fine."

- 她愣说我**一条臭鱼弄腥了一锅汤**

  一条臭鱼弄腥了一锅汤 "One bad apple spoils the barrel." For example, "他们全班就出了她一个害群之马，一条臭鱼弄腥了一锅汤。 "She was the black sheep of the class; and one bad apple spoils the barrel."

- 她**凭什么**呀?

  凭什么 (凭 [ping] base on; take as the basis) "What is the basis of this?" It is often used with an unpleasant tone. For example, 你凭什么这么说? "What are you basing your words on?" 凭什么我就得听他的? "Why should I listen to him?"

- 她**一个领导**, 总不该没事儿找事儿吧。

  ...一个... "Since ... is a ...." This is a shortened form for ...是一个..., in which the verb 是 is omitted. In the pattern, ... refers to a person; "..." refers to his or her position, and the rest of the phrase describes the appropriate actions for that position. For example, 我一个穷学生, 怎么买得起这么贵的车? "I'm a poor student, so how can I afford such an expensive car?" 他一个经理, 就不该那么不负责. "As a manager, he shouldn't be so irresponsible."

- 她一个领导, 总不该**没事儿找事儿**吧。
  没事找事 To ask for trouble." For example, 那个酒鬼一喝醉了酒就没事儿找事儿。"That drunkard goes asking for trouble whenever he gets drunk."

- 她就借口我**泡病号**, 磨洋工, 把我骂得狗血淋头。
  泡病号 (泡 [pào] dawdle; 病号 [bìnghào] person on the sick list) "Call in sick to avoid work." For example, 他们公司泡病号的太多, 怎么能不赔钱呢? "Too many people at their company call in sick to skip work; how can they not lose money?"

- 她就借口我泡病号, **磨洋工**, 把我骂得狗血淋头。
  磨洋工 (磨 [mó] dawdle, waste time) "Slack off." For example, 磨洋工的甭想拿奖金。"Those who slack off will not get bonuses."

- 她就借口我泡病号, 磨洋工, 把我骂得**狗血淋头**。
  狗血淋头 (骂 [mà] verbally abuse, scold; 淋 [lín] pour, drench) Also, 骂得狗血喷头, "Pour out a flood of invective against …," "let loose a stream of abuse against …." For example, 我只出了一个小错, 他就骂得我狗血淋头。"Although I made only a small mistake, he went on a tirade against me."

- **一个巴掌拍不响**, 还是让人家抓住你的辫子了。
  一个巴掌拍不响 (巴掌 [bāzhǎng] palm, hand) "You can't clap with one hand." It means: "It takes two to quarrel." For example, 一个巴掌拍不响, 他不可能无缘无故就骂你。"It takes two to quarrel. There's no way that he would attack you for no reason at all."

- 一个巴掌拍不响, 还是让人家**抓住你的辫子了**。
  抓辫子 (辫子 [biànzi] plait, braid, pigtail) Also as 揪辫子。 Literally: "To grab someone's queue." It means "To take advantage of somebody's weaknesses." For example, 他老抓别人的辫子,

所以人人恨他。 "He loves to attack the weaknesses of others, so everyone hates him."

- 可我是个**老病号**
  老病号 "To be on the sick list." For example, 哪个公司也不愿意雇老病号。 "No company wants to hire someone who's always sick."

- 她再**霸道**也不能不让人得病吧!
  霸道 ([bàdào]) "Overbearing," "high-handed," or "unreasonable." For example, 别看他在公司里挺霸道, 回到家里可是个好丈夫。 "Although overbearing at the company, he is a very good husband at home."

- 她这是**杀鸡给猴儿看**。
  杀鸡给猴儿看 Also 杀鸡吓猴. Literally, "kill the chicken to frighten the monkey." It means: "To make an example of someone." For example, 为了杜绝迟到, 公司用了杀鸡给猴看的办法, 把迟到最多的工人给开除了。 "In order to end tardiness, the company made an example of someone, and fired the employee who was late most often."

- 急了我就**豁出去**给她来个躺倒不干, 让她抓瞎去。
  豁出去 (豁 [huō] crack, give up) "Go ahead regardless," or "be ready to risk everything." For example, 反正也晚了, 咱们就豁出去晚到底吧。 "Since we are late already, let's go ahead regardless of how late we are."

- 急了我就豁出去给她来个**躺倒不干**, 让她抓瞎去。
  躺倒不干 (躺倒 [tǎngdǎo] lie down) Literally, "to lie down and do nothing." The context meaning is: "to refuse to work." For example, 这几天, 公司的活儿多得干不完, 老板警告说:

"谁躺倒不干, 谁别拿年终奖金。" "These few days there is too much work to finish at the company. The boss warned us that anyone who refuses to work will not get a year-end bonus.'"

- 急了我就豁出去给她来个躺倒不干, 让她**抓瞎**去。
  抓瞎 (抓 [zhuā] seize, stress; 瞎 [xiā] blind, no purpose) "To be stumped," "To be at a loss." For example, 考试前一定要早复习, 免得临时抓瞎。 "It's better to review early before a test, rather than be stumped at the last moment."

- **别价**, 万一她狗急跳墙, 把你炒了鱿鱼, 你喝西北风去不成?
  别价 (价 [jie]) A colloquial expression: "Don't." For example, " 我把这把伞拿去用用。" "别价, 我马上要用。" "Let me borrow this umbrella" "Don't. I'm using it right now."

- 别价, 万一她**狗急跳墙**, 把你炒了鱿鱼, 你喝西北风去不成?
  狗急跳墙 "Do something desperate." For example, 咱们不要把他惹翻了, 免得他狗急跳墙。 "Let's not provoke him, lest he do something desperate."

- 别价, 万一她狗急跳墙, 把你**炒了鱿鱼**, 你喝西北风去不成?
  炒鱿鱼 (炒 [chǎo] stir-fry; 鱿鱼 [yóuyú] squid) A colloquial expression for "to fire." For example, 他上班才三个月就被老板炒了鱿鱼。 "He got fired by his boss after only three months."

- 别价, 万一她狗急跳墙, 把你炒了鱿鱼, 你**喝西北风**去不成?
  喝西北风 Also as 吃西北风. Literally: "drink the northwest wind." It means: "live on air" or "have nothing to eat." For example, 再不找工作, 等你这点儿钱花完了, 可就得喝西北

风了. "If you don't find a job, you'll spend the little money you have, and starve."

- **大丈夫能伸能屈,** 我劝你这次就跟她说两句软话, 息事宁人得了。
  大丈夫能伸能屈 (伸 [shēn] stretch; extend; 屈 [qū] bend) Literally: "A real man can both bend and stretch." This expression encourages the listener to turn the other cheek. For example, 我不在乎, 大丈夫能伸能屈嘛! "I don't care. A real man turns the other cheek."

- 我劝你这次就跟她**说两句软话,** 息事宁人得了。
  说软话 (软 [ruǎn] soft; weak) "Spoke to express apology," "ask pardon," or "show sympathy." 软话, "soft words." For example, 他特别要面子, 从不说软话。 "He is very self-conscious and never admits doing anything wrong."

- 她那个人**不知好歹**
  不知好歹 (歹 [dǎi] bad, evil, vicious) Also 不识好歹, "To be ungrateful." For example, 你帮了他的忙, 他不但不感谢你, 还埋怨你, 真不知好歹。 "You helped him and he turns around and blames you. He is so ungrateful."

- 你俩**不对付**也不是一天两天了
  不对付 Also 不对, a colloquial expression for "be in disagreement" or "be at odds." For example, 他们俩虽然是亲兄弟, 可是一直不对付。 "Even though those two are brothers, they have always been at odds."

- 我干脆**打开天窗说亮话**
  打开天窗说亮话 "To speak frankly." For example, 咱们今天谁也别瞒谁, 打开天窗说亮话, 把问题彻底解决了。

"Let's not hide anything from each other; let's speak frankly, and resolve the problem once and for all."

- 告诉她, 要是再出口伤人, 我就跟她**对着干**
  对着干 "To oppose." For example, 他们俩关系不好, 什么事都对着干。 "Those two have a bad relationship and oppose each other at every turn."

- 真要**撕破脸**整你, 你能得了好儿吗?
  撕破脸 "Put aside all considerations of face"; or "not spare somebody's face." For example, 夫妻之间应该相互敬重, 千万不能撕破脸。 "A husband and wife should respect each other, and never say things that can't be taken back."

- 真要撕破脸**整你**, 你能得了好儿吗?
  整… "Fix …." "Make … suffer." … refers to a person. For example, 他们头儿老整他, 所以他想换个工作。 "His boss is always making him suffer, so he wants to change his job."

- 真要撕破脸整你, 你能**得了好儿**吗?
  得了好儿 A colloquial expression for 得到好处 "gain profit." For example, 今天的工作要是干不完, 谁也甭想得了好。 "If we do not finish our job today, it will be bad for anyone."

- 我也知道**吃小亏占大便宜**的理儿
  吃小亏占大便宜 "To take a small loss for a big profit." For example, 他常说: 吃小亏占大便宜; 什么小亏都不吃的人也占不到什么便宜。 "He always says it is good to take a small loss for a big profit. Those who refuse to risk anything will never get anything in return."

- 可她**小题大作**, 实在太气人了。
  小题大作 "Make a fuss over a trifle." "Make a mountain out of a

molehill." For example, 我就出了这么一点小错, 你就别小题大作了。"I made only a small mistake. Please don't make a big fuss over nothing."

- **好男不和女斗,** 忍一忍, 咽下这口气吧.
  好男不和女斗 (斗 [dòu] fight, struggle against) "A gentleman does not fight women." For example, 和太太吵架的时候, 想想 "好男不和女斗" 这句老话, 气就消了。"When fighting with your wife, think of the old saying, 'a gentleman does not fight women,' and cool down."

- 好男不和女斗, 忍一忍, **咽下这口气吧**。
  咽下这口气 (咽 [yàn] swallow.) Literally: "swallow your angry." The context meaning is "You'd better hold your anger and put up with it." For example, 今年的年终奖又没我的。我实在咽不下这口气。"This year there's no bonus for me, again. I just can't take it this time."

- **君子报仇十年不晚,** 这次我就先饶了她。
  君子报仇十年不晚 (报仇 [bàochóu] revenge; avenge) "Revenge is a dish best served cold." For example, 你着什么急呀? 君子报仇十年不晚, 以后再整他。"Why hurry? Revenge is a dish best served cold. Get him later."

——■——

CONVERSATION B:

Simplified

两个女友在聊天, 说丈夫和儿子的事。

兰芬:　看你的眼睛**又红又肿**, 气色也不好, 怎么啦?

美英: **嘻,别提了**! 我老公**仗着**多挣了几个钱,背着
我养小秘,恨得我牙痒痒。前天居然把情人领
家来,**让我给撞上了**。

兰芬: 那可够不象话的,你怎么办?

美英: 气得我使劲冲他喊: **"你给我滚!"**

兰芬: 你得劝劝他,可别再这样了。

美英: 有什么可劝的? 我真**恨不得**宰了他!

兰芬: **看你说的,**一日夫妻百日恩,再说你们孩子都这
么大了。**看在他是你丈夫的面子上**,你还是劝
劝他,**没准儿拨对了哪根筋**,他就回心转意了。

美英: 什么夫妻不夫妻的,你不知道,我现在是离也
离不了,过也过不下去,真把我难受死了。实
话跟你说吧,要不是为了儿子,我早跟他离了。
兰芬: **唉,家家都有一本难念的经**。说到儿子,
我那不争气的儿子可把我气死了。他**放着正
经事不干**,动不动就赌钱,这不,昨天又让公
安局给抓起来了,真可恨。

美英: 你对儿子是**恨铁不成钢**,和我不一样。

兰芬: 你儿子那么好,**说真的**,我还挺羡慕你的。丈
夫可以说离就离,这儿子可不能说不要就不
要了吧。

美英: 儿子哪能不要呀! 好好说说他吧。

兰芬：　光说有什么用? 这些年**我骂也骂了,打也打了,他还是照样儿赌**. 现在他也大了,我干脆不管他了,听天由命吧.

美英：　**你那不是把他害了吗? 气归气, 恨归恨, 管还是得管**. 你想想,**你不管谁管**?

兰芬：　公安局的也说,我管也得管,不管也得管,谁让他是我儿子呢.

———■———

Two girlfriends are chatting about their husbands and sons.

Fen: Look at how puffy and red your eyes are; your color isn't too good either. What's going on?

Ying: Oh, I don't want to talk about it! My husband, just because he made a few bucks, got a mistress behind my back. I hate him so much! The day before yesterday he actually brought her home, and I ran into them!

Fen: That's horrible, what did you do?

Ying: I was so angry I shouted at him with everything I had: "Get the hell out!"

Fen: You have to talk to him, and make him stop acting like this.

Ying: What is there to talk about? I wish I could kill him!

Fen: Look what you're saying, you guys are married, after all. Besides, your son is so big already. For the fact that he's your husband, go talk to him. Maybe you'll hit on something, and he'll change his ways.

Ying: I don't care if he's my husband or not. You don't know, right now I can't leave him and I can't stay with him, it feels terrible. Truth be told, if it weren't for my son, I would've left him long ago.

Fen: Every family has its list of troubles. Talking about sons, that no-good son of mine is going to be the death of me. He doesn't do anything gainful, gambles all day, and look, yesterday he got himself arrested by the police. What a mess!

Ying: What you're feeling about your son is disappointment; it's different for me.

Fen: You have such a nice son, really, I admire you quite a bit. A husband you can just leave, but a son, you can't just disown him.

Ying: How can you disown your son! You should talk to him.

Fen: What use is there in talking? All these years I've yelled and screamed and even beaten him, but he goes on gambling. Now that he's grown up, I've stopped worrying about him; it's his life now.

Ying: Aren't you abandoning him? You can be angry, you can hate him, but you still have to care for him. Think about it; if not you, then who?

Fen: The police station said so, too; it's my business no matter if I want it or not, because he's my son.

Traditional

兩個女友在聊天, 說丈夫和兒子的事。

蘭芬:　看你的眼睛**又紅又腫**, 氣色也不好, 怎麼啦?

美英： **嘻,別提了**! 我老公**仗著**多掙了幾個錢,背著
我養小秘,恨得我牙癢癢。前天居然把情人領
家來,**讓我給撞**上了。

蘭芬： 那可夠不象話的,你怎麼辦?

美英： 氣得我使勁沖他喊:"**你給我滾!**"

蘭芬： 你得勸勸他,可別再這樣了。

美英： 有什麼可勸的? 我真**恨不得**宰了他!

蘭芬： **看你說的,**一日夫妻百日恩,再說你們孩子都這
麼大了。**看在他是你丈夫的面子上**,你還是勸
勸他,**沒準兒撥對了哪根筋**,他就回心轉意了。

美英： 什麼夫妻不夫妻的,你不知道,我現在是離也
離不了,過也過不下去,真把我難受死了。實
話跟你說吧,要不是為了兒子,我早跟他離了。

蘭芬： **唉,家家都有一本難念的經。**說到兒子,我那
不爭氣的兒子可把我氣死了。**他放著正經事
不幹**,動不動就賭錢,這不,昨天又讓公安局
給抓起來了,真可恨。

美英： 你對兒子是**恨鐵不成鋼**,和我不一樣。

蘭芬： 你兒子那麼好,**說真的**,我還挺羨慕你的。丈
夫可以說離就離,這兒子可不能說不要就不
要了吧。

美英： 兒子哪能不要呀! 好好說說他吧。

蘭芬： 光說有什麼用? 這些年**我罵也罵了,打也打了,
他還是照樣兒賭。**現在他也大了,我乾脆不管
他了,**聽天由命吧。**

美英: **你那不是把他害了嗎? 氣歸氣, 恨歸恨, 管還是得管。** 你想想, **你不管誰管**?

蘭芬: 公安局的也說, 我管也得管, 不管也得管, 誰讓他是我兒子呢。

———◼———

词语注释

- 看你的眼睛**又红又肿**，气色也不好，怎么啦？
  又...又... "Be both ... and ...." Here 又 is used to introduce multiple adjectives. For example, 又快又好, "fast and good." 又香又脆 "sweet and crispy." 又红又肿, "red and puffy."

- **嗐,** 别提了!
  嗐 ([hài]) Interjection, "alas," expressing sadness, regret or remorse. For example, 嗐, 他怎么病得这么厉害! "God, why is he so ill?"

- 嗐, **别提了**!
  别提了 "You don't want to know," "You can hardly imagine." For example, "你怎么这么伤心啊？" "别提了, 我先生上星期去世了。" "How come you are so sad?" "You don't want to know; my husband died last week."

- 我老公**仗着**多挣了几个钱, 背着我养小秘,
  仗着 (仗 [zhàng] rely on) "Rely on"; "depend on." For example, 他常仗着他爸爸的势力欺负人。"He often bullies people through the power of his father."

- 前天居然把情人领家来, **让我给撞上了**。
  让我给...了 A colloquial pattern that conveys the same meaning

as 让我...了, "I ... it." ... is a verb or verb phrase. 给 is often used before the predicate verb in a passive sentence for emphasis. For example, 今儿早上我弟弟不肯去上学, 让我妈给骂了一顿。 "This morning my younger brother wouldn't go to school, and he was criticized by my mother."

- 气得我使劲冲他喊: "**你给我滚!** "
  你给我... "You'd better." This is an imperative phrase. One meaning of preposition 给 is "for" or "to." For example, 你给我们唱个歌好吗? "Will you sing a song for us?" 他给她送去了一束花。 "He sent a bunch of flowers to her." However, 你给我 is a colloquial imperative sentence pattern and usually used in an angry, threatening or compelling tone. For example, 你给我老实点儿! "You'd better behave yourself!"

- 气得我使劲冲他喊: "你给我**滚!** "
  滚 ([gǔn]) "Get out." When used in the imperative, it connotes anger. For example 你滚开点儿! 少跟我啰嗦! "You get out! Don't trouble me!"

- 有什么可劝的? 我真**恨不得**宰了他!
  恨不得 (恨 [hèn] hate; regret) Also as 恨不能, "if only one could." For example, 我恨不得马上回家。 "If only I could go home right now."

- **看你说的**, 一日夫妻百日恩, 再说你们孩子都这么大了.
  看你说的 "What are you saying!" This is a colloquial pattern that is often used to show disagreement and mild criticism. For example, 看你说的, 我哪有那么大本事。 "What are you saying, how could I ever do that?"

- **看在他是你丈夫的面子上**, 你还是劝劝他

  看在...的面子上 Literally, "for the sake of ..." It often means: "for the sake of the relationship between you and ...." For example, 看在老朋友的面子上, 你就帮他一把吧。 "For the sake of your old friend, you should help him."

- **没准儿**拨对了哪根筋, 他就回心转意了。

  没准儿 (准 [zhǔn] norm; accurate) "Probably"; "who knows." For example, 这件事没准儿能成。 "Maybe it will work." 他那个人, 说不来没准儿又来了, 说来没准儿倒不来。 "Being the kind the person he is, maybe he will come, maybe he will not."

- 没准儿**拨对了哪根筋**, 他就回心转意了。

  拨对了哪根筋 (拨 [bō] move with hand; 筋 [jīn] muscle; tendon) This expression means "to manage to convince someone," with the connotation that it is unlikely, but not impossible. For example, 你试试看吧, 要是拨对了哪根筋, 他大概就愿意来了。 "Why don't you try? If you manage to convince him, he might agree to come."

- **唉**, 家家都有一本难念的经。

  唉 ([āi]) An interjection: "Oh." "Ah." "Alas." A sigh of sadness or regret. For example, 唉, 她的小孩得了白血病。 "Alas, her kid got leukemia."

- 唉, **家家都有一本难念的经**。

  家家都有一本难念的经 (念 [niàn] read aloud; study; 经 [jīng] scripture) "Every family has a skeleton in the cupboard." "Every family has its own problems." For example, 不要老看着别人好, 家家都有一本难念的经。 "Don't envy others; every family has its own problems."

- 他**放着正经事不干**, 动不动就赌钱
  放着...不... "To put ... aside and not ... it." The second "..." is a verb and the first "..." is its object. This pattern is usually used with a tone of dissatisfaction or blame. For example, 她放着现成的饭不吃, 去饭馆了。 "She put her food aside and didn't eat it, eating out instead."

- 你对儿子是**恨铁不成钢**, 和我不一样。
  恨铁不成钢 (铁 [tiě] iron; 钢 [gāng] steel) "To be frustrated by one's lack of ability." For example, 老师批评我们是恨铁不成钢。 "The teacher lectured us because he was frustrated by our lack of ability."

- 你儿子那么好, **说真的**, 我还挺羡慕你的。
  说真的 "No kidding." For example, 说真的, 他就是会说十几种外语呢! "I'm not kidding, he really is able to speak more than a dozen foreign languages!"

- 这些年我**骂也骂了, 打也打了, 他还是照样儿赌**。
  ...也...了, ...也...了, 还是... "After ... and ..., still ...." In this pattern, in the first and the second phrase, each "..." is a verb, and each phrase contains the same verb. For example, 这家伙吃也吃了, 喝也喝了, 还是不给干活。 "After eating as well as drinking, this guy still refused to work."

- 现在他也大了, 我干脆不管他了, **听天由命吧**。
  听天由命 (由 [yóu] follow, obey; 命 [mìng] lot, fate) "Leave it up to fate." For example, 医生都说治不了他的病, 他只好听天由命了。 "The doctors all said they can't cure him, so he can only leave it up to fate."

- **你那不是把他害了吗?**

  你那… This is a double-subject colloquial pattern that is often used to express opinion. In the pattern, 那 usually refers to some thing that 你 did, which is introduced in the context; and … is often a comment. To generalize the pattern, we can replace 那 by 这, and replace 你 by other personal nouns or pronouns, such as 老王, 李明, 你们, 我, and 他. For example, 我这也是为了你们好。 "I am doing this for your own good."

- **气归气, 恨归恨, 管还是得管。**

  … 归…, … 归…, … (归 [guī]) Also as: …是…, …是 …, …. When 归 and 是 are interchangeable, the pattern means: "Although … and …, …." In the pattern, both the first and the second "…" are verbs; and the third "…" is a clause. For example: 看电视归看电视, 玩游戏归玩游戏, 别忘了作作业。 "Watch TV, and play games, but don't forget to do your homework." 对他批评归批评, 处罚归处罚, 关心还是要关心。 "Criticize him, punish him, but we still need to care for him."

- **你想想, 你不管谁管?**

  你不…谁…? "If you do not …, then who will …?" This is a rhetorical question, and … should be a verb. It means: "You should certainly …." For example, 他是领导, 他不负责谁负责? "He is the leader; if he doesn't take responsibility who will?"

VOCABULARY

头儿	tóur	head; chief
干架	gànjià	quarrel; come to blows

腥	xīng	fishy
总	zǒng	anyway
从来	cónglái	always; at all times
霸道	bàdào	domineering; overbearing
长远打算	chángyuǎndǎsuàn	long-term plan
息事宁人	xīshìníngrén	make concessions to avoid trouble
白费口舌	báifèikǒushé	waste one's words; speak to the wind
忍气吞声	rěnqìtūnshēng	swallow an insult; submit to humiliation
出口伤人	chūkǒushāngrén	speak bitingly; offend by rude remarks
顶头上司	dǐngtóushàngsi	one's immediate (or direct) superior
权	quán	right; power; authority
忍	rěn	bear; endure; tolerate
饶	ráo	let somebody off; forgive
肿	zhǒng	swelling; swollen
气色	qìsè	complexion; color
挣	zhèng	carn; make
背着	bèizhe	behind somebody's back
养	yǎng	support; provide for
恨	hèn	hate
痒	yǎng	itch; tickle
居然	jūrán	unexpectedly; go so far as to
情人	qíngrén	sweetheart; lover
领	lǐng	lead; bring

撞上	zhuàngshang	discover by chance; catch somebody in the act
冲	chòng	towards
宰	zǎi	slaughter; butcher
一日夫妻百日恩	yīrìfūqībǎirì'ēn	A day together as husband and wife means endless devotion the rest of your life
回心转意	huíxīnzhuǎnyì	change one's views; come around
离	lí	divorce
不争气	bùzhēngqì	be disappointing
正经事	zhèngjǐngshì	serious affair
动不动	dòngbudòng	frequently; at every turn
赌钱	dǔqián	gamble
羡慕	xiànmù	envy
公安局	gōngānjú	Public Security Bureau

EXERCISES

A. Fill in the spaces with the appropriate words or phrases:

没事找事　　磨洋工　　一个巴掌拍不响
躺倒不干　　豁出去　　杀鸡给猴儿看　　找茬儿
狗血淋头　　泡病号　　一条臭鱼弄腥了一锅汤

1　我今天_____了，就是把我开除我也不怕。

2　我这些日子在家_____呢, 好几天没去上班了。

3　干活儿的时候, 我有多大力就用多大力气, 从来
不_____。

4　他们公司老板不喜欢他,一直想_____解雇他。

5　既然问题已经解决了,咱就别提它了,省得_____。

6　平常总是他骂别人,这回他可被别人骂了个_____。

7　她这个人,工作一忙就请病假,_____。

8　那个老板就爱用_____的办法吓唬人。

9　你光说他不对,_____,你要是没错哪会跟他打起来?

10　他一个人用毒品坏了大家的名声,_____。

B. Choose the expression from the following list that best corresponds to the underlined words or phrases:

> 炒鱿鱼　　凭什么　　他一个　　愣说　　可不
> 不知好歹　抓辫子　　老病号　　霸道　　别价

1　我说那本词典不好,他说:"就是,有用的词常常查不到。"

2　我们老师可不讲理了,他批评学生的时候不许学生解释。

3　那篇文章是我写的,可是老师非说我是抄的。

4　他太不注意健康,结果年纪不大就成了请病假最多的人。

5　"时间到了,她还不来,咱们开始吧。""别开始,再等等她。"

6　在这儿,你要是不想被解雇,就得好好干。

7　你们为什么把他抓起来? 总该说说为什么吧!

8　我们公司老板特别会找工人的错,所以人人都怕他。

9　我为你好,你还骂我,真是不懂得好坏。

10 <u>他是个大学教授</u>,怎么会张口就骂人呢?

C. Fill in the spaces with the appropriate words or phrases:

大丈夫能伸能屈　狗急跳墙　对着干　小题大作
吃小亏占大便宜　咽下这口气　抓瞎　喝西北风

1 他对人很好,所以他要作什么,从来没人和他_____。

2 我的护照和机票都找不到了,这下我可_____了.

3 警察抓那个小偷时,那个小偷_____,把警察打伤了.

4 我只迟到了三分钟,老板就_____,要扣我工资.

5 快过年了,咱们得留点儿钱,总不能_____过年吧?

6 你哪儿斗得过警察? 你还是_____,把罚款交了吧.

7 _____,这次你就忍一忍吧,别跟他吵了.

8 他懂得_____的道理,所以常常故意吃点儿小亏.

D. Choose the expression from the following list that best corresponds to the underlined words or phrases:

得了好　不对付　君子报仇十年不晚　整人
撕破脸　说软话　打开天窗说亮话　好男不和女斗

1 那个公司的老板很会<u>故意给人找麻烦</u>。

2 你们班那么多同学,有没有和你<u>不好</u>的?

3 这次我就是把工作丢了,也不能让他<u>占便宜</u>。

4 每次和他太太吵完架,都是他先<u>说对不起</u>。

5 同事之间要尽量客气,不能为一点小事就<u>吵架</u>。

6 你只要和太太吵架, 就是你不好, 因为<u>男的就不该跟女的吵</u>。

7 这次他打伤了我, 我先不理他, <u>以后有机会再报仇</u>。

8 要想解决这个问题, 咱们最好都<u>把话说明白</u>。

E. Fill in the spaces with the appropriate words or phrases:

给打破了　别提了　面子　　嗐　　唉
听天由命　哪根筋　恨铁不成钢

1 "你的病好点儿了吗?" "＿＿＿＿＿＿,越来越不好了."

2 我问他这次考试考得怎么样? 他说: "＿＿＿＿＿＿, 别提了, 又没及格."

3 她问我怎么又迟到了, 我说: "嗐,＿＿＿＿＿＿, 我那辆车又出毛病了."

4 我已经尽了最大努力, 结果怎么样, 只有＿＿＿＿＿＿了.

5 那些父母骂孩子都是因为＿＿＿, 不是恨自己的孩子.

6 你的茶杯让我＿＿＿＿＿＿, 你看, 我买了一个新的赔你.

7 看在他是你老朋友的＿＿＿＿＿＿上, 你就再借一次钱给他吧.

8 你再劝劝他, 说不定拨对了＿＿＿＿＿, 他就愿意读书了.

F. Choose the expression from the following list that best corresponds to the underlined words or phrases:

你那不是　　说真的　　没准儿　　你给我
看你说的　　谁教课　　又大又甜　　滚

1 老李气得对小张大喊: "<u>走开</u>! 我不想再看见你了!

2 别看我老和他吵架, <u>其实</u>, 我可尊敬他了。

3 "我肯定找不到工作。" "<u>你怎么这么说</u>! 你也太没信心了!"

4 天气预报也有不准的时候, <u>说不定</u>明天不下雨呢。

5 这个店卖的水果特别好, 你看, 这苹果<u>不但大, 而且甜</u>。

6 这么冷的天去游泳, <u>你是不是</u>等着生病啊?

7 今天晚上, <u>你必须</u>把作业作完才能睡觉!

8 你是老师, 你要是不教课<u>让什么人教</u>?

G. Choose the expression from the following list that best corresponds to the underlined words:

实话对你说吧　　恨不得　放着　还是　　仗着
吃归吃, 喝归喝　家家都有一本难念的经

1 他<u>因为</u>自己学习成绩好, 总是看不起别的同学。

2 我这工作累死人了, <u>我真希望</u>明天就换一个工作。

3 别看我表面上挺高兴, <u>跟你说实话</u>, 我心里难过极了。

4 你别以为只有你的日子难过, 其实<u>每家都有每家的难处</u>。

5 那个人很怪, 他<u>有</u>教授不当, 非要去饭馆炒菜。

6 今天咱们<u>可以随便吃, 随便喝</u>, 可是谁也不能酒后开车。

7 他非要儿子学钢琴, 他儿子学也学了, 练也练了, <u>可就是</u>没兴趣。

ANSWER KEY

Exercise A (Dialogue 1)

1   豁出去
2   泡病号
3   磨洋工
4   找茬儿
5   没事找事
6   狗血淋头
7   躺倒不干
8   杀鸡给猴儿看
9   一个巴掌拍不响
10 一条臭鱼弄腥了一锅汤

Exercise B (Dialogue 1)

1   可不
2   霸道
3   愣说
4   老病号
5   别价
6   炒鱿鱼
7   凭什么
8   抓辫子
9   不知好歹
10 他一个（…一个…）

Exercise C (Dialogue 1)

1   对着干
2   抓瞎
3   狗急跳墙
4   小题大作
5   喝西北风
6   咽下这口气
7   大丈夫能伸能屈
8   吃小亏占大便宜

Exercise D (Dialogue 1)

1   整人（整…）
2   不对付
3   得了好
4   说软话
5   撕破脸
6   好男不和女斗
7   君子报仇十年不晚
8   打开天窗说亮话

Exercise E (Dialogue 2)

1   唉/嗐
2   嗐/唉
3   别提了
4   听天由命
5   恨铁不成钢

6 给打破了（让我给…了）

7 面子（看在…的面子上）

8 哪根筋（拨对了哪根筋）

Exercise F (Dialogue 2)

1 滚

2 说真的

3 看你说的

4 没准儿

5 又大又甜（又…又(B)）

6 你那不是（你那…）

7 你给我（你给我…）

8 谁教课（你不…谁…）

Exercise G (Dialogue 2)

1 仗着

2 恨不得

3 实话对你说吧

4 家家都有一本难念的经

5 放着（放着…不…）

6 吃归吃, 喝归喝（… 归…, …归…, …）

7 还是（…也…了, …也…了, 还是…）

———■———

CULTURE NOTES

When you read in Chinese, you might often see the Chinese character, 命. One group of meanings represented by 命 is "life," "lot," "fate," and "destiny." Following are some words and expressions that contain 命 with these meanings:

命定   determined by fate; predestined

命根子   one's very life; lifeblood

命运   destiny; fate; lot

薄命   (usually of women) born under an unlucky star; born unlucky

奔命	rush about on errands; be kept on the run
偿命	pay with one's life
短命	die young; be short lived
革命	revolution
活命	earn a bare living; scrape along; eke out an existence; <formal> save sb.'s life; life
救命	save somebody's life
卖命	work oneself to the bone for sb.; die (unworthily) for
没命	lose one's life; die; recklessly; desperately; like mad; for all one's worth
拼命	risk one's life; defy death; go all out regardless of danger to one's life; exerting the utmost strength; for all one is worth; with all one's might; desperately
饶命	spare somebody's life
人命	human life
丧命	meet one's death; get killed
舍命	risk one's life; sacrifice oneself
生命	life
寿命	life span; life
送命	lose one's life; get killed; go to one's doom
算命	fortune-telling
逃命	run (or flee, fly) for one's life
玩儿命	gamble (or play) with one's life; risk one's life needlessly
性命	life (of a man or animal)
要命	drive sb. to his death; kill; confoundedly; extremely; awfully; terribly; a nuisance
挣命	struggle to save one's life
致命	causing death; fatal; mortal; deadly

谋财害命 murder somebody for his money

疲于奔命 be kept constantly on the run; be tired out by too much running around; be weighed down with work

死于非命 die an unnatural (or a violent) death

听天由命 submit to the will of Heaven; resign oneself to one's fate; trust to luck

亡命之徒 desperado

一命呜呼 die

. 第十五章 .15 .

你这人有病啊?
大家都看不下去了

QUARRELING

CONVERSATION 1:

Simplified

在一辆很挤的公共汽车上, 两个背着书包的中学生吵了起来。

女: 挤什么呀! 别挤啦!

男: 没见这么多人呀? 怕挤**打的**去!

女: 你这人**有病**啊? 人家越躲, 你越往上靠! 什么**德行**!

男: 看你那德行样儿! 好像谁**希罕**你似的, **也不撒泡尿照照自己**!

女: 好好儿跟你说话, 别**给脸不要脸**! **讨厌**!

男: 又是 "不要脸", 又是 "讨厌", 还算好好儿说话! **倒挺会往自己脸上贴金**的, 真**不是东西**!

332

数落 to be lectured, criticized, wrung out by someone (see page 339.)

On a very crowded bus, two middle school students wearing backpacks start arguing.

Girl: What are you pushing for! Stop pushing!

Guy: Don't you see all these people? If you can't stand pushing go call a cab!

Girl: What the hell's wrong with you? The more I back up the more you push! How disgusting!

Guy: Look at yourself! You think I like you, go take a piss and look at yourself!

Girl: I'm trying to talk to you; don't act shamelessly when people treat you with respect! Jerk!

Guy: There's "shameless" and there's "Jerk," and you call that trying to talk to me? You're pretty good at making yourself look good, asshole.

女:　缺德! 你是东西, 你是**什么东西! 你才不是东西呢! 少跟我犯混!**

男:　你才犯混呢! 你才**浑蛋**呢! 真**他妈的**!

乘客甲: 别说脏话! 别骂人!

乘客乙: **行了**, 行了, 都少说一句吧。

售票员: 大家往里边儿走走。下一站, 建国门到了。

———■———

Traditional

在一輛很擠的公共汽車上, 兩個背著書包的中學生吵了起來。

女:　擠什麼呀! 別擠啦!

男:　沒見這麼多人呀? 怕擠**打的**去!

女:　你這人**有病**啊? 人家越躲, 你越往上靠! 什麼**德行**!

男:　看你那德行樣兒, 好像誰**希罕**你似的, **也不撒泡尿照照自己**!

女:　好好兒跟你說話, 別**給臉不要臉! 討厭**!

男:　又是 "不要臉", 又是 "討厭", 還算好好兒說話! **倒挺會往自己臉上貼金**的, 真**不是東西**!

女:　缺德! 你是東西, 你是**什麼東西! 你才不是東西呢! 少跟我犯混!**

男:　你才犯混呢! 你才**渾蛋**呢! 真**他媽的**!

Girl:	Dick! Who the hell are you! You're the asshole! Don't mess with me!
Guy:	You're the one messing! You the one messing! Damn it!
Pass. A:	Don't cuss! Don't yell!
Pass. B:	Okay, okay, both of you back off.
Conductor:	Everyone move in. Arriving at the next stop, Jianguomen.

———————■———————

乘客甲: 別說髒話! 別罵人!

乘客乙: **行了**, 行了, 都少說一句吧。

售票員: 大家往裏邊兒走走。下一站, 建國門到了。

———————■———————

词语注释

- 怕挤**打的**去呀!
  打的（的 [dī] taxi）"Hail a taxi"; "take a taxi." For example, 现在出租车多了, 打的比以前方便多了。"There are a lot of taxis nowadays; taking them is a lot easier than before."

- 你这人**有病**啊?
  有病 "sick" or "mentally ill." Often used to mock a person with the connotation that he or she is unbalanced. For example, 你是不是有病? 说话怎么颠三倒四的。"Are you ill? Why are you spouting nonsense?"

- 什么**德行**!
  德行 Also as 德性, "disgusting" or "shameful." This expression is used to ridicule somebody's appearance, behavior, conduct, or manner. For example, 看你那德行, 还想当军官呢! "Look how disgusting you are, and you want to be an officer!" 那个家伙真德行。 "That fellow is really disgusting."

- 好像谁**希罕**你似的, 也不撒泡尿照照
  希罕 Also as 稀罕, "cherish"; "value" Often used with a negative connotation or in rhetorical questions. For example, 我才不稀罕你的钱呢! "I don't care about your money at all."

- 好像谁希罕你似的, **也不撒泡尿照照**
  撒泡尿照照 "You should make some water and look in it!" 撒泡尿, colloquial form for "piss." 照照, abbreviation of 照照镜子, "look in the mirror." This is an insult about the target's appearance or character. For example, 看你那德行, 也不撒泡尿照照, "You are so disgusting! Why don't you make some water and look in it!"

- **别给脸不要脸**! 讨厌!
  给脸不要脸 给脸 means to "give face," to show respect to someone. 不要脸 means "shameless" or "brazen." For example, 别给脸不要脸! "Don't be shameless when I try to save your face." 我不说话了你还吵个没完, 你这个人怎么给脸不要脸。 "I've stopped talking but you continue to yell; why are you such an ass when I'm trying to smooth things over."

- 别给脸不要脸! **讨厌**!
  讨厌 "Repugnant," "disgusting," or "disagreeable." For example, 他对女孩子总是动手动脚的, 真讨厌! "He is always fresh with girls. How repulsive!"

- **倒**挺会往自己脸上贴金的, 真不是东西!
  倒 It is used to focus on the meaning that is contrary to what is expected or thought. For example, 他个子不高, 干起活来倒很有力气。 "He is short, but he's a good worker."

- 倒挺会**往自己脸上贴金**的, 真不是东西!
  往自己脸上贴金 "Promote oneself." 贴金 literarilly: "to cover with gold foil." For example, 别往自己脸上贴金了! "Oh, stop blowing your own trumpet."

- 倒挺会往自己脸上贴金的, 真**不是东西**!
  不是东西 Also as 不是个东西. 东西 means "thing," and when 东西 refers to a person, it contains a negative connotation. The expression 不是东西 is often used in criticizing or rebuking. For example, 他真不是东西! "He is a real asshole!" 我们头儿可不是个东西了! "Our boss is a horrible jerk!"

- 缺德! 你是东西, 你是**什么东西**!
  什么东西 The expression is used as a curse, but does not contain any "dirty" words. For example, 你是什么东西 is similar to "You bastard." 他居然打他老妈。什么东西! "He even hit his old mother; what a scoundrel!"

- 你是什么东西! **你才不是东西呢**!
  你才···呢 This pattern is used to indicate an emphatic tone. For example, 你说我不懂音乐, 你才不懂音乐呢! "You said that I know nothing about music. In fact it is you who knows nothing about music." 她才不会信你的话呢。 "She will absolutely not trust what you say."

- **少跟我犯混**
  少··· "Stop …!" In this pattern, 少 is used as a verb with the

meaning "stop" or "quit." For example, 少废话! "Stop talking rubbish!" 少来这一套! "Cut it out!" "Quit that!"

- **少跟我犯混**
  犯混 A colloquial expression meaning "to act up." For example, 那孩子犯起浑来, 谁说都不成。 "When that kid starts acting up, he won't listen to anybody."

- **你才浑蛋呢!**
  浑蛋 ([húndàn]) Also written as 浑蛋 ([húndàn]). "Bastard." For example, 你这个混蛋! 滚开! "You bastard! Get away!"

- **真他妈的!**
  他妈的 A commonly used curse. According to context, its meaning is similar to the following English expressions: "Damn it." "blast it." "To hell with it." "Gosh." "Hell." "God damn you." For example, 他妈的, 这车坏了。 "Damn it. The car died !"

- **行了,行了,都少说一句吧。**
  行了 "Okay." Used to express dismissal, and is similar to 得了 or 算了 when being used to smooth over an argument. For example, 行了,行了,别再说了。 "Okay, okay, that's enough."

CONVERSATION B:

Simplified

小张和小王是一个国营单位的雇员。他们在议论同事李刚的事。

小张: 哎, 你听说没? 今天咱这儿的人都在传李刚和王兰的事儿呢, 他们**那个**了。

小王: 哪个了? 你说什么哪?

小张: 你怎么连这都不明白? 就是**发生关系**了, **上床**了。

小王: 李刚怎么这么**胡闹**? 自己有老婆孩子还乱搞。

小张: **谁说不是啊**! 早就听说他和他们头儿**有一腿**, 王兰正是他们组的头儿。

小王: 这事儿是怎么传出来的?

小张: 昨天他老婆来单位跟他打架, 就传开了。

小王: 她也太不给李刚**留面子**了。

小张: 就是。开头两人还就是**拌嘴**, 他老婆说他 "气人", "可恶", 是 "忘恩负义" 的 "白眼儿狼"。

小王: **当着**同事的面让老婆这么**数落**, 这让李刚的**脸往哪儿放**?

小张: 她是气**极**了, **不管三七二十一**了。李刚本来**理短**, 可是**脸上又挂不住**, 就**回了几句嘴**。他老婆更生气了, 就大骂起来, 骂他 "浑蛋", "王八蛋", "畜牲", 还骂王兰 "婊子"。

小王: **好家伙**, 这些骂人话可不该在办公场合说。那李刚受得了吗?

小张: 他也**急了眼了**, 连脏话都用上了。那种话, 旁边听的人都**受不了**。

小王: 那后来是怎么收场的呢?

小张: 大家都**看不下去**了, 最后叫保安把他老婆架出单位才**完事儿**。

Zhang and Wang are employees at a state-owned department. They're discussing the affairs of their coworker, Gang.

Zhang:	Hey, have you heard? Everyone's talking about Gang Li and Lan Wang today; they've been at it.
Wang:	At it? What are you talking about?
Zhang:	How can you not get it? They've been seeing each other—they slept together.
Wang:	How can Gang Li screw around like that? He's got a wife and kids and he still causes trouble.
Zhang:	Nobody's disagreeing with you! I've heard from way back that he's got a thing with his boss, and Lan Wang happens to be their group's boss.
Wang:	How did this get out?
Zhang:	Yesterday his wife came to the department and had a fight with him, and now it's out.
Wang:	She's left Gang Li with no face.
Zhang:	That's right. At first the two of them were just arguing, his wife called him "annoying," "damnable," and an "ungrateful social climber."
Wang:	Being wrung out by his wife in front of his coworkers like that, how can Gang Li stand it?
Zhang:	She was enraged, and didn't care any more. Gang Li was in the wrong, but he couldn't stand losing face like that, so he talked back. His wife got even more mad, and started screaming at him, calling him "bastard," "asshole," "animal," and she also called Lan Wang a whore.
Wang:	Oh man, you can't use that kind of language at work. How could Gang Li take it?

Li: He went crazy, too, and started cursing, too. That kind of language, even the people listening couldn't stand it.

Wang: So how did it end?

Li: Everyone couldn't keep watching, and in the end they had to call security to drag the wife out of the building.

———————

Traditional

小張和小王是一個國營單位的雇員。他們在議論同事李剛的事。

小張: 哎, 你聽說沒? 今天咱這兒的人都在傳李剛和王蘭的事兒呢, 他們**那個**了。

小王: 哪個了? 你說什麼哪?

小張: 你怎麼連這都不明白? 就是**發生關係**了, **上床**了。

小王: 李剛怎麼這麼**胡鬧**? 自己有老婆孩子還亂搞。

小張: **誰說不是啊**! 早就聽說他和他們頭兒**有一腿**, 王蘭正是他們組的頭兒。

小王: 這事兒是怎麼傳出來的?

小張: 昨天他老婆來單位跟他打架, 就傳開了。

小王: 她也太不給李剛**留面子**了。

小張: 就是。開頭兩人還就是**拌嘴**, 他老婆說他 "氣人", "可惡", 是 "忘恩負義" 的 "白眼兒狼"。

小王：　當著同事的面讓老婆這麼**數落**，這讓李剛的**臉往哪兒放**？

小張：　她是氣極了，**不管三七二十一**了。李剛本來**理短**，可是**臉上又掛不住**，就**回了幾句嘴**。他老婆更生氣了，就大罵起來，罵他"渾蛋"，"王八蛋"，"畜牲"，還罵王蘭"婊子"。

小王：　**好傢伙**，這些罵人話可不該在辦公場合說。那王剛受得了嗎？

小張：　他也**急了眼了**，連髒話都用上了。那種話，旁邊聽的人都**受不了**。

小王：　那後來是怎麼收場的呢？

小張：　大家都**看不下去**了，最後叫保安把他老婆架出單位才**完事兒**。

———————

词语注释

- 他们**那个**了。
  那个　Can be used in place of certain words as an euphemism. Here it refers to "having an affair." For example, 你刚才说的话有点太那个了。"What you said was just too ...you-know-what." The connotation is that the subject is taboo."

- 就是**发生关系**了，上床了。
  发生关系 "having an affair." For example, 他才结婚不久，就和别人发生了关系。"He had an affair not long after he got married."

- 就是发生关系了，**上床**了。
  上床 One meaning is: "To sleep with someone." For example, 他们认识的当天就上床了。 "They slept with each other on the day they met."

- 李刚怎么这么**胡闹**?
  胡闹 "Run wild"; "make trouble." For example, 他昨天喝醉了胡闹，把玻璃窗打碎了。 "He got drunk yesterday and made trouble, and broke the window."

- **谁说不是啊**，早就听说他和他们头儿有一腿
  谁说不是啊 When 谁, or "who," is used in a rhetorical question, it usually indicates "no one." Here, the rhetorical question "Who's going to disagree?" connotes "No one disagrees." For example, 谁不知道今天是除夕呀? "Who doesn't know that it's New Year's today?"

- 早就听说他和他们头儿**有一腿**,
  有一腿 A colloquial form for "having an affair." For example, 谁不知道他和他的秘书有一腿。 "Who doesn't know that he's having an affair with his secretary?"

- 她也太不给李刚**留面子**了。
  留面子 "Do somebody a favor to save his (or her) face." For example, 你们是老朋友，你总得给他留点儿面子。 "You two are old friends, so you'd better help him save face."

- 开头两人还就是**拌嘴**
  拌嘴 A colloquial word for "bicker," "quarrel," or "squabble." For example, 他们俩虽然是好朋友，但常常拌嘴。 "Even though they're good friends, they often argue."

- 当着同事的面让老婆这么**数落**,这让李刚的脸往哪儿放?

  数落 ([shǔluo]) A colloquial word that means "to scold somebody by listing his faults." For example, 今天约会我又去晚了,让我女朋友数落了一顿。 "Today I was late for my date again, and I got wrung out by my girlfriend."

- 当着同事的面让老婆这么数落,这让李刚的**脸往哪儿放**?

  脸往哪儿放 Literally, "where to put somebody's face." It is a rhetorical question that denotes losing face or being embarrassed. For example, 你在会上当着我的下级喊我小名,叫我的脸往哪儿放? "You called me by my nickname in front of my subordinates at a meeting; how was I supposed to react?"

- 她是气极了,**不管三七二十一**了。

  不管三七二十一 "Regardless of the consequences"; "casting all caution to the winds"; "recklessly." For example, 你怎么能不管三七二十一就把所有的钱都买了一种股票呢? "How could you cast all caution to the winds and put all your money into one stock?"

- 李刚本来**理短**,可是脸上又挂不住,就回了几句嘴。

  理短 "Have no justification"; "be in the wrong." For example, 他自知理短,就先说了声"对不起"。 "Knowing that he was in the wrong, he started off by saying 'sorry.'"

- 李刚本来理短,可是**脸上又挂不住**,就回了几句嘴。

  脸上挂不住 "Unable to stand the loss of face." For example, 昨天他没做作业受到老师批评时,脸上挂不住,跑出了教室。 "Yesterday he did not do his homework, and when the teacher criticized him, he felt very embarrassed and ran out of the classroom."

- 李刚本来理短, 可是脸上又挂不住, 就**回了几句嘴。**
  回嘴 "Retort"; "talk back"; "scold back." For example, 父母说他时他从不回嘴。 "When his parents scold him he never talks back."

- **好家伙**, 这些骂人话可不该在办公场合说。
  好家伙 An interjection that is used to express surprise or admiration. "Good God"; "Good Lord"; "Good Heavens." For example, 好家伙, 你居然一晚上记了三百多个生词! "Good God, you memorized over 300 vocabulary words in one night!"

- 他也**急了眼**了, 连脏话都用上了。
  急眼 A colloquial expression for "get angry"; "fly into a rage." For example, 你这个人也太爱生气了, 跟你开个玩笑你就急眼了。 "You get angry way too easily; I make a joke and you get pissed off."

- 那种话, 旁边听的人都**受不了**。
  受不了 "Cannot stand"; "cannot endure." For example, 我累得受不了了。 "I'm so tired that I can't take it anymore."

- 大家都**看不下去了**
  看不下去 "Cannot bear the sight anymore"; "cannot stand by and watch." For example, 我儿子做手术时, 虽然医院让在窗外看, 可我一见他出血, 就看不下去了。 "Although I was allowed to watch my son's surgical operation from the window, I just couldn't bear the sight anymore when I saw his blood."

- 最后叫保安把他老婆架出单位才**完事**儿。
  完事 "Be settled." For example, 你搬家搬了一个礼拜了, 现在完事儿了吧? "You have been moving for a week; have you finished now?"

VOCABULARY

挤	jǐ	crowd; push against; squeeze
躲	duǒ	hide (oneself); avoid; dodge
似的	shìde	as; as if
好好	hǎohǎo	nicely
脏话	zānghuà	bad language; speaking rudely
骂人	màrén	curse; swear; call names
国营	guóyíng	state-operated; state-run
雇员	gùyuán	employee
议论	yìlùn	talk; discuss
传	chuán	spread
打架	dǎjià	fight; quarrel; wrangle
气人	qìrén	annoying
可恶	kěwù	hateful; detestable
忘恩负义	wàngēnfùyì	devoid of gratitude; ungrateful
白眼狼	báiyǎnláng	supercilious wolf
气急败坏	qìjíbàihuài	flustered and exasperated
王八	wángba	tortoise; (offensive) cuckold
王八蛋	wángbādàn	bastard; son of a bitch
畜牲	chùsheng	animal; beast
婊子	biǎozi	prostitute; whore
场合	chǎnghé	occasion; situation
收场	shōuchǎng	wind up; end up; stop
保安	bǎoān	security personnel
架	jià	take somebody away forcibly

EXERCISES

A. Fill in the spaces with the appropriate words or phrases:

给脸不要脸　行了,行了　不是东西　德行　讨厌
撒泡尿照照　你才错了呢　什么东西　他妈的

1　天天都这么堵车,真_____! 烦死人了。

2　你看看你,买东西不排队,还老骂 "_____"。

3　他也不想想自己什么_____,还想当班长呢!

4　快别提他了,他是_____,不值得一提。

5　我已经说对不起了,你还没个完,别_____。

6　_____,你不用说了,全按你的意思办好啦。

7　他可_____了,离婚以后从来不付孩子的生活费。

8　他还想上哈佛大学? 他最好先_____再说。

9　什么? 你说我错了? _____!

B. Choose the expression from the following list that best corresponds to the underlined words or phrases:

浑蛋　　有病　　打的　　倒　　　少
稀罕　　犯浑　　往自己脸上贴金

1　你刚说完行又说不行,你是不是<u>病了</u>?

2　今天下这了么大的雪,不但不冷,<u>还</u>挺暖和的。

3 那个<u>坏蛋</u>,抢了东西不说,还把人也打伤了。

4 我不是<u>喜欢</u>你有钱,我是喜欢你有才。

5 有什么话好好说,<u>别</u>动手动脚的!

6 她儿子动不动就<u>瞎闹</u>,她一点儿办法也没有。

7 <u>坐出租车</u>方便,坐公共汽车便宜,各有各的好处。

8 别看他人不怎么样,可是挺会<u>吹自己</u>,所以找了个好工作。

C. Fill in the spaces with the appropriate words or phrases:

看不下去　谁说不是啊　留面子　受不了　　那个
发生关系　脸往哪儿放　有一腿　不管三七二十一

1 你看他俩多亲热,准是_____了；都是有家的人,真不像话!

2 这个新老师留的作业又多又难,真让人_____。

3 他妈病危他都不管,邻居们_____,把老太太送进了医院。

4 要不是发现他和秘书_____,他太太也不会和他离婚。

5 现在在中国多数人还是觉得男女结婚前不应该
_____。

6 中国人特别重视面子,所以说话做事都注意给别人_____。

7 你别当着孩子的面数落你先生,要不然,他的_____?

8 跟他讲也讲不清楚,咱干脆_____,干起来再说。

9 "你有病就该休息。" "_____,可我忙得休息不了."

D. Choose the expression from the following list that best corresponds to the underlined words or phrases:

急了眼   胡闹   理短   上床   拌嘴

好家伙   数落   回嘴   完事   脸上挂不住

1 你们的官司打了几个月了,现在<u>打完</u>了没有?

2 他跟我说过,他最不爱听他妈妈没完没了地<u>说</u>他。

3 这件事情谁<u>没道理</u>已经挺清楚了,不用再多说了。

4 你是有太太的人,怎么也不应该再和别人<u>发生关系</u>。

5 我妈说,就象牙免不了咬着舌头一样,夫妻也免不了<u>争吵</u>。

6 按中国的老习惯,如果大人说孩子,孩子不能<u>表示不同意</u>。

7 孩子再怎么<u>不听话</u>也是孩子,不值得生这么大的气。

8 <u>我的天</u>,你真能吃,你一个人吃得比我们全家都多。

9 老李批评了她几句,她觉得<u>丢脸</u>,就跟老李吵了起来。

10 他脾气可不好了,要是<u>生了气</u>,谁他都敢骂。

———■———

ANSWER KEY

Exercise A (Dialogue 1)

1 讨厌
2 他妈的
3 德行
4 什么东西
5 给脸不要脸
6 行了,行了（行了）
7 不是东西
8 撒泡尿照照
9 你才错了呢（你才… 呢）

Exercise B (Dialogue 1)

1 有病
2 倒
3 浑蛋
4 稀罕
5 少（少…）
6 犯浑
7 打的
8 往自己脸上贴金

Exercise C (Dialogue 2)

1 那个/有一腿
2 受不了
3 看不下去
4 有一腿/那个
5 发生关系
6 留面子
7 脸往哪儿放
8 不管三七二十一
9 谁说不是啊

Exercise D (Dialogue 2)

1 完事
2 数落
3 理短
4 上床
5 拌嘴
6 回嘴
7 胡闹
8 好家伙
9 脸上挂不住
10 急了眼（急眼）

▮ CULTURE NOTES: DIRTY WORDS – TABOO LANGUAGE

To the Chinese, "Dirty Words" (脏话) are considered undesirable or offensive, and there is a strong prohibition against using them. Using dirty words in public is not only an insult to the audience, but is also an insult to the speaker. As in many cultures, in Chinese swear words are mainly related to sex, to animals considered dirty, and to certain beliefs.

Swear terms conveying dissatisfaction, anger, or insult can be roughly divided into three categories based on where one speaks and with whom. The first category of words is used when one speaks to an acquaintance (family member or relatives, friends and colleagues) in public. 不象话 (unreasonable); 讨厌 (disgusting); 可恶 (abominable); 缺德 (wicked); 不是东西 (less than human, implies less worth than an object); 什么东西 (less than human, compares the level of a person to that of an object); etc. The second category is those words used to verbally abuse, to curse, or to insult. Well educated people will not use these words, and those who do only use them only when consumed with fury: 不要脸 (shameless); 不是人 (not human); 畜牲 (animal); 混蛋 (son of bitch); 王八蛋 (bastard); 他妈的 (damn); 婊子养的 (son of a whore); etc. The third category comprises those words that should be prohibited on any occasion at anytime—such as: 操 (fuck); 操你妈 (fuck your mother); etc.

Index 1

. Index 1 .

•

Aᴸᴾʜᴀʙᴇᴛɪᴄᴀʟ

•

Index 2

•

BY CHAPTER

•

Index 3★

•

ALPHABETICAL

•

*Indexes 3 and 4 contain more than 80% of level 3 and level 4 colloquial items listed in the *Outline of Chinese Proficiency Level and Grammar Level* (汉语水平等级标准与语法等级大纲), which was drawn up by the office of China's central government that is in charge of teaching Chinese as a foreign language (国家汉办).

Index 4★

•

BY CHAPTER

•